THE

SCRIPTURAL EXPOSITIONS

OF

DR. AUGUSTUS NEANDER,

COMPLETE IN ONE VOLUME.

TRANSLATED FROM THE GERMAN

BY MRS. H. C. CONANT.

I. THE EPISTLE OF PAUL TO THE PHILIPPIANS.

II. THE GENERAL EPISTLE OF JAMES.

III. THE FIRST EPISTLE GENERAL OF JOHN.

New York:

LEWIS COLBY AND COMPANY,

122 NASSAU STREET.

1853.

THE

EPISTLE OF PAUL

TO THE

PHILIPPIANS,

PRACTICALLY EXPLAINED,

BY

DR. AUGUSTUS NEANDER.

TRANSLATED FROM THE GERMAN

BY

MRS. H. C. CONANT.

NEW YORK:
LEWIS COLBY & CO.,
122 NASSAU STREET.

1853.

INTRODUCTION.

In offering the following work of Neander to the American public, some brief explanation of its character seems to be necessary. Many, who have only heard of the author as one of the most profound scholars and thinkers of the age, might otherwise be deterred from reading it, by the supposition that it was merely a work of learned criticism. Such, however, is far from being the case. It was the beginning of a series of popular practical commentaries, intended to embrace the more important portions of the Bible. Next to the Epistle of James, which was completed, and a translation of which we expect shortly to present to the public, were to follow the Epistles of John, then the Gospels, the Psalms, &c., as rapidly as the public duties of the author would allow. The surpassing excellence of the beginning makes us deeply lament the loss to the church, through the recent death of the great and good Neander, of so rich an addition to its means of understanding the Scriptures, and one so happily adapted to the wants of common Christians. This, however, does not impair the value of the separate parts, each division being complete in itself;

and we cannot but rejoice that, as he was not permitted fully to carry out his plan, he should have executed a part so appropriate as the closing labor of his life. Had he foreseen that these were to be his last words of counsel to his brethren in Christ, he could nowhere have found freer scope for all he wished to say for their instruction, comforting, and edification, than in a commentary on the Epistle to the Philippians. One might almost believe, such a fulness of pious feeling pours through its pages, that he had some such presage. Whether this were so or not, doubtless He to whom all events are known guided him in the selection; and we may receive it as the dying legacy of one of the greatest Christian teachers with which God has ever blessed his church. May its instructions sink deep into the heart of the church, and bring forth fruit to the honor and glory of God!

In reading this commentary, one cannot but be forcibly struck with the strong affinity between the character of Paul and that of his expounder. Different as were their outward circumstances and course of life, Neander seems to have had, in his own nature and spiritual sympathies, a perfect key to those of the Apostle. Hence it is that he has surpassed all others in giving the spirit of this Epistle. The grandeur of Paul's spiritual conceptions, his personal aspirations, his inward conflicts, his magnanimity, tenderness, and humility, his all-absorbing love for Christ and for man, are delineated with a life and power which only a kindred soul in the writer could have inspired. His very manner bears the same stamp of resemblance. Impatient of the niceties of minute criticism, he breaks through the mere outward form, the shell of words and phrases, into the very heart of the Epistle; and develops its contents, not by a petty weighing of particles, but by one broad, extended view of the whole scope of the Apostle's design and meaning. This he illustrates from Paul's history and character, his present circumstances and those of the infant churches; and the whole glows with the light and warmth of a deep personal experience of the Gospel. Thus, though the work is rich in the results of a learning as profound as it was various, the earnest and intelligent, but unlearned reader, can pursue his way unimpeded by any obtrusive lumber of scholarship. It is indeed a beautiful illustration of what his friend and colleague, the evangelical Strauss, says of him in his funeral discourse: "He did not despise human knowledge; he sought for it with unwearied diligence; he was a master in it; but he laid all the surprising treasures of his learning at the foot of the cross." To edify the members of Christ's body was with him a greater object, than to make a vain parade of his own superiority; as to be one with Christ was to himself, personally, an immeasurably greater object than all human learning or honor.

One characteristic of the work, which adds greatly to its practical value, has also a special interest as showing the author's character under a new aspect;—we mean the comprehensive and accurate knowledge it exhibits of men and their relations. It shows that he was no mere recluse scholar, buried in the past, with no eyes nor ears for the living world around him. It is indeed a problem, how a man who so seldom went beyond his study and his lecture room, whose own relations to society were so few, and his associations almost exclusively among the learned, could have gained so much acquaintance with human nature, and with the various forms and phases of Christian experience. The solution is to be found in the fact, that Neander had a heart as well as intellect; a heart gifted by nature with the largest human sympathies, and from early life penetrated by the spirit of Christian benevolence. Man his brother, man whom God had created and for whom Christ had died, was to him an object of unspeakable interest, and nothing was unimportant which affected his character and prospects. Hence, from the little that he mingled with men he learned much of man; and he applies the inspired instructions with a discrimination and point, which show that no generic differences in human character had escaped him. It is a matter of no little interest, to know what views of man were received from this study by a mind like Neander's. It is plain that he cherished no high-wrought notions of the natural goodness and perfectibility of the race. Yet he did not turn from the weak and erring being with philosophic contempt, or thank God that he was not as other men are. His was the earnest, penetrating scrutiny of a Christian philanthropist, seeking to know his brother's wants in order that Christian love might supply them. Though he was no believer in inherent human goodness, he was a firm believer in the efficacy of the great remedy for man's moral diseases. Hence the clearer perception of his ruined and lost state, only awoke more strongly the love which yearned to bring relief. The spirit of Neander's life and writings furnish sufficient proof, if proof were still wanting, that the clear recognition of man's entire moral perversion is the basis for all true love of humanity. His practical wisdom, as well as the tenderness of his heart, are beautifully exhibited in his treatment of the yet immature believer. The germ of divine life, planted in a human heart, is an object which engages all his interest. The causes which may obstruct its free development, as found in the various forms of self-deception, in the power of early prejudice, and not less in the over-hasty zeal or unchristian harshness of brethren, are touched with admirable skill. If his lessons of rigid self-scrutiny, trying as by fire every thought and motive of our own hearts, and of a fraternal charity, quick to discern and acknowledge and tenderly to cherish the faintest signs of grace in others, were carried into practice by every disciple of Christ, who can doubt the speedy increase of spiritual life, of unity, and of moral power in the church!

Another not less interesting point is the simply scriptural character of his theology, of the exhibition here given of the essential doctrines of the Gospel. Christ, the Crucified and the Risen, as the one foundation of the church, the living root from whom proceeds all spiritual life and growth; man as a sinful and lost being, depending for regeneration and sanctification on the influences of the Holy Spirit; the utter insufficiency of human works as the ground of salvation; a holy life as the necessary fruit of holy love; these, no man since Paul has more eloquently enforced than Neander. In developing Paul's theology, deep religious experience supplied to him that light, for the lack of which so many have misunderstood and perverted the meaning of the great Apostle. The natural man, and the spiritual man, designate with him radical distinctions of character. The tendencies of the natural man, however beautiful his social and even religious virtues to human view, are yet, as springing from self and ending in self, radically wrong; the tendencies of the spiritual man, as springing from God and ending in God, are radically right. But the spiritual man, and the perfect man, are not with him interchangeable terms. The Christian life is an unceasing conflict with inward depravity; that we persevere in this conflict to the end, the only reliable proof that we belong to Christ. The Christian's standard of character is perfection, is Christ; his ever increasing sense of unlikeness to this faultless model, the strongest evidence that he is becoming more and more assimilated to it. This sense of unlikeness, while it humbles and stimulates, does not disquiet the believer; for his confidence and his affections are placed on a nobler object than self, were it in a state of absolute perfection. The incarnate Word, the brightness of the Father's glory and the express image of his person, once humbled in humanity, now reigning in divine glory, is the centre of all his aspirations and hopes, the life of his life, his all in all. An affecting proof of Neander's personal consciousness of these truths, was given on the evening of his last year's birth-day. His pupils having, as is customary in German universities on such occasions, honored their beloved teacher with a torch-light procession and a eulogistic address, he replied by a pathetic confession of human weakness, and spoke of himself as a sinner needing forgiveness through the blood of Christ. The whole course of his inward and outward religious life corresponded fully to this expression. "As to be a Christian," says Strauss, "nothing but a Christian saved by grace, was all his desire in his inward experience, so in his calling he desired only to be a servant of Christ." The love of Christ to his people, as developed in the past history of the church, was his most interesting subject of contemplation. In his hands, Church History became not a mere record of the mistakes of the human spirit, but primarily, a record of the miracles of the love of Jesus. And often, says his friend, his voice trembled and his whole heart gushed forth, when narrating individual experiences of grace, exemplifying the love of Christ. What a beautiful illustration of his own favorite maxim, "It is the heart that makes the Theologian!" The modesty of his Theology is not less marked than its scriptural character. Our knowledge of God and divine things, though all-sufficient for our present need, in his view is necessarily fragmentary and imperfect; "to be cast aside when we are raised to the full vision of the life above, as the conceptions of childhood are cast aside by the mature man." How habitually this conviction was present to his mind, is pleasingly illustrated by the circumstance, that when called on for an autograph to accompany his engraved portrait, he wrote for the purpose the words: "Now we see through a glass darkly, but then face to face."

The closing scenes in the life of this eminent servant of Christ, seem like the reflection of that conflict which he so admirably depicts in the heart of Paul, between the longing to depart and be with Christ, and the desire still to live that he may labor for the salvation of his brethren. To labor for Christ was, as with Paul, his life on earth. Apart from this work, life had no value, no significance. While he lived he must labor; and even after the hand of death had touched his long diseased body, he still strove to compel its services in his appointed calling in God's kingdom. This calling was one which enlisted all the energies and affections of his soul. To be the instructor of youth in the Holy Scriptures, and the historian of the Church, was a high destiny; and his devotion to it had all the ardor of a ruling passion. His history he had now brought down to the period of the Reformation; and with a mind unimpaired by age or disease, and glowing with his theme, he was about entering on the development of that central epoch of modern Christianity, when the summons came to lay aside the earthly for the heavenly. How his heart clung to his life-work, is affectingly shown in the sketch of his last hours by his attached friend and pupil Rauh. We give the substance of the account.

He was at his desk in his lecture room, on Monday, when the attack came upon him. Inúred to pain, and accustomed to master it by his powerful will, he persevered in completing the exercise; though the broken tones of his voice, at times almost inaudible from debility, forced upon his affectionate auditors the conviction expressed in the touching language of one of their number: "This is the last lecture of our Neander!" He reached home in a state of great exhaustion. But after some slight refreshment, he immediately resumed his usual afternoon employments. For three successive hours, though often interrupted by increasing weakness, he dictated on his Church History. Late in the afternoon, the symptoms of dangerous illness becoming more and more marked, his anxious sister insisted that he should give himself rest. But he could not be persuaded to quit his work. "Nay, let me go on!" he exclaimed: "can every day-laborer work as much as he will, and would you deny it to me!" At length he was obliged to yield, and allow himself to be conveyed to bed. The next morning he was forced, by the increased violence of his malady, to consent that his usual lecture should be deferred; "but," as he expressly added, "only for to-day!" From this time it was an incessant struggle for supremacy between the mind and the body. In the afternoon, he called imperatively for his reader;* and blamed his over-anxious friends for having sent him away, and thus interrupted his progress in a work with which he was engaged, Ritter's Palestine. He then listened to the reading of the newspaper by another pupil, with earnest attention; selected what he wished to hear, and commented on this and that of its contents, till at length a heavy slumber overpowered him. The next day also, the daily paper being read to him as usual, the mention of some occurrence in the Church drew from him an exclamation of humorous contempt at the modish spirit of the day; an expressive shrug indicated his dissatisfaction at another. This day he experienced a little relief, from the refreshment of a more quiet night, which encouraged his desponding friends. But on Friday evening the last ray of hope was extinguished. Paralysis, the result of his exhausting disease, seized upon the kidneys. The fatal hiccough set in, and allowed not a mo-

* An affection of the eyes, which had increased almost to blindness, had for some two years rendered such assistance necessary.

ment's sleep. This scene of distress continued four hours, without mitigation. Groans were forced from him by the extremity of his anguish; and he was heard praying in a weak and plaintive tone, which drew tears from every eye, "Oh God! that I might sleep!" But the energy of his spirit was not yet quenched. The next afternoon, though in an agony of pain, the longing to be again at work in his great calling seemed to awaken in full force. He insisted that he would no longer be confined in bed; and with a feverish impatience, never seen in him before, ordered a servant to bring his clothes that he might rise. A pupil who was at hand vainly tried to soothe him. Even his sister's entreaties were of no avail, till she said to him: "Remember, dear Augustus, your own words to me, when I resisted the physician's orders, —'It is all from God, and we must yield cheerfully to his will!'" "True," he gently replied in an altered tone; "it all comes from God, and we must thank him for it!" Through all the variations of his sickness, his wonted tender consideration for his friends did not forsake him. He would not allow his pupils to neglect their duties in order to attend upon him; watched lest his sister should not take needful rest, and received every slight service with the most touching gratitude. Even when scarcely able to speak, from pain and weakness, he would make the utmost effort to express his thankfulness. One little characteristic trait deserves to be mentioned. His large income, always devoted more to others than himself, was yet insufficient for his multiplied charities, so that he was often perplexed and distressed when he found a new object of compassion which he had not the means of relieving. He practised the most rigid economy in his own personal expenses, that he might have more for others. Every luxury was in his view a robbery of the poor. So fixed were his habits in this respect, that when a little champagne was offered him during this last sickness, he promptly refused it with the expression, "O that is a foolish indulgence!"

The final scene is one most characteristic of the man, as well as one of the most striking ever witnessed in the chamber of death. A wine bath had been prepared for him, as a last resort. Refreshed and strengthened by it, he was borne from the darkened room where he had lain hitherto into his study, that cheerful little apartment opening to the sun, which had been so long the workshop and the paradise of the man of thought. Here for nearly twenty years he had studied and written. From this spot had gone forth those great works which have delighted and instructed Christendom. With thirsty glances he drank in the full golden sunlight, of which he was always so fond.* A spoonful of choice wine being offered him, he did not reject it,—"a significant omen,"

* In this also, "a child of the light," as he sportively called himself (ὀπαδὸς τοῦ ἡλίου) a few days before. "This I have,"—said he on that occasion,—"in common with the emperor Julian; but that," he added, "Strauss must not know!"

says Rauh, "that the old order of things approached its end." Ere long he murmured dreamily, as if at the close of a long fatiguing walk with his sister, "I am weary; let us now make ready to go home!" Just then the rich sunset glow, pouring through the window, lighted up the shelves from which looked down upon him the masters of thought, with whom for so many years he had held silent but high and endearing communion. Raising himself by a sudden effort from his pillow, he commenced a regular lecture upon New Testament exegesis. Soon a new image passed before his restless fancy. Imagining himself at the weekly meeting of his beloved *Seminarium*, surrounded by his fondly attached theological pupils, he called for the reading of a dissertation, shortly before assigned, on the material and formal principle of the Reformation. He then dictated the titles of the different courses of lectures to be delivered by him during the next session; among them, "The Gospel of John, from its true historical point of view." His last thoughts amid the struggles of death, were devoted to the great labor of his life. Beginning at the very passage of his Church History where sickness had arrested his progress, he resumed the thread of thought, and in spite of interruptions, continued to dictate in regular periods for some time. At the close of each sentence he paused, as if his amanuensis were taking down his words, and asked, "Are you ready?" Having closed a division of his subject, he inquired the time. Being told that it was half-past nine, the patient sufferer repeated once more: "I am weary; I will now go to sleep!" Having by the aid of friendly hands stretched himself in bed for his last slumber, he whispered in a tone of inexpressible tenderness, which sent a strange thrill through every heart: "Good night!" It was his last word. He immediately fell into a sleep, which continued four hours; when his great spirit, in the quiet of a Sabbath morning, passed gently into the land of peace.—What a commentary on his own exhortation so lately uttered; that "the Christian should ever remember that here all is fragmentary, nothing reaches completion; that even service in the cause of Christ on earth, is but the beginning of an activity destined for eternity; that we must therefore not be so absorbed, even in labors consecrated to God, as to be unprepared to obey, at any moment, the summons to the higher life and service of Heaven!" He was so prepared, that when his ear caught the summons, he could drop the great labor of his life unfinished, lay himself down quietly upon his bed, and with a child-like "Good Night" to those whom he left behind, *slumber over* (as the German beautifully expresses it) into that higher life of heaven.

Before closing, the translator would beg of those conversant with the author's manner in the original, as favorable a judgment of her work as justice will allow. They can best appreciate the difficulty of the task. It has been her aim, not merely to give a faithful rendering of the author's ideas, in an easy English style, but to reproduce them, so far as possible, in their original form and mould. The elephantine march of his style suits, as no other could, to the great burden of his thoughts; which, moreover, are so combined and *massed* together, that not only would the manner be lost by much breaking up of his sentences, but the connection and relation of the different parts be seriously impaired.

H. C. C.

ROCHESTER, N. Y.
Sept. 1851.

EPISTLE OF PAUL

TO

THE PHILIPPIANS.

If the Spirit of God has revealed to holy men of old the word of truth, that they might proclaim it for the salvation of mankind; if God has revealed himself through their lives, their discourses, their writings, as the depositaries of his Spirit; this is not to be regarded merely as an isolated fact belonging solely to the past. To us as living members of the body of Christ, as partakers in that fellowship of his Spirit, which unites the instant of the present with the whole progressive development since the first outpouring of the same Spirit by the glorified Son of man, to us, this should be no external, no foreign thing. The past must become to us the present. We need no further revelations. On the contrary, it must be to us as if the Lord had himself at this moment spoken to us, inasmuch as he has given us the instruction required for all the higher necessities of the present; as if he had himself said to us all which it concerns us to know, in order to find consolation under present sufferings, the means of certain victory in all conflicts, the clue to guide us out of all the perplexities of a distracted age safely to our goal. For the attainment of this object, we must carefully investigate the precise historical conditions and relations under which these depositaries of the Divine Spirit spoke and acted. We must transfer ourselves into that past time, so as to live, as it were, in the midst of the circumstances under which these holy men acted, and in reference to which they spoke. The objects of divine wisdom in its guidance of the Church, we perceive in this, viz., that divine truth has been revealed to us, not in a law of the letter, not in a digested summary of specific articles of faith, but in this historical embodiment, in this application to individual cases, to specific historical circumstances and social relations, imparted through the instrumentality of individual men, who lived as depositaries of divine truth among their fellow-men; who, in the common intercourse of human life, testified of and revealed the divine, speaking and acting as men, each in his own peculiar human manner, though hallowed indeed by the Spirit of God. Thus was divine truth to be brought humanly near to us. Thus to our own spiritual activity, under the guiding and quickening influence of the Spirit of God, without whom nothing divine can be received or understood, was to be left the work of investigating the divine in its connection with the human; from the particular to deduce the universal; and again, by an application of this to the peculiar circumstances of the age and society in which we live, to reconvert it into the particular for ourselves; to detect in that which was said or done by the organs of Christ's Spirit, under the peculiar circumstances of the past, whatever is applicable for our use to the circumstances and relations of the present. Whilst, therefore, an humble dependence on that Divine Spirit, who alone leads into all truth, and unlocks the depths of his word, is an indispensable condition to the right understanding and application of the Divine Word in its human embodiment; so also is a careful attention to all the human relations. The word of God allows no slothful hearers; it demands all the powers of the mind and soul. Only thus can its treasures be brought to light. If we fail of discovering these treasures, and lament over the want of light to illumine the darkness of the present state, it is because we have not met the required conditions. We have none to reproach but ourselves. We may here apply those weighty words of our Lord, adapted no less to stimulate and encourage diligent inquiry, than for warning and rebuke: "He that hath, to him shall be given."

In an especial manner is this true of the Letters of the Apostles. In these we should find far more to instruct, edify, and guide us in all the relations of life, if we thus weighed the import of every word. May the Spirit of the Lord enlighten and guide us, that we may in this manner understand, and learn to apply, one of the noblest epistles of the Apostle Paul, written as no other could write, and presenting to our eyes the living image of the Apostle to the Gentiles!

First, then, we must bring before our view the peculiar circumstances and relations, under which Paul wrote this epistle. Zeal for the salvation of the heathen world had drawn upon him the extremest persecution of the enraged Jews, who grudged to the Gentiles an equal participation and equal privileges with themselves, in the kingdom of God. To this was owing his apprehension at Jerusalem, his long imprisonment in Cesarea Stratonis, and finally, through his appeal to Cæsar, his captivity at Rome. The issue of his fate was still uncertain. In his imprisonment, he was far less occupied with anxiety for his own life, than for the welfare of the churches, scattered through various regions, who through the dangers which beset their Apostolic teacher might become unsettled in their faith, deprived, as they were, of his personal guidance in this dark and troubled period. Through his pupils and associates in the preaching of the gospel, who now formed the living link between him and these churches, and through his letters, must the want be supplied. Among these churches was that of Philippi in Macedonia. It was the first church which Paul had founded in that country. Its members had been witnesses of the ignominy and suffering endured by Paul, on account of the gospel, as recorded in the Acts of the Apostles. They had witnessed the example he gave of boldness in the faith, of devotion to the Lord, of triumphant enthusiasm in his service, his joyfulness in suffering, and the wonderful deliverances wrought for him by the Lord. This had served, in a special manner, to give greater depth and ardor to their love for him, who was ready to sacrifice all that he might bring them the glad tidings of salvation. They followed the example of their faithful teacher. As yet, indeed, Christianity had not drawn upon itself the attention of the Roman civil power; nor had it become an object of persecution through the state laws, as from its opposition to the national religion must soon be the case, under a civil constitution with which this was intimately interwoven. Accordingly no general persecution had arisen, and the churches in most regions enjoyed peace. In this respect, however, Macedonia formed an exception. Here, from the very first, the malignant hatred of the Jews, who were scattered in great numbers through the commercial cities, had been excited against the preachers of the gospel, and all who embraced it; and they had not wanted means for producing discord between the believers and their fellow-citizens and associates among the heathen. Although no civil laws as yet existed against Christianity, still there were means by which the heathen could, in many ways, disquiet and injure its new converts, distinguished by their life and conversation in so striking a manner from themselves. In the history of modern missions the same thing is repeated, in the intercourse between the new converts and their former heathen associates. The church at Philippi remained steadfast under all these persecutions. Their faith and love had been approved thereby. Neither could they be unsettled in their faith, by the persecutions which had now befallen their Apostolic teacher. They were conscious of that higher fellowship with him under all his conflicts and sufferings. His sufferings, and the dangers which hung over him, but added new fuel to their love and sympathy. To manifest this to him they had sent one of their own number, Epaphroditus, who might also bring back to them more exact information of his circumstances. We know that although the right had been given to the Apostles, by the Lord, to depend for their temporal necessities upon those for whose spiritual welfare they labored, yet Paul never availed himself of this privilege. As the attracting and recovering grace of the Lord had been exhibited towards him in so peculiar a manner; as it had transformed him from the bitterest persecutor into the preacher of the gospel; he felt himself constrained to do more than others, called by Christ in the ordinary way, and gradually fitted for his service, and to forbear the exercise of a right to which he was equally entitled with them. Thrust, as it were, by force into the work, he would, by more abundant labor, endurance, privation, manifest his unconstrained love for his appointed calling.—(1 Cor. ix. 17–19.) It is to be accounted his gift, growing out of his peculiar nature sanctified by the Holy Spirit, that he was able to number himself among those whom Christ pronounces blessed, for having forborne marriage for the kingdom of God's sake. Not that he would call them blessed on account of the state of celibacy, in and for itself; as if Paul could claim any advantage over Peter, who in a marriage consecrated by the Lord, labored for the advancement of the same cause; but on account of the spirit which led them to abstain from marriage, that love which would offer up all to the kingdom of God. It was this which animated Paul, and impelled him to contemplate as a duty whatever might, under his special circumstances, serve for the advancement of his work, and to undertake it with joyful zeal.

It was for this also, that amidst the labors of preaching, he sustained himself with his own hands as a tent-maker. He experienced in himself the truth of the Lord's words, "It is more blessed to give than to receive." In order to avoid every appearance of self-seeking, and to take from the opposers among the Jews and Judaizing Christians every occasion of suspicion, he himself assumed the whole charge of his temporal support. Still the church at Philippi were moved, by their heartfelt love to him, to anticipate his wants; and knowing how difficult he must often find it to earn a maintenance, they had several times sent sums of money for his necessities. Paul, though he sought no gift, yet, in view of the feeling which prompted it, could not reject the free-will-offering of love. This church had now once more manifested in this way their active sympathy for Paul, by sending to him Epaphroditus. This circumstance, and what he learned through their messenger of the condition of the Philippian church, occasioned the writing of this epistle. Its object was to express to the church at Philippi his gratitude and love; to relieve their anxiety respecting his own situation; to give them a view of his Christian state and temper in the midst of his conflicts and dangers; and to bestow upon them the counsels and encouragements suited to their peculiar circumstances.

We must now, therefore, direct our view to Paul's situation in his imprisonment at Rome; to his demeanor in his captivity, as the mirror of the state of his soul, so far as we can learn it from this letter; and to his counsels to the Philippian church, in reference to their peculiar relations, as furnishing suggestions applicable in numerous ways to similar circumstances.

Looking first then at Paul's situation, we shall perceive that this was adapted to produce great variations of feeling. He had given his public testimony for the Lord Jesus, and had made his own defence. This defence had produced the general impression, that it was not as a disturber of the public peace that this imprisonment had befallen him, nor for any other crime; but only as the preacher of a religion hated by the Jews.* Against this new faith, as we have already remarked, there existed as yet no state law. If now Paul could triumphantly establish his innocence in this respect, it would seem that his safety was

* Chap. i. 13

secured. But the Roman civil laws ever regarded an individual as in some degree criminal, who should seduce the citizens and subjects of the empire to apostasy from the state religion; and should attempt to make proselytes to a new faith, which, if not condemned by an express law, was yet in its nature opposed to the religion of the state, and was not of the number recognized by it as tolerated religions. Paul's case was, therefore, by no means so simple a one. Many difficult questions were involved in it. At times, the impression made by his public defence would awaken in him the expectation of a happy deliverance, and that he might be permitted to visit the churches founded early in his ministry, and among these the church at Philippi. Again, the prospect of death was before his mind. What then? Do we find his soul divided between fear and hope, despondency and joy, dependent upon the external impression of these changeful circumstances, as is wont to be the case with others in like situations? No; one deep undertone of cheerful tranquillity, of surrender to the will of the Lord, pervades the whole epistle. We see the man, whose confidence rests on an immovable foundation unaffected by change of circumstances, a foundation which no waves or storms can shake. He is certain that, in one way or another, the Lord will conduct him through these conflicts triumphantly to a glorious end.* With joyful confidence, he approaches the termination of a life singly consecrated to one holy service. He is conscious of not having labored in vain, as a faithful preacher of the truth, which he sees bringing forth fruit in the churches. These, as for instance the church at Philippi, are the living memorial of his devoted labors for the Lord, as he himself expresses it in this epistle; the witness that he has preached the word of the Lord in purity; his glory before the Lord when, at the day of judgment, that shall be by Him brought to light which was here concealed; when much, which here seemed to be somewhat, shall be exposed in its nothingness; and when much, that was misjudged and condemned by the world, shall be acknowledged by the Lord as his own. How nobly does this spirit of Paul express itself in the words of this epistle, where he exclaims:† "And even if I be offered‡ upon the sacrifice and priestly service of your faith, I joy and rejoice with you

* Chap. i. 19, 20. † Chap. ii. 17, 18. ‡ Literally, poured out.

all; in like manner should ye also joy and rejoice with me." We must endeavor to make clear the full import of these weighty words.—The Lord Christ is the one Mediator, between God and the sinful human race redeemed by him. Through him all, who believe on him and enter into fellowship with him, are taken out of the ungodly world and consecrated as a holy community to God. Thus do they all become one priestly generation. There is no longer the distinction of Priests and Laity. All are become, through him and in fellowship with him, what he himself is,—Priests before the God of Jesus Christ who is also their God, before his Father who is also their Father. Their whole life is a priestly calling; as Paul represents it, Rom. xii. 1, "a reasonable service," that is, a spiritual worship proceeding from the rational nature, the soul. Herein the whole spiritual life manifests itself as a God-devoted, to God presented self-sacrifice; every inward and outward act as done in fellowship with Christ, as performed in his name, pervaded by his Spirit, enstamped with his image, a thank-offering and a praise-offering of the redeemed, well pleasing in the sight of God. This being true of all the acts of each Christian in his proper vocation, Paul regards as his own priestly calling the Apostolic work; as his own acceptable offering to God, the faith planted by him among the Gentiles and the Christian life of the converted heathen world. It is in this sense he speaks, in these words to his Philippian brethren, of "the sacrifice and priestly service of their faith" as his offering to God. It was customary, moreover, to pour out wine upon the altar, a so-called libation, as a seal of the offering. Paul, foreseeing that his own blood might be poured out in his priestly office of proclaiming the Gospel among the heathen, that he might be called to testify to what he preached in the very face of death, and to put the seal of martyrdom upon his life's work, here speaks of the outpouring of his own blood as a libation,—an offering of himself upon the sacrifice. Thus, with joyful confidence, the Apostle advances towards so glorious a consummation of his work. Far from needing solace from others, he could call on the Philippians to rejoice with him. Uncertain whether he was to finish his captivity by the martyr's death, or whether his life would be preserved to labor still for the advancement of the kingdom of God upon the earth, he was prepared for both, submissive in either case to the divine will. The will of the Lord was his will. The result would show, in what way it was the purpose of the Lord to make his life most subservient to His own glory. He was in a strait betwixt two,—longing to depart, out of the conflicts of the earthly life, into the peace of the spirit's heavenly home; from where the Lord is seen only by the eye of faith, to where in blissful nearness he becomes an object of sight. Although Paul was certain even in this his earthly life of union with the Lord, he was far from feeling himself satisfied with what he already enjoyed. Not merely from external conflicts had he learned, that this is not the land of peace promised to the Christian, and sought for by his longing spirit. To those internal conflicts, yet more severe, which the life of faith must ever sustain, he was no stranger. Herein also had his Saviour led the way; he who cried "My soul is exceeding sorrowful even unto death!" and, "My God, my God, why hast thou forsaken me!" One of his sore trials he calls "a thorn in the flesh;" comparing it to the anguish inflicted by a thorn fixed and rankling in the flesh. It was the painful experience of his own human weakness, in contrast with the revelation of the divine glory, which at times was imparted to him. Thus was he taught to distinguish what is divine and what is human, what belongs to this life and what to the life beyond. Thus too was he to learn, that the land of heavenly peace, after which the renewed spirit sighs, is not to be found on earth. Although Paul, as his life and his epistles testify, had made great advances in personal sanctification, yet he was far from wishing to separate himself from the number of those, who as sinners seek in Christ for justification; far from holding himself to be a sinless saint. He knew well that he had still to maintain the conflict with sin, and that he must persevere in that conflict faithfully to the end, if he would stand before the Lord. We need only to hear his own professions, as when warning the Corinthians against a false security he writes (1 Cor. ix. 27): "But I keep under my body, and bring it into subjection; lest, having preached to others, I myself should be a cast-away." By these words he describes his unceasing conflict with himself, lest after having brought others to salvation by the preaching of the word, which through the indwelling divine power works independently of the preacher, and brings forth fruit to eternal life, he should himself be overcome by temptation and fall short of that goal to which he has conducted others. The figure, of which Paul here makes use, is taken from the boxing combats of the ancients. The body is represented as the antagonist with whom the boxer contends; implying a still continued resistance of the body, once the servant of sin, against the divine life in the spirit. Paul describes himself as one, who by unremitting effort makes his body, the organ of sanctification entrusted to him, serviceable to himself as the servant of Christ. This conflict with the body of sin, inasmuch as the whole outward life of man manifests itself in the body, designates in general the entire conflict still to be waged by the spiritual against the fleshly man, by the new man against the old;—and this in the case even of a Paul. Thus Paul, instructed by his rigorous self-examination, is far from supposing when he contemplates his own life, that he has already reached the limit of heavenly perfection, or that he could build his confidence thereon as if it were a life of perfected sanctification. "Not as if I had already attained, or were already perfect," is his own beautiful expression of his conviction, in a passage of this epistle which we shall presently consider. Paul, then, was conscious that the blessings pronounced by the Lord: "Blessed are they who hunger and thirst after righteousness, for they shall be filled!" "Blessed are the pure in heart for they shall see God!" were not as yet completely fulfilled in him, but were still, in a certain sense, a promise looking into the future. Moreover, although Paul had been elevated, in his perception of divine things, above others of his own time and of all time; although he could claim that single higher revelations, over and above that which was to be the subject of general proclamation, had been vouchsafed to him; yet he well knew that all this was but partial and fragmentary, far from that completeness of knowledge before whose light all which is called in this life higher perception, prophecy, the gift of tongues, shall vanish away. He reckons himself among those, whose knowledge of divine things is like objects obscurely reflected in a mirror, where much still remains uncertain; a knowledge which, in relation to that of the eternal world, is as the knowledge of the child, to that of the mature man. He was fully conscious, that when he should be raised to the full vision of the life above, that which he knew of divine things in this life must be cast aside by him, as the mature man casts aside the conceptions of childhood. The twilight of the earthly life of faith did not satisfy the aspirations of his soul, which thirsted after knowledge; and he longed to pass into that pure day of heavenly clearness, where our knowledge of God and divine things will be inward, immediate, a direct perception of that which is present, a knowing as we are known. We see then that, in all these respects, Paul was penetrated with the full consciousness that the hope which has reference to the future, not less than the present exercise of faith, constitutes the life of the Christian. Apart from this undoubting prospect into the future, the whole Christian life seems to him an effort without aim, a chase after a phantom, a deceptive show; as he expresses it 1 Cor. xv. 19, "If in this life only we have hope in Christ, we are of all men most miserable." For the life of others is directed towards some aim, higher or lower, of the sensual or spiritual life, which may actually be attained on earth. But the life of the Christian, with all its conflicts, labors, and privations, has reference to an object which has no reality, if it be not found in the eternal life of the future. It is from this point of view that Paul reproaches the proudly secure Corinthians, with having lost the consciousness of this distinction between the present and the hereafter, between the conflict of the earthly and the triumph of the eternal life. In their spirit and conduct they seemed as if already in possession of all riches, enjoying full satisfaction, the contentment of all necessities, with no farther warfare from within or from without. With this he contrasts the wholly different image of the Apostle's life (1 Cor. 4:8). "Ye are," says he, "already become full, ye are already become rich, ye reign without us." They were in spirit and conduct, as if the kingdom of Christ had with them already reached its consummation; and they, as partakers therein, had attained to all riches, to the satisfaction of all their desires. And would this were so, says he; would they had already attained to this participation in the perfected kingdom of Christ; for then, assuredly, the Apostles would not have been excluded therefrom, nor would their circumstances be such as they now are. Thus he holds up before them his own life of conflict, in contrast with their false security, their unauthorized and groundless exultation. (1 Cor. iv. 9–13.)

Thus there was reason sufficient even for Paul, though rejoicing in conflicts for Christ's sake, and finding therein his glory, still to long after that perfect union with the Lord in the life to come. In earlier years, indeed, we find him constantly referring to the contrast between the earthly life of faith, and the consummation not to be enjoyed till the resurrection. But at a later period, especially from the date of his second epistle to the Corinthians, we remark in him an ever increasing consciousness, that, as a necessary result of the inseparable union of believers with their Lord, both in his sufferings and his exaltation, they also shall on their departure from the earthly existence enter at once on a higher life of vision, into a higher, more undisturbed fellowship with Him. Thus in the fifth chapter of the second epistle to the Corinthians, he in this view represents the abiding in the flesh as an absence from the Lord, that is, from the immediate vision of Christ; while the state which follows, entered through death, through the laying off of the earthly life, is a being at home with the Lord—(2 Cor. v. 8). He expresses the same conviction in this epistle to the Philippians. Christ is his life.* He distinguishes life in this sense from his life in the flesh.† Christ is his true life; he has no life except in him, none apart from him. In him that which alone he calls life, has its being; it has its root in union with Him. And as Christ, having laid aside human infirmity, having risen and ascended to Heaven, now reigns triumphant in the Divine Life, living in the power of God a life exalted above the reach of death; so also is this true of the life of the believer, as being one with His own, yea one with Himself. And hence Paul concludes, that although even now, while abiding in the flesh, he has Christ for his true life; yet death is for him gain, inasmuch as through the laying off of the earthly existence, this true life, which has its being in Christ, shall be freed from the checks, hindrances, and disturbances by which it is still clogged, and shall attain to its complete development. He knows, that with his departure from the earthly life, will commence his "Being

* Chap. i. 21.

† Ver. 22.

with Christ"* in that more perfect sense, his presence with Him as an object of immediate vision. Hence this is the goal of his desires.

But there are two mistakes, against which the example of the Apostle warns us, viz.: the declension, on the one hand, of that longing after the blessedness to come, which, as we have seen, is inseparable from the very nature and essence of the Christian life; and on the other, such a one-sided morbid predominance of this desire, as to weaken the exercise of patient submission to the will of the Lord. As to the first, we remark, that it is not alone in the enjoyment of earthly gratifications, which we should ever remember are in their nature transitory and but a shadow and pledge of those higher, eternal, heavenly joys, that the Christian may suffer the loss of this heavenward desire. Even his activity, in a calling entrusted to him for the promotion of the kingdom of God, may likewise so absorb him as to obscure the consciousness that he has here no abiding home, that his native country is in Heaven. He labors as if this work upon earth, which is but the beginning of a higher activity destined for eternity, were to be consum-

* Chap. i. 23.

mated here, as if it were already the work of eternity. Hence the thought that here all remains fragmentary, that nothing reaches completion, nothing attains to its end, withdraws itself from him; and death surprises him in the midst of his labors, consecrated though they be to God, as an unexpected unwelcome guest, who finds him unprepared. He is called away before he has finished his account; and instead of following joyfully the summons to a release from the sufferings of time, his heart clings fast to that earthly scene of labor which he too reluctantly quits, to those happy results of his labors on which he has set too high a value. Here may be applied the admonition of the Lord: "Rejoice not that the spirits are subject unto you, but rather rejoice that your names are written in Heaven." This heavenward longing is ever the salt of the Christian life, amidst all sorrows, all joys; in every season of repose, in every labor. But on the other hand, this very desire, in itself perfectly right, but needing to be restrained by submission to the holy will of God, and by fidelity to the calling appointed us in this earthly life, becomes itself an error when it oversteps these boundaries. Thus arises a one-sided direction of feeling, an impatient haste for the call, which should be waited for with a steadfast unfaltering patience. In this undue, all-engrossing longing after the eternal, the importance of the earthly life and of its duties, connected as they are with the eternal, is forgotten. Earthly joy, and earthly labor, lose the proper value assigned them in the divine arrangement. That which the goodness of God has given us for the moment, as an earnest and a preparation for the higher joys of the future, is impatiently and unthankfully contemned. The consciousness is wanting, which should be ever present with the Christian, that for the redeemed united in fellowship with Christ, even here below, the earthly of whatever name, whether it consist in receiving or in doing, whether it be enjoyment or labor, is transformed into the heavenly. The temper of mind, which Paul's words exhibit, holds the just medium between these two extremes. The longing after the life of eternity, after the immediate society of the Lord, continues to be the ground-tone of his soul, which no other can overpower. Through all the pressure of his labors in the service of God, this longing after the heavenly rest is not smothered, is not crowded from his heart. But he is far from an over-hasty impatience, which cannot await the end of the earthly conflict; far also from that more refined selfishness, which cannot endure to strive and labor longer for the salvation of others, and be still deprived of the quiet enjoyment of heavenly blessedness. Though to depart from the earthly life, and to be present with the Lord in a perfect personal union, be the goal of his desires; he is yet ready to deny this desire, the offspring of what is noblest in man, in order to labor still upon the earth and to strive for the salvation of his brethren. If it may serve for the advancement of the work entrusted to him by the Lord, he is willing yet longer to forego the object of his wishes, and to be still a wanderer upon the earth. Love to his brethren, who may need him for their salvation, enables him to present this offering willingly; and thus drawn hither and thither by these two directions of his desires, he remains submissive in either event to the will of the Lord. But one desire remains fixed and unwavering, to which all others must yield, viz.:—That Christ may be glorified through him, be it by life or by death. Let us hear his own noble words:— "As I earnestly expect and hope, that in nothing

I shall be put to shame; but that with all boldness, as at all other times so also now, Christ may be glorified in my body, whether it be by life or by death. For Christ is my life, and death is gain. But if my life in the flesh is fruitful for my work, —then I know not which to choose. For I am in a strait betwixt the two; desiring to depart and to be with Christ, for this is far better."* Still he gives that the preference, which may most subserve the welfare of the churches which he has founded; and hence he adds: "But to abide in the flesh is more needful for your sake." His love to the churches inspires him, at this moment, with the confident expectation (which indeed as he well knew might prove illusive, but which as we have reason to believe, was fulfilled by his release from his first imprisonment at Rome) that God would again restore him to their society, for the strengthening of their faith and the furtherance of their joy. "And having this confidence, I know that I shall remain, and shall continue with you all, for your furtherance and joy in the faith; that your glorying on my account may abound in Christ Jesus (i. e. the exulting joy which Christ should bestow upon

* Chap. i. 20–23.

them by the restoration of Paul to their society)—through my coming again to you."

We here observe in Paul the example of submission to the divine will, both in doing and in suffering, in self-sacrifice and self-preservation. Surrendering his own will, he is ready for whatever God may appoint, be it life or death, as may best promote the work committed to him. Filled with longing after the home of heaven, he yet seeks not death. For the good of the churches he willingly remains on earth. Only in the faithful performance of the duties of his calling is death to him a divine gift, to be joyfully received from the hand of his Heavenly Father. Thus, in life and in death, it is alike the same operation of self-denying love. This example of Paul has primary and immediate reference to the martyr's death, the genuine Christian martyrdom purified from all admixture of fanaticism. But is it not also applicable to death under all circumstances, and in the ordinary course of nature? In that case too, there may be either that spirit of selfish impatience, which, though it ventures not presumptuously to sever the thread of the earthly life, is not willing to endure it longer; or that selfish love to the earthly life, which clings to this with its whole strength, which cannot let it go when the call of God requires. Thus, in both these respects, does Paul's example of a love consecrated to God in self-sacrifice and self-preservation, find an application here. Thus should each Christian become, in respect to living and dying, one with him in spirit, though his calling may not lead to the martyr's death.

Furthermore, we here observe in Paul that higher degree of self-renunciation, which manifests itself not in the relinquishment of temporal earthly interests, which could have no attraction for a Paul, but in the relinquishment of the higher interests of the immortal spirit. It is a heavenly aspiration, which enkindles the lofty soul of the Apostle. His desires reach beyond the narrow limits and perplexities of the earthly existence after the immediate vision of Christ, in him to find the full satisfaction of all the wants of the higher life. This to his spirit would be the highest good. Yet even this he foregoes. He is ready to relinquish what is dearest to himself, to forego the satisfaction of that heaven-born desire, to abide still longer in the strange country, to labor still upon earth, striving and suffering for the welfare of others. What is best for the churches, for the furtherance of God's kingdom upon the earth, is more to him than what is best for himself. Now this example is not to be restricted to its merely literal application to a precisely similar case, viz.: when one who is penetrated with longing for the heavenly father-land, is yet obliged to bear the load of the earthly life for the welfare of others. It may in its spirit be applied to every case, where the Christian is called on to relinquish a course of life most favorable to his own spiritual interests, a life of tranquil and collected thought consecrated to devotion; and to plunge into a whirl of business, toil, and conflict alien to the higher inclinations of his soul, but where he is appointed to labor because the salvation of others requires it. In this respect also, Paul furnishes for our imitation an example of self-denying love, which shuns no sacrifice for the good of others. How often have Christians, who should be the salt of the earth, by withdrawing themselves from its corruption acted in contrariety to this example!

Let us present still another view in which all Christians have an interest. While Paul stands thus between life and death, whereon is his confidence grounded? He, if any one, was a faithful laborer in the work of the Lord. He was conscious of having labored more than all others in the proclamation of the gospel. But he knew at the same time that this was not his own work, but the grace of God accomplishing all through him; as he himself says: "I have labored more abundantly than they all; yet not I, but the grace of God which was with me." When higher considerations demanded his self-justification, against suspicions which might shake the confidence of the churches in him, he could indeed recount what he had done and suffered above others for the cause of the Lord (2 Cor. xi. 22, 23). He could appeal to the memorials of what he had endured in the cause of Christ, in whose fellowship he suffered, and whom he followed in his sufferings; to the marks enstamped in his body by the Lord himself (such as soldiers and servants were accustomed to bear) as proofs that he was Christ's servant. (Gal. vi. 7). Still, when looking towards the close of his earthly course, he reviewed his life so abundant in labors and sufferings for the Lord, as it now spread out before him, he felt that he could not rest his confidence on what he had himself done. All seemed marked with imperfection. He was constrained to forget what he had already accomplished, and to fix his eye upon what still remained for him to do. It was with him a law, to forget what was already done, what lay behind, and to press continually forward towards the prize of the heavenly calling. It may, at first view, seem strange, that Paul expresses himself so doubtfully on the great point, whether he shall attain to the victor's crown of life, shall share in the blessedness of the resurrection. It seems to be in conflict with that divine confidence which breathes through the whole epistle, and which he expresses elsewhere in regard to the object of his hope ; as e. g. in 2 Tim. iv. 8 : "I have fought a good fight, I have finished the course, I have kept the faith." But this conflict belongs to the nature of the Christian life, and is ever recurring in the experience of the believer. Does the Christian look away from himself to his Redeemer, to the delivering grace assured to him, the unchangeable word of promise ; the goal towards which all his efforts tend, seems then an object of perfect certainty. Does he, on the other hand, test his own life by the standard of perfect holiness; his confidence then finds no firm ground. Defects and blemishes present themselves everywhere to his view; and this all the more the farther he has advanced in holiness, the more his sight has been sharpened by the power of the Holy Spirit, to recognize the model of divine holiness in its application to himself, to test by comparison with this pattern his inner and outer life in its nakedness and poverty, to penetrate into the hidden windings of his own heart. Hence Paul expresses himself so doubtfully in reference to what he is in himself, and has himself accomplished. What he has performed seems to him nothing, and he only looks forward to that which remains to be done. He is penetrated with the consciousness, that he is yet far from having attained perfection. But the ground of his confidence is this—that Christ has taken him into fellowship with himself, that Christ has apprehended him; and hence he hopes, that as he has been apprehended of Christ, he also shall apprehend the prize set before him by Christ. He knows that Christ, by whom he has been apprehended, will not leave unfinished the work he has himself begun in him; but, if he truly surrenders himself to his hands, will conduct it through all conflicts to a glorious completion. Let us hear his own brief, expressive words: "Not as though I had already attained, or were already perfect; but I follow after, if I may apprehend that for which I am apprehended of Christ Jesus." So important does Paul deem it to set forth, in the clearest light, this truth drawn from his own self-consciousness and from his Christian experience, and to bring it home to the Christian as a warning against self-satisfaction, self-righteousness, and spiritual pride! Hence he adds yet again: "My brethren, I count not myself to have apprehended. But this one thing I do; forgetting the things which are behind, and reaching forth unto the things which are before, I press towards the mark for the prize of the high calling of God in Christ Jesus." Paul was conscious in himself of the utter insufficiency of man's own righteousness, not merely of that to which the vital principle is yet wanting, that which precedes regeneration and exists independently of Christianity; but of that also which possesses already in faith the true element of sanctification, without having as yet brought this to complete development and realization. Hence, the only immovable ground of his confidence is Christ, by whom he has been apprehended; and whom he, surrendering himself wholly to his hands, seeks ever more to apprehend and to appropriate as his own. Looking away from himself to Christ, his assurance is complete; looking back upon himself, he must doubt and waver; and thus he is driven to look away from himself, and to cling more and more firmly to Christ, from whose love nothing can separate him. It is the righteousness of God in Christ which alone avails for him, and is all-sufficient for him; as expressed in the words of this epistle, "The righteousness which is of God by faith." To him Christ is all. All centres in this one point, that we enter into his fellowship and make it more and more our own; that we follow him by bearing the cross, thus following him as crucified for us; that in fellowship with him we die to sin, to self, and to the world; following him in the entire renunciation of selfish and earthly interests, not shunning to partake in the fellowship of his sufferings; and following him also as the RISEN ONE, experiencing in ourselves the power of his resurrection—the resurrection to an imperishable and divine life above sin, death, and nature, proceeding from him to us, inasmuch as he has apprehended us and we apprehend him. So Paul expresses it, in a passage which we must more particularly consider hereafter: "That I may know him and the power of his resurrection and the fellowship of his sufferings, being made conformable unto his death; if by any means I might attain unto the resurrection of the dead." We have already explained how the Apostle could here express himself with so much apparent doubtfulness, consistently with his divine assurance of faith.

It was the greatest joy of the Apostle, that his imprisonment must necessarily serve for the furtherance of the Gospel; since it was becoming more and more known, that no guilt of any kind could be imputed to him, that it was but his zeal for the faith which he preached that had drawn upon him all his sufferings. A cause, to which a man like Paul felt constrained to offer up everything, could not fail to command attention. To this was added the impression necessarily made upon those, who were witnesses of the enthusiasm with which he testified in behalf of the Gospel, of his steadfastness, and of his whole course of life. The knowledge of this had spread, as he intimates, by means of the soldiers from the imperial guard (the *castris praetorianis*) who held watch by turn in his dwelling, among their comrades and from these still more widely. Other Christians were stimulated by Paul's example to preach the Gospel with similar zeal, and to bear their testimony with like fearlessness. Thus increased the proclamation of the truth.

But Paul himself makes a great distinction among these preachers of the Gospel. Thus, when expressing his joy at the increasing promulgation of the Gospel, he says, "Some indeed preach Christ from envy and strife; but others also from good-will: the one out of love, knowing that I am set for the defence of the Gospel." The latter, he means to say, connect with their love to the Gospel also love to himself. They know that they can cause him no greater joy, than by laboring that the Gospel may be promoted by his imprisonment; for they well know that this is the one object of his life, and that he himself regards it as the divinely appointed end of all that he is to do and to suffer in life. "But the others," he proceeds to say, "out of party spirit, not sincerely, supposing to add affliction to my bonds." The first is clear. But who are those who sought, by the preaching of the Gospel, to add affliction to Paul's imprisonment, and whom he charges with insincerity? We must here take into view what he afterwards says in reference to this distinction, viz. that by the one class Christ was preached in truth, by the other only in appearance. Are we to suppose that these men, without personal love to the Gospel, without personal conviction of its truth, preached Christ for no other reason than to add to the hardship of Paul's situation, and to bring him into greater danger by the wider extension of the Gospel in Rome; thus rendering him, as the origin of it all, more obnoxious to the Roman civil power? It appears at once how unnatural, and intrinsically improbable, is such a supposition. If they could thus bring Paul into greater peril, they would by so doing plunge themselves into equal danger. Can it be imagined that one would play so hazardous a game, simply from hatred to another? He who at that time did not himself believe in the Gospel, must be enlisted against it; and would certainly not have given himself up to the business of preaching it, merely as the means to another end. We must seek, then, another explanation of this difficulty. When it is said of an individual that he preaches the Gospel only in appearance, this need not be understood as necessarily meaning that he has no concern whatever in regard to the subject of his preaching; that he has no personal interest in it, no conviction of its truth, that he makes use of it only as a means to another end. It may mean that he preaches it, not in its purity and completeness, but mingled with foreign elements; that although an interest in it cannot be denied him, yet this is not perfect and unalloyed. In this sense it might be said of such an one, that he does not preach the Gospel sincerely. Paul might therefore express himself thus, in regard to persons who testified of the Gospel of Christ from real conviction; yet did not preach the whole, unmixed, pure Gospel in its completeness, but an adulterated, mutilated Gospel. And when, moreover, he says of such, that they were actuated by party zeal and hatred against him, desiring to add new affliction to his sufferings; it is not necessary to understand by this, that their witness for the Gospel was mere pretence, a form of hypocrisy to which the circumstances of the time afforded no occasion and no ground; but that their ruling motive in preaching was not pure love to the Lord, that it was their aim, consciously or unconsciously to themselves, by their manner of preaching to give offence to Paul, and to raise up for themselves a party against him.

If now we look farther into the history of the development of Christianity in this its earliest period, and investigate more minutely, in the history of the Apostolic church, the peculiar relations and opposing influences under which Paul's labors were prosecuted, we shall soon be in a position to determine with greater exactness what we have here remarked in general. We know that Paul had to contend with opposers, to whom all that has here been said is applicable. There were those who did indeed acknowledge and preach Jesus as the Messiah, but a Messiah in the Jewish sense; who acknowledged him, not as that which he has revealed himself to be, the only ground of salvation for man; who in connection with the one article of faith, that Jesus was the Messiah promised in the Old Testament, still adhered to the Jewish legal position; who understood nothing of the new creation of which Christ was the author, and to whom faith in Jesus as the Messiah was only a new patch upon the old garment of Judaism. These were the opposers, with whom we so often find Paul contending in his Epistles. Of such he might justly say, that they preached the Gospel not purely and sincerely, but only in appearance; for they were indeed far more concerned for Judaism than for Christianity, and their converts became rather Jews than Christians. Of such he might also say, that they sought to form a party against him, and to add affliction to his bonds; for these persons everywhere seem chiefly animated by jealousy of Paul, through whom the Gospel was preached to the heathen world as freed from all dependence upon Judaism, and standing upon its own foundation. They oppose themselves to him on all occasions, contest his Apostolic dignity, seek to encroach on his sphere of labor, to draw over the people from him to themselves, from that pure and complete Gospel to their own mutilated one. And it need not surprise us to meet such even in Rome; for Paul's Epistle to the church at Rome, written some years previous to his imprisonment there, shows us in this church, consisting chiefly of Gentile converts, a small party of such judaizing Christians who were in conflict with the rest. It was a matter of course, then, that when the pure Gospel in the sense of Paul was preached by the one party, the other, provoked to rivalry, should rise up in opposition and seek to give currency to their own corrupted form of the Gospel.

We must now endeavor to understand fully Paul's position towards these opposers. Rightly understood, it will furnish an important rule for our own application in many cases. In the first place, it is clear that these men were personal enemies of Paul; and that in their efforts to promote the Gospel, their object was to frustrate the labors of the Apostle, and to form a party of their own in opposition to him. What self-renunciation must it then have required, to enable Paul to rise so entirely above this personal relation, that forgetting the design against himself he can rejoice with his whole heart that the One Christ, whom it is his sole desire to glorify, is preached, even though it be by his personal enemies! Thus everything pertaining to self gives place to that all-absorbing love to the Lord, and to those for whom He gave his life. How rare are the examples of a love so heaven-like, so purified from all selfishness! One may even be animated by real zeal for the cause of the Lord, and yet that zeal be impaired by personal considerations. If others, who from unfriendly designs against him personally labor to frustrate his efforts, are used as instruments for the promotion of the same holy cause,—he cannot rejoice over it. That this is accomplished not through himself, but through those who are acting against him, weighs more with him than the common interest of Christ's cause; and instead of giving him joy, it becomes a source of vexation, jealousy, and envy. He is not concerned alone that Christ should be preached, but that He should be preached through him; or at least through his followers, through those who in every respect harmonize with him, and acknowledge him as their teacher in Christianity. Least of all can he endure it, when Christ is preached by those who take a hostile attitude towards himself; whose most zealous effort it is to lessen his reputation, to throw suspicion on him as a teacher, to draw men away from him. To this course of conduct, which we so frequently observe among men, the Apostle's self-denying zeal forms the most striking contrast. He acted in accordance with the principle which he himself lays down in 1 Cor. iii. 21, showing in what light the preachers of the Gospel should be regarded. "Let no man," says he, "glory in men;" the highest, the only concern is the honor of Christ, and the salvation of believers.

Thus would the case be easily understood, and thus might Paul's conduct serve as a pattern for us, if it were merely a matter of personal variance and not a strife respecting the nature of the doctrine itself. But, as we have already seen, this was by no means the case. It is a false form of doctrine, placing itself in competition with the preaching of Paul and in opposition to it, a mutilated and corrupted Gospel that is here spoken of. Those opposers, it is true, acknowledged Jesus to be the Christ, but not in the sense in which Paul received him. It was not in his full character as the sole ground of salvation, the central point of the whole Christian life, as he was regarded by Paul. Hence, we might naturally suppose, Paul could not rejoice that Christ was preached through them, since it was not in his pure complete character. And indeed, we see Paul dealing elsewhere quite differently with such persons. How indignantly does he combat them in the Epistle to the Galatians! He does not acknowledge them as preachers of the same Gospel; he declares that there is no other Gospel than that preached by him; that they do but pervert the Gospel of Christ. In opposition to those who would connect with the Gospel the righteousness of the law, he says: "If righteousness come by the Law, then has Christ died in vain" (Gal. ii. 21). And in this Epistle also he expresses himself, as we shall see hereafter, with equal severity in regard to this false tendency. How then is Paul's manner of speaking in this passage, to be reconciled with what he says in those other cases? It is only necessary to discriminate carefully the different relations, presupposed by this diversity of judgment and conduct. Paul manifests this warmth of displeasure, only in cases where the Gospel had already gained a foothold among the Gentiles, and where that judaizing tendency threatened to pervert it, by intermingling so much of Judaism as wholly to obscure its peculiar nature. For it could only cause him grief, that the blessing of which a people were already in full possession, should be marred and taken from them. But it was otherwise here, where he speaks in relation to the heathen who as yet knew nothing of Christianity. Those preachers bore witness at least to the fact, that Jesus had appeared to found the kingdom of God in man; they testified of his history, the facts of his life, his resurrection, his ascension to heaven; although they did not themselves comprehend, nor were able to unfold to others, how much was involved in all this. Now Paul could not but rejoice that the common foundation of the Gospel, a knowledge of the person and history of Christ, should be made known to those who as yet had heard nothing of them. This was the first thing; the starting-point from which all the rest must proceed. If this personage, these facts, became once known and could be made objects of attention, here was a basis for still further labors. If Christ, the crucified, the risen, the ascended Christ, could but once be known and acknowledged, those who had gone thus far might, from this starting-point, be led onward to find still more in him; might be assisted to search deeper and deeper into the inexhaustible riches which are in Christ. Paul could therefore rejoice that Christ was preached, even though it was in this defective manner; though the doctrine of Christ were not presented in its purity and completeness. There are, it must be remembered, different degrees in the knowledge of Christ. More or less may be found in him. We must therefore deal with no one as an enemy, because he has at first but little; but must help him on from this point that he may gain more, that he may become conscious of those greater treasures, which he needs but rightly to develop out of that which he has already received; "till," as Paul expresses it in the fourth chapter of the Epistle to the Ephesians, "we all come to the unity of the faith and of the knowledge of the Son of God, unto a perfect man, unto the measure of the stature of the fulness of Christ." Paul's conduct, in this case, is in accordance with the principle indicated by Christ himself. When the disciples met with one, who attributed to Christ's name a power whereby evil spirits might be cast out, they refused to allow the use of that name by one who had not as yet become his professed disciple, and who had not made common cause with them by uniting himself to their company. But Christ rebuked them, in those memorable words: "He who is not against us, is on our part." "Not to be *against* Christ" contained in itself the germ, from which the positive, "to be *for* Christ," might yet be developed. Though he did not as yet know Christ as the Apostles knew him, though he was still ignorant of the true significance and power of this name, and connected many errors with his belief in its efficacy; still it was a germ of faith not to be despised, a germ from which more might develope itself and be developed. It was a point of connection, from which one who had gained so much could be led still farther. It needed only that he should be brought to perceive what was implied in this, what must be presupposed in the strange efficacy of the invocation of Christ's name. Who must HE be, from whose name such power proceeds! In what relation must He stand to the kingdom of evil, when his name exercises such sway over evil spirits! It is clear that he who had once acknowledged so much was already in a position, from which, with patience and love, he might be conducted farther and farther in knowledge and faith. From him who as yet was only not an opposer of Christ, who knew and recognized Christ in some single point of view, might be formed by building upon that which he had already attained, a positive disciple of Christ. But he might also, if not thus dealt with, if too much was required of him with his present attainments, be wholly repelled. Not only might he be hindered from farther progress by such harsh treatment, but be unsettled in regard to what he had already gained; and thus the germ of truth, in its yet imperfect development, might be wholly destroyed. Against such a course we are warned by those words of Christ; and with these Paul accords when he rejoices that Christ was preached and acknowledged, even though in an obscured and defective manner.

We have already, before we saw clearly the relation which these opposers held to Paul, and regarding them merely in general as his personal enemies, felt ourselves constrained to acknowledge him as a model of self-denying zeal for the cause of Christ. We are now, after a more full and careful development of this relation, called upon to contemplate this great model under a new light. It implies a love purified from selfishness far above what is common, to be able to recognize and with joy to acknowledge the work of the Lord, when performed through the agency of a personal enemy. But the power of this purified and exalted love reveals itself under still another view, when the truth lying at the basis of even an erroneous representation of the Gospel is recognized and welcomed; when the seed of truth is not rejected and spurned on account of the error, even though this may oppose itself to a purer, more complete, unmutilated conception of the Gospel as preached by ourselves, but is welcomed as one step towards the farther advancement of the Gospel. But how seldom do we find a like example! One who is capable, it may be, of joyfully welcoming the work of the Lord when advanced by means of a personal enemy, might yet not be able so far to forget self as to accept with cordial love, and to use for the common cause of the Lord, the truth lying at the bottom of the errors promulgated by his opponent, especially when in direct opposition to the pure truth which he is himself conscious of preaching. How different would it have been in the church, how many divisions might have been avoided, how many who have labored only to oppose each other might have labored together for the spread of the Gospel; how many who have hardened themselves in their errors, and have lost by degrees even so much of divine truth as they had embraced, might from that partial view have been led farther and farther in the knowledge of the truth, and have been gradually made free from the bondage of error; if Christians, instead of demanding everything at once, with the impatient zeal of a love not sufficiently purified from self, had been more observant of the various grades of faith and knowledge, and had nurtured them with a forbearing charity!

The principle here expressed and acted on by Paul admits of numerous applications. But to what form of Christian labor is the immediate reference here? To that which most exactly corresponds to Paul's peculiar vocation, that where the first concern is to establish the church upon the one foundation, which is Christ; we mean the missionary work. Here should all, after Paul's example, fix their aim upon this single point, to make CHRIST everywhere known, to testify only of Him. Here, then, should the strife respecting differences in the form of representation and differences of creed find no place; and amidst all diversities on these points, there should be a union of labor for the one object of proclaiming Christ.

/hatever differences may exist on other points, ιould all be made an offering to his cause. To ιch one it should be matter of rejoicing that ırough others also, and even such as in his view ave a less perfect knowledge of Christ, He, the reat centre of all, is made more and more widely nown. We may apply this example of Paul in still another view. There are times in which the church, even where it is already firmly established, is called on to exercise anew a missionary activity; times in which the ideas and tendencies to which Christianity first gave being and currency, though still exerting their influence upon society, yet deny their connection with Christianity, and even array themselves against it. Such are times of wide-wasting apostasy; when the culture, which has grown up under the fostering care of Christianity, rises up in opposition to it,—an opposition which may, however, have been first called forth by the impure mixture of human institutions with Christianity. Such periods occur in the history of all religions, when reason, matured to self-dependence, disunites itself from the faith under whose guardianship it has been nurtured. Nor could Christianity escape this fate.

It is subject to the same laws and conditions as all things human; and distinguishes itself only in the manner in which, by virtue of its divine nature and character, it rises victorious from all such conflicts. For whilst other religions find in such conflicts their grave, to Christianity they prove but the transition points to a resurrection, in increased purity and glory, in the energy of a renewed youth. In such times, as well as in periods of missionary labor, does the principle "that CHRIST alone be preached" find anew its application. The sole concern then is, that Christ should first of all be brought near to the souls estranged from him, that he may draw them to himself and make them subject to him. Here too, all cannot be achieved at once; but gradually, from the common relation to the one Christ, must the way be opened for a union among souls reclaimed to him from the most diverse forms of error. Here must Paul's example of magnanimous denial of self be our guide. Here every one, who is animated by the same spirit with the Apostle, must rejoice if "in every way CHRIST is preached," even when he cannot but feel that the manner leaves much to be desired.

Still another trait of Paul's Christian character

is presented to us, in his manner of accepting the gifts sent to him by the Philippian church. There is in the natural man a false striving after independence and self-reliance; a pride of self-will, which not seldom decks itself with noble names, the influence of which is to make one ashamed to accept from others gifts of which he stands in need, lest he should humble himself before them. A still worse development of the same radical fault of the natural man is seen, when the gifts indeed are accepted and enjoyed, but there is a disposition to forget them again, to shun the remembrance of them, to acknowledge no indebtedness to others through fear of seeming dependent, of humbling one's self before them. But the Apostle is penetrated by the consciousness, that all are related to each other as the members of one body, and should abide in this mutual dependence upon one another as members under one head, Christ Jesus. He knows that the growth of the whole body, from the one head which guides animates and connects all the members, can only then be truly promoted, when all the single members are ready, as instruments of the one head, mutually to sustain and forward each other in spiritual and in temporal things, to work together in love and unity. This is beautifully expressed by Paul in the Epistle to the Ephesians (iv. 15, 16): "That we grow up into him in all things, which is the head, even Christ; from whom the whole body fitly joined together, and compacted by that which every joint supplieth, according to the effectual working in the measure of every part, maketh increase of the body unto the edifying of itself in love." Christ is here presented as the one to whom the whole development must tend; the aim of all is to grow up into true fellowship with him, to receive him wholly into themselves, to become full of him. He is equally the one, from whom the whole growth up into him can alone proceed; from whom issue all the vital energies, the living juices; from whom alone all the members can receive life and direction. Christ so works upon the whole body, that by means of the different members through which his vitalizing influence flows, using each in its appropriate manner, he works through the whole. And hence the growth, proceeding from him and tending up to him, can truly prosper only when all the members alike yield themselves to him; and under his guidance, in mutual dependence and mutual influence upon each other, abide together in closest union. The Christian should ever bear in mind, that our various necessities, and the means of supplying them, are distributed in varying modes and proportions through the different members, in order to keep them in a state of mutual dependence and reciprocal influence; so that no one may break loose from his connection with the whole, thinking to maintain an existence by himself, and that mutual necessities may serve continually for the furtherance of mutual love. The Christian will not be ashamed, therefore, of a dependence upon others springing from such a connection; but will recognize it as the law naturally arising from the relation of the members to one another. As he who gives rejoices in having received from God means which he may use for the aid of the other members; regarding it as a loan for this purpose from their common Lord, as a medium for the manifestation of that love which the Spirit of God has poured into the hearts of believers, that being the mark by which the disciples of the Lord, the members of his body, are to be known: so he that receives rejoices far less in the brief temporal service of the gift, than in the heavenly temper expressed in the bestowal,—in the love, that vital principle of the church, which manifests itself therein. He knows that it is for the highest good of the giver himself; who thus, by deeds of love, sows in the earthly life what he shall reap in life eternal; who thus manifests in his works the spirit which makes him meet for life eternal. So Paul represents the Christian relation, in his own manner of accepting the gifts of the Philippian church, when he says: "I rejoiced in the Lord greatly that now at length your care for me hath flourished again,"—rejoiced, that now after long-endured privation, they are placed once more in a condition to fulfil the wish they had ever felt, to care for his temporal wants;—"because ye have ever cared for me, but ye lacked opportunity. Not that I speak in respect of want." And in conclusion he says: "Not because I desire a gift, but I desire fruit"—the fruit which springs for them out of such manifestations of love—"which may abound to your account"—may be laid up for life eternal.

Again: Paul here gives us a model of the genuine Christian character, in his demeanor in respect to external things. The Christian, in the power of the Lord through which he is able to do all things, proves his independence of the world, and his supremacy over it, by his ability to endure joyfully all the privations which the Lord lays upon him, in the circumstances of his lot, in what is required of him by his calling. His soul, filled with the divine life, cannot be bowed down by earthly want. Subjected to privation, he so much the more feels and proves his inward mastery of the world. But the Christian is far also from that self-imposed mortification of the flesh, in an imaginary spirituality, which nevertheless only serves for the satisfaction of the fleshly mind; for in the Holy Scriptures, all which does not proceed from the divine Spirit, all which comes from our own will, therefore every form of vanity and spiritual pride is ascribed to the flesh. (Coloss. ii. 23.*) He is far from imposing upon himself privations, in order thereby to merit any-

* This passage, incorrectly translated by Luther, stands thus in the original: "which (namely, the principles spoken of in vss. 21 and 22) have indeed a show of wisdom in self-chosen spirituality and humility and mortification of the body, but have no worth, serving only for the satisfying of the flesh." Ex. MSS.

thing before God or man, though submitting joyfully to those which God lays upon him; but accepts with humble gratitude whatever God may bestow upon him above what is required for his absolute wants. The Christian's greatness is ever built upon humility. His independence of the world, his supremacy over it, consists in just this, that in every condition of want or abundance he is the same, neither depressed by want nor seduced by prosperity into worldliness and vain-glory; that he uses both alike in order to make known that divine life by which he is raised above the world. This is the spirit which Paul here exhibits when he says, that though he needs not the Philippians' gifts of love, he still rejoices in that love which prompted them; and when to this he adds the testimony, that he has accustomed himself to all changes of condition; that he knows how to adapt himself equally to all circumstances, whether of want or abundance, through the power of Him who animates him. "I have learned," says he, "in whatsoever state I am, therewith to be content. I know both how to be abased, and I know how to abound; in every respect and in all things I am fully instructed, both to be full and to be hungry, both to abound and to suffer need. I can do all things through Christ which strengtheneth me." Such is true Christian fortitude and greatness of soul, whose basis is humility.

SECTION SECOND.

After having thus carefully considered Paul in his then existing circumstances and temper of mind, let us now turn our attention to the state of the Philippian church, and to what Paul has to say in reference to this, by way of warning and counsel for the future.

We will first take a general view, and from this pass to particulars.

It is customary with Paul to commence his letters, with a recognition of whatever is praiseworthy in the church to which he is writing. In this appears his wisdom as a spiritual guide. The confidence of men is far more easily won, and a hearing secured for whatever one has to say in the way of admonition and rebuke, if it appears that he nowise overlooks or undervalues what is good in them, that he does not willingly find fault, but is ready to acknowledge every real excellence with cordial approbation. Good and bad, moreover, stand frequently in close connection with each other. The good lies at the foundation; but the evil mingles its disturbing influence with the good, and hence it is through the latter that we can best reach and remedy the former. It is in the clear perception of this relation, and in the skilful use of it for the correction of error, that Paul manifests his wisdom. Of this a striking example is furnished in the first epistle to the Corinthians. Thus Paul regards whatever of real value he finds already existing in the churches, not as something produced in them from themselves and by their own agency, but wrought in them by the Spirit of God, that Spirit which has begun to transform them into new men. Hence he feels himself constrained to thank God for that which He has wrought in their hearts and in their lives by his grace, before he offers to Him the prayer, that what He has already wrought in them He will more and more purify, carry it forward, and bring it to perfection. Upon the good which already exists in them he builds the hope, that they will ever continue to advance in goodness, even unto perfection. Not indeed upon the good as a work of man can he rest such a hope. He knows too well the weakness of man, too well how subject is everything human to constant change. But this is the ground of his hope, that in this beginning of the Christian life he sees not the work of man but the work of God. He thus builds his hope upon the truth and faithfulness of God, who will certainly carry forward what He has begun, through all conflicts and trials, safely to its consummation. It is not God's way to do things by halves. Thus too does Paul begin his letter to the Philippians; thanking God for their living fellowship in the gospel from the beginning up to the present hour; and then expressing the confidence, that He who has begun in them the good work will also carry it on to its completion. In this it is indeed always presupposed by Paul, that they likewise will do what belongs to them, by yielding themselves to the power of God which works nothing without man, albeit man without it can work nothing; as in the eleventh chapter of the epistle to the Romans (v. 22), he represents the continued manifestation of God's goodness in men as conditioned on their continuing in His goodness, and thus susceptible of the grace of God by truly yielding themselves up to its influence. It is on this connection between the divine and the human he founds the exhortation, "to work out their salvation with fear and trembling; for," he adds, "it is God who worketh in you both the willing and the doing, of his own good pleasure." It is here assumed that the salvation of man is conditioned upon his own conduct. He is himself to work out his salvation. And yet Paul always represents the salvation of man as something which can be accomplished only through the grace of God, as the work of God in man. But he adds, in this passage, a more exact designation of the temper of heart with which they should work out their salvation, viz., "with fear and trembling." This would not be appropriate if he were speaking of what lay merely in the hand of man, in which case all would depend upon his own strength. It is because Paul is conscious of the weakness and insufficiency of all human strength, because he presupposes that man can do nothing without God, and must constantly watch over himself, lest through his own fault he lose the aid of divine grace, without which all human efforts are in vain; it is for this reason that he designates this temper of mind as one of fear and trembling, as the feeling of personal accountability and helplessness, of insecurity and instability in ourselves, by which we may be ever admonished to continual watchfulness, and to ever-renewed waiting upon God as the fountain of all our strength. Hence, as the ground of such an admonition, he appeals to this consciousness that we can of ourselves do nothing, that it is God who alone bestows upon us the power to will and to perform what is needful to our salvation; that all, indeed, depends upon his sovereign will. This feeling of dependence, the ground-tone of the Christian life, is ever to be maintained. It is this which must combat the presumption of a vain human self-reliance, which, finding itself deceived in the result, so easily gives place to dejection and despair.

All the admonitions which Paul gives the Philippians in reference to the Christian walk, are comprehended in this one; that they should "walk in a manner worthy of the Gospel of Christ." And what is required of them in their position, in the midst of a corrupt world, he points out in chapter ii. 15–16. Inasmuch, he says, as they are called to live as children of God in the midst of a corrupt world, they are called to maintain unsullied, amidst all the defilements of surrounding pollution, that divine life of which, as children of God, they have become participants, and to show forth its glory in contrast with the perverse generation in which they live. The terms "crooked and perverse," in which Paul describes this wicked generation, have reference to the perversion of the original godlike nature, which can be restored only through the new creation. So also, as children of God, they are to shine as lights, as radiant luminaries in the world of darkness. Whilst all around them is darkness, here alone shall all be light. So indeed does Christ say to those who belong to his kingdom, that they are to be the lights of the world, just as He is the Sun who sends his light into this dark world, its light in the highest and only true sense. Thus what He is, is communicated to those who enter into fellowship with him, and they too through him become the light of the world. This light shines in the holy walk of Christians, and thereby do they testify of Him who is light itself, and in whom is no darkness; thereby do they glorify him and lead others to acknowledge and honor him; as Christ himself has said: "Let your light so shine before men, that they seeing your good works may glorify your

Father which is in Heaven." They are to testify of that which is life, to show forth the true life in this world of death.* Everything which men, in accordance with the revelation of the law written in their consciences through the impulses of their moral nature, are accustomed to account moral and virtuous, belongs also to the peculiar stamp of this new divine life, in which the children of God manifest themselves as such. All must find its fulfilment here; only that is done away which proceeds from the disturbing influence of sin; as Christ says, that he "came not to destroy but to fulfil." Hence it is the conclusion of Paul's exhortation,† that their minds be directed only to "what is true"—(true and good being in the biblical sense one and the same, the truth here appears as that which penetrates and gives direction to the whole life; all has its root in the truth, the true is the divine)—to "what is becoming, what is upright, what is chaste, what is lovely, what is of good report, whatever is virtue and whatever is praise." Thus it is implied by Paul, that the divine life must manifest itself in an amiable form before men; and he ap-

* As in some MSS. "holding forth the true life."

† Chap. iv. 8.

peals to what they had learned from his instructions, and had witnessed in the example of his own life. Although, as we have seen above, he was far from holding his life to be entirely pure and perfect, yet he could with confidence assume the essential correspondence between his life and teachings, and that his conduct did not give the lie to his instructions. And thus he was able, without untruth or self-exaltation, to hold up to the Philippians the example of his own course among them as an admonition to them. Self-exaltation is the less to be attributed to him here, as he was himself fully conscious, that whatever in his own conduct he proposed as their example was only the work of grace, the fruit of the new creation in him. So may the Christian when made aware, by a comparison of his earlier and later life, of having gained the victory over the old nature in any of its sinful tendencies, be fully conscious of this and freely rejoice over it; for this is no self-exaltation. He knows that it is not to his own nature or his own strength that he is indebted for it; that the Spirit of God, the Spirit of Christ has wrought this in him; and therefore the consciousness of his victory only impels him to praise and to thank Him, through whose power he has attained it. And at the same time, he feels himself constrained to acknowledge how much still remains for him to contend with, and with the Apostle, whose words we have quoted, to forget what is behind and press continually forward.

The church at Philippi, as we have already remarked, had been called to endure many forms of persecution. It was necessary that Paul should exhort them to steadfastness under these trials. How then does he express himself? It is important for us to bring this out clearly, for it is applicable to all the conflicts which Christianity has to encounter in all times. They should in no wise suffer themselves to be terrified by their adversaries;* "which to them is an evident token of perdition, but to you of salvation and that of God. For to you it is given, for the sake of Christ—not only to believe on him—but for his sake to suffer also." What is the full import of these words? This is best shown by contrast. Had the opposers of the gospel succeeded in terrifying the Philippians, it would thereby have been made manifest how much these opposers could effect, what power

* Chap. i. 28, 29.

they possessed; the weakness of the Philippians would have appeared, and the cause which they served might have seemed an impotent one. Or it might have seemed merely a contest between man and man, their opponents being the stronger and they the weaker party. Their demeanor would have been a testimony, how much was still wanting to them of that divine power which was to manifest its efficacy in believers; how much, therefore, they still lacked of the genuine life of faith. But while they did not suffer themselves to be terrified by those who warred with weapons of the flesh, this was a proof that they were in the service of a divine cause, victorious over all human opposition; that a power of God wrought in them against which no human force could avail. The conflict with their adversaries served but to test and to approve their faith, and their power through faith. It was a proof of the vanity of their opposers' efforts; even as Christ reckons it as one of the works of the Holy Spirit, to lead men to the conviction that the Prince of this world has been judged, and hence can accomplish nothing farther through his instruments (Jno. xvi. 11). Thus through them is this power of the Holy Spirit manifested. So far, it was an evidence of the condemnation drawn upon themselves by those who warred in the service of the Prince of this world. But for the Philippians, it was for that very reason a certain proof, a pledge, of their salvation; for the faith which remains steadfast in conflict is indeed assured of salvation. It was the pledge that the power of God, through which they were able to hold themselves unterrified by their adversaries, would also lead them through all conflicts to final salvation; as in the works of God one thing answers to another, one guaranties the other. And thus Paul gives special prominence to the thought, that this is not of man; that it is no illusive human proof, but a factual proof given by God himself. It is one part of this proof, that to them it was given of God to suffer for Christ's sake. For whoever follows Christ in his sufferings, must needs follow him also in his glorification. Paul had said, "for Christ's sake;" intending at first only to say, "for Christ's sake to suffer." But he would bring out the full meaning of this with a stronger emphasis. He therefore interrupts himself, and says, "not merely to believe on him, but for his sake to suffer also." He who believes in Christ is, so far as his faith approves itself to be genuine, certain of the blessedness of heaven. But it is also requisite that this faith approve itself to be genuine, by assuring its possessors against all fear of their adversaries; and by giving them the power to follow Christ in his sufferings, as in general its office is, in all things, to bring them into fellowship with Christ. And therefore, although with faith in Christ, as the root of all else pertaining to the Christian life, all else is given so far as regards the principle whence it springs, the germinating power which produces it; yet to suffer for Christ is more than merely to believe on him, inasmuch as through these sufferings the power of faith makes itself manifest, approves itself to be genuine. For one might suppose himself the possessor of that genuine faith, and yet the result, when he was found to shun a participation in the sufferings of Christ, would prove the contrary. In another view, indeed, suffering is of less account than faith. For there might be a suffering too, which was not true Christian suffering, as not proceeding from the life of faith, that faith which works by love. As Paul says in 1 Cor. xiii. 3; "And though I give my body to be burned, and have not charity, it profiteth me nothing." The same is true, in general, of the relation of faith to the entire course of Christian life in its outward manifestation, of the relation of faith to good works. It everywhere finds an application, in a greater or less degree, in respect to the relation of the inward to the outward, of the internal feeling to its manifestation in action.

The Christian life is no instinctive, unconscious one. It follows not feeling alone; but demands, everywhere and in all things, an intelligent discrimination between what is of God and what is not, in respect to all the relations of life; between what accords to the will of the Lord, to the spirit and nature of Christianity, and what is in contrariety thereto. It cannot subsist, cannot fulfil its mission, without a considerate conscious process of scrutiny and discrimination. As flesh and spirit are still coexisting in the Christian, and are ever in conflict with each other; so the power of discriminating what proceeds from the one or the other, what is in accordance with the one or the other, is continually needed, in order that the Christian may not yield to the suggestions of the flesh, when he thinks he is acting according to the impulses of the spirit. Of such a testing and discriminating process there was especial need, in churches established in the midst of the Pagan or Jewish world; since there, Christianity, contending with existing customs relations and views of life which were the product of another spirit and principle, was now first to bring into existence a new creation, in which Christ should be all in all. Here of course the question must often arise: What does Christianity require? In what respects does the heathen or Jewish point of view stand opposed to it? Wherein may the Christian conform himself to the world, wherein may he not? For this reason Paul, in his practical admonitions to this church, desires for them especially increase in knowledge,* in the faculty of perception; that they might test things which differ, the good and the bad, the true and the false, that thus they might avoid the one and choose the other. Paul assumes that, for this work, the diligent exercise of the faculty of perception is necessary; that such a power of discernment is the fruit of unremitting exercise of the Christian judgment. In like manner in the epistle to the Hebrews (v. 14), it is accounted one of the attributes of the state of Christian maturity, that, through

* Chap. i. 9.

the exercise of the organs of spiritual perception, a readiness had been attained for distinguishing good and evil. But if, on the one hand, there are objects of knowledge and judgment where all depends on the exercise of the understanding, where he who is most practised in thinking possesses also the best judgment, and is most fully guarded against error; yet in regard to the objects which the Apostle has in mind, those pertaining to moral duties, this is by no means the case. In general, we shall often find how much the judgment is here biassed by the direction of the will. The mistakes which lie at the basis of action, and errors in conduct, arise not so much from defect in the thinking faculty, as from selfish inclinations which sway the judgment. And this is particularly the case with Christianity, which assigns wholly new objects as the aim of life. To know what is in harmony with it, LOVE must be the controlling and directing principle of the whole life. The more entirely one is animated by love, the more will his moral judgment be in harmony with Christianity. A soul, however well practised in thinking, will miss the right, if not thus quickened and the eye of the spirit made single by love. To this we must add, that Christianity is no mere law of the letter, which establishes only single general rules of duty, according to which all single cases of conduct are to be determined; but it is a law of the Spirit, which makes known to each individual his peculiar mission in life, that very one which the Lord has appointed him to fulfil, and what is needed for its fulfilment. No one can prescribe to another, what from his standpoint, under his appointed relations, it is his duty to do; but it is LOVE, that spirit common to all, which makes known to each in particular what is duty for him, and in reference to this leads him to make the necessary discrimination. To love, therefore, Paul here gives the first place, and ascribes to its quickening presence the knowledge and capacity required for distinguishing the good and the bad, the true and the false; as he himself expresses it, "that your love may more and more abound in all knowledge;" meaning, that *therein* its effect is seen,—that increase of knowledge in the fruit of more abundant love. But as here the theoretical proceeds from the practical, the new direction of the judgment from the new direction of the will, of the moral disposition; so is the theoretical in like manner to react upon the practical, the enlightened judgment upon the conduct. Hence Paul adds, as the object to be thus attained, that they should continue "pure and irreproachable" in their Christian walk, until all shall appear before the Lord; "being filled with the fruit of righteousness, which is by Jesus Christ, to the glory and praise of God." Thus Paul here designates righteousness, not as something to be gradually acquired; but on the contrary, it is presupposed as something inherent in their fellowship with Christ, flowing out to them from him, as produced in them by his Spirit. He contemplates the entire Christian life as the fruit of this righteousness; not speaking, as in other passages, of single fruits in single works, but of the whole Christian course in its connected unity as one fruit, and that the fruit which is produced by Jesus Christ. That from him all proceeds, that through him all is accomplished, is the very thing which gives to such a life its peculiar stamp. This it is which is truly well-pleasing unto God, and by which God is truly glorified, even as the whole life of Christ was a glorifying of God in our nature. But it is also clear from what has been said, that though, as a whole, the Christian life is thus represented as a fruit of righteousness produced by Jesus Christ, yet with this are presupposed many different stages of development, many separate results of the reciprocal working of the practical and theoretical, of the moral disposition and the judgment, as necessary to the production of this sum total; just as the fruit of the tree, to follow the image chosen by Paul, does not attain to its full form and maturity at once, but through many preparatory stages in the natural process of development and growth.

We have already observed Paul's manner of contemplating the church as a whole consisting of various members, whose growth is dependent on the harmonious co-operation of all. But many hindrances stood opposed to this harmonious action; and these could only be overcome gradually by the subduing power of the Christian spirit. Only by degrees, and through the power of that spirit, could this higher unity be formed out of the conflicting elements existing in the church. Some of these originated in national differences, in the modes of thought peculiar to those of Jewish or of pagan parentage. From these arose those opposite leading tendencies, of which we shall speak more particularly hereafter. There was also the difference of rank and wealth, which threatened to impair the spirit of oneness and equality in the Christian body. And, finally, there were differences arising from peculiarities in constitution and mental endowments, all which had been brought by Christianity into its service. Hence the diversities in the operations of the Holy Spirit, animating these different natural gifts; and hence too the diversity of spiritual gifts, and of offices connected with them, in the church. From all these diversities collisions might arise, disturbing the unity and harmony of the church; each might wish to magnify what was peculiar to himself, and thus self-exaltation and disunion follow, occasioning strife among the members. Here then, in order to secure that unity in the church which belongs to its nature, all must be harmonized by the victorious spirit of love. It is clear how important and necessary, under these relations, were Paul's reproofs and admonitions, his warnings against self-exaltation and disunion, his exhortations to humility and harmony. Let us examine this point more particularly. If they would make his joy complete,* they must be of the same mind,

* Chap. ii. 2, 3.

having the same love, being of one accord, of one mind; nothing must be done through party spirit or vain ambition, but in humility each must esteem others better than himself. But how are we to understand this? One's judgment of another is not within the control of his own will. How can he esteem his brother higher than himself, if this is not in accordance with the truth; if he cannot but perceive in himself excellencies which are wanting to the other, and defects in the other from which he is himself free? How can it be required of him to do violence to his judgment? Is he to practise deception upon himself? Is humility to be grounded upon falsehood? Most certainly not. If one should endeavor to work himself into such a judgment of others in comparison with himself, or should express such a judgment without really thinking so, this would be mere hypocrisy in a grosser or more refined form. But there is here pre-supposed, as resulting from the full development of the Christian life, a pervading temper of heart, of which such a judgment of one's self in comparison with others is but the necessary and natural expression. The Christian's love will lead him first of all to discern what is good in another, to discover even in his blemishes his peculiar gifts, that in which he is really superior to himself; while, on the other hand, through a self-scrutiny sharpened by the Spirit which quickens him, he detects with rigorous exactness his own faults. And this self-rigor, united with love, will give leniency to his judgment of whatever may obscure the divine life in others. Thus a readiness to take such a position, in respect to others, as is here represented, will not be a mere casual thing with the Christian, something produced in him from without by external influence; but is the spontaneous result of the internal process of Christian development. And this manner of viewing one's self, in relation to others, will appear likewise in his whole conduct in regard to them. The idea is of course excluded that one should make himself the centre of all, referring everything to himself, and thus regarding all others as existing but for him. It is clear how greatly others will in this way rise in his estimation. This spirit of love and humility will manifest itself in his deportment towards others; and hence it is added: "Look not each one upon his own things, but also on the things of others." Let each one be ready to subordinate his own interest to that of others, to deny himself for the welfare of others. Paul says, "also," although the form of the first clause would not lead us to expect such a limitation. But he adds this "also" because it is not his aim wholly to exclude the care for our own interests, but only to oppose the tendency to make this predominant, to allow it to swallow up all else. Of course he here speaks only of human, worldly interests, which one is bound to sacrifice for the best good of others; for in regard to that which is the highest and properly real interest of each one personally, his own soul's welfare, the cultivation of the inner man for the life of eternity, no such contrariety can exist, no such requirement of self-denial can be made. But does this seem to conflict with what we have previously remarked of self-denial in reference even to the higher interests of the spirit? By no means. The true, the highest interest of the spirit, that it should be ever growing in self-denying love, in purification from all selfishness, thereby becoming ever more meet for the kingdom of God and eternal life, this must always be promoted by such sacrifices, even in reference to what we call the higher interests of the soul, which yet are not its highest interest. In reference to such a temper and course of conduct, Paul now presents, as the type and pattern, Him after whom the whole Christian life in its spirit and conduct should be moulded, CHRIST HIMSELF. "Let the same mind be in you which was also in Christ Jesus: who, being in the form of God, did not eagerly claim equality with God;* (so, we think the Greek is more truly expressed than in Luther's version;) but emptied himself, taking the form of a servant, being made in the likeness of men; and being found in fashion as a man, he humbled himself, becoming obedient unto death, even the death of the cross. Therefore also hath God exalted him over all, and hath given him a name which is above every name, that in the name of Jesus every knee should bow, of beings in heaven and upon the earth and underneath the earth, and every tongue confess that Jesus Christ is Lord to the glory of God the Father."

That we may rightly understand the use here made of the example of Christ, as the model after which the Christian life is to be formed, we must

* In his appearance on earth, as understood by Neander; see page 103, line 3.—TR.

first endeavor to bring the model itself clearly and distinctly before our minds. Before the eye of the Apostle stands the image of THE WHOLE CHRIST, the Son of God appearing in the flesh, manifesting himself in human nature. From the human manifestation he rises to the Eternal Word (as John expresses it), that Word which was, before the appearance of the Son of God in time, yea, before the worlds were made; in whom before all time God beheld and imaged hinself; as Paul in the Epistle to the Colossians calls him, in this view, the image of the invisible, i. e. of the incomprehensible God. Then, after this upward glance of his spiritual eye, he descends again into the depths of the human life, in which the Eternal Word appears as man. He expresses this in the language of immediate perception, beholding the divine and human as one; not in the form of abstract truth, attained by a mental analysis of the direct object of thought. Thus he contemplates the entrance of the Son of God into the form of humanity as a self-abasement, a self-renunciation, for the salvation of those whose low estate he stooped to share. He whose state of being was divine, who was exalted above all the wants and limitations of the finite and earthly existence, did not eagerly claim this equality with God which he possessed; but, on the contrary, he concealed and disowned it in human abasement, and in the forms of human dependence. And as the whole human life of Christ proceeded from such an act of self-renunciation and self-abasement, so did his whole earthly life correspond to this one act even to his death; the consciousness on the one hand of divine dignity which it was in his power to claim, and on the other the concealment, the renunciation of this, in every form of humiliation and dependence belonging to the earthly life of man. The crowning point appears in his death,—the ignominious and agonizing death of the cross. Paul now proceeds to show what Christ attained by such self-renunciation, thus carried to the utmost limit, by such submissive obedience in the form of a servant; the reward which he received in return, the dignity which was conferred upon him.

Here too is presented the universal law, laid down by Christ himself, that whoso humbles himself, and in proportion as he humbles himself, shall be exalted. Now it is of itself apparent that He who, according to Paul's teaching, was in his own nature elevated above all, the first-born over the whole creation, He through whom and in whom all was created, could not as such be exalted. But, as already intimated, it is the image of the One Christ uniting in himself the divine and human, which is here before the mind of Paul. Of this Christ in humanity it might be predicated, that He is as man exalted above all,—the glorified Son of man. And this his exaltation subserves no selfish interest. He finds his exaltation in the salvation of fallen beings. This was its end, in this indeed it should consist, that by the universal acknowledgment of Him as Lord and Saviour and subjection to Him as such, God might be glorified in Him and through Him; glorified in the triumphant establishment of his kingdom. What application then is to be made of this example, in the connection in which the Apostle introduces it? As Christ aimed only to subserve the salvation of men, so should Christians be ready to labor thus for the salvation of their brethren. As Christ offered up all for the salvation of men, so should Christians also be ready to offer up all for the salvation of their brethren; to give up everything for others, in order to secure their highest welfare;

thus in self-humiliation and self-renunciation following their Lord. So shall the life of the Christian too, from its first spiritual beginning, from the first act of faith, be a continuous self-abasement and self-renunciation. And this being the ground and condition of Christ's exaltation as the Son of man, so shall the same be, for believers who thus follow Christ, the ground and condition of their exaltation, till they come to share the full glory of Him whom they follow. We may compare this with a similar development of the same thought by Paul in 2 Cor. viii. 9, where he says of Christ: "Though he was rich, yet for our sakes he became poor." To the "being rich" corresponds the "being in divine form," the "being equal with God," in the passage before us; to the "becoming poor," the self-renunciation and self-abasement in the human servant-form, in its full extent as exhibited above. In the passage just quoted, this is used as an exhortation to that benevolence which sacrifices its own, subjects itself to privations, in order to relieve the necessities of others. It is based on the general thought, arising from a contemplation of the life of Christ, that each one should be ready to give up and to renounce all that he has for the highest good of others; the beneficent and condescending spirit of self-denying Christian love, which pervades the whole Christian life in all its acts. And in this general form is the thought conceived in the passage before us. It is this which characterizes Paul as a moral teacher; that with him the specific is in all cases carried back to the highest, deepest, most comprehensive; that his special admonitions, in regard to the Christian life and character, have for their basis the general fundamental ideas of the whole Christian life, all centering in the example of Christ.

The church at Philippi needed the Apostle's admonitions and warnings, especially in reference to the obstacles with which Christianity, in its process of development, then had chiefly to contend. This process has in every age its peculiar obstacles to overcome; and it would be easy to show a certain affinity between these opposing influences, although different periods give rise to different forms. But here an important distinction is to be made. There may be spiritual tendencies and teachings, which come into direct conflict with the peculiar essence of Christianity; a case where no reconciliation is possible, but the choice must be for the one or for the other; and where the decision for the pure Christian tendency, must manifest itself in firm adherence to the one and steadfast rejection of the other. Somewhat different is it with those tendencies, which unite with the sincere acknowledgment of Christian truth only a slight remaining influence of former views, and which form in their successive stages the gradual transition to pure Christian truth. This is especially true of the obstacles, with which Christianity had then to contend in its process of development. As it was from Judaism the transition was made to Christianity, so did the first important obstacle to its process of development, arise from the intermixture of views brought from the Jewish standpoint. It is to these views that the distinction above stated must be applied.

Such a predominance of the Jewish spirit did exist, through which the consciousness of the peculiar nature of Christianity was essentially repressed and stifled. Jesus was indeed outwardly acknowledged as the Messiah; but there was wanting the true import and power of such a conviction. He was made, after the Jewish conception, a carnal Messiah with carnal hopes. As Christ, after the miracle of the loaves, said to those who followed him with false views (John vi. 26), that it was not because they had seen the miraculous signs,—tokens of the manifestation of the divine in the world of sense, intended to point to a nature in itself divine made known through these tokens,—that not for these did they seek him, but because they had eaten of the loaves and were filled, that only sensual want attached them to him; so in these Jews of whom we are now speaking, there was the same lack of the divine sense, of the feeling of higher, inward, spiritual need. With them too it was only a mere sensual want, which led them to believe on Jesus. And though they differed from the Jews to whom Christ spoke in this respect, that they were not led by this similar fleshly tendency to open opposition against Jesus as the Messiah, but sought on the contrary to be outwardly united to him, yet no important advantage was thus gained. For while the former would not believe on a Jesus, who did not satisfy their physical necessities; the latter, believing in Jesus as the Messiah, yet made him nearly such an one as those had desired, and such as Jesus refused to be. With this one article, of faith in Jesus as the

Messiah in the sense here given, they united, as we have already seen, a strict adherence to the entire legal position. Not Jesus the Messiah was to them the sole ground of salvation; but in the observance of the whole Law, and in circumcision, they sought for righteousness and salvation. Not the righteousness which comes from within, from faith, was the object of their desire; but a righteousness which comes to man from without.

It is clear that where an opposition of this kind existed, there could be no agreement, no reconciliation. The true Christian spirit alone could make the decision, between a carnal or a spiritual Messiah; between a righteousness grounded on faith in the Redeemer alone, or in the Law and its works; between the transformation effected by the divine life, working from within the reformation of the whole man, or a mere external change in outward conduct; between God's work or man's work, humble acceptance of divine gifts, humble surrender to Jesus as the Saviour, or a carnal Messiah with the admission of the desert of one's own works. It was because the question for the new churches was of just such an unconditional opposition, between what was Christian and what was unchristian, that Paul felt himself obliged to present the case so strongly, and to testify so earnestly against those erroneous views. "Beware of dogs" (the term in the original expressing the shameless effrontery of these opposers of the truth); "beware of evil workers" (those who would supplant the Christian by the Jewish stand-point); "beware of the concision." But how is it that Paul here speaks of circumcision, which he nevertheless regarded as a divine ordinance for a specific period, in so contemptuous a manner? Circumcision was in his estimation a divine seal, by which the theocratic people were separated, as the divinely consecrated race, from the nations abandoned to idolatry and its attendant abominations, for the purpose of conducting to that fellowship with God which should one day embrace all humankind. To him it was, as he says in the Epistle to the Romans, an outward symbol of the new relation to God, into which Abraham entered by virtue of his faith (Rom. iv. 11); and emblematical of that inward spiritual circumcision, the circumcision of the heart in the spirit, of purification from the excrescences of sin, which alone constitutes a true people of God, through which alone the conception of a people of God can find its realization. But if now, as was the case with those Judaizers, justification and salvation were sought in this outward circumcision, as such; if indeed to faith in Jesus as the Messiah, who in his true character was the author of all righteousness, circumcision was to be added as something higher, as the real source of true righteousness; then was Paul bound to expose, in the most emphatic manner, the utter worthlessness of such an external act in reference to the object to be attained. No words could seem to him too strong to represent the perverseness of such a view as this; which could ascribe that to the external and sensuous, which can only be produced from within, by virtue of what is wrought within upon the spirit, through the imparting of a divine life. Hence he calls circumcision, in opposition to such an over-estimation of it, a concision, a self-mutilation; and in the Epistle to the Galatians, with a similar contemptuous allusion to the abuse of this abrogated rite, he expresses the wish that those who made so much account of circumcision would practise it to what extent they pleased on themselves, provided they would but leave other Christians in peace. Certainly that which seems to Paul as something so unchristian and perverse, and excites in him so much indignation, must have reference not merely to circumcision, that single peculiarity of Judaism, but to everything external and sensuous regarded as a ground of justification, of sanctification, of salvation; for, as such, it stands in direct opposition to that worship of God in spirit and in truth, which springs solely from the inward act of faith. This contrariety to the true Christian principle is expressed in the succeeding words, "For we are the circumcision." That is, they are not the truly circumcised, but their miscalled circumcision is a mere excision, a self-mutilation. We are those who really deserve this name; we Christians are the truly circumcised; "we," he adds in proof of the assertion, "who serve God in the spirit, and glory in Christ Jesus, and have no confidence in the flesh." We must endeavor to develop the meaning of these weighty words. "To serve God in the spirit," forms the direct opposite to a worship of God connected with sensible, external, earthly things, and dependent thereon; a worship which has not its spring in the spirit within; as when one supposes that he can honor

God by receiving circumcision or by any external legal works, be they religious or moral, by any single acts whatever of external worship.

The true worship of God, on the contrary, Paul describes as one which proceeds from the spirit; meaning by this only such as can proceed from the renewing and sanctifying of the human spirit, by nature estranged from God, through the Holy Spirit which Christ alone imparts. Only thus can the spirit of man, being led back to fellowship with God and made a temple of God, become the sanctuary where God is worshipped aright; and then the whole life and conduct of the spirit is one act of divine worship. But as the redemption attained through Christ is here presupposed, as faith in the Redeemer and fellowship with him is the root and fountain of all, Paul therefore connects therewith the "glorying in the Lord;" i. e. glorying in such a manner as excludes all pride of human glory; a glorying in self-abasement; a glorying, to wit, only in Christ and in that which we are in him, which has its ground in him, for which we are indebted to him, and hence (what is but the counterpart of this) not placing our confidence in anything human. Paul presents his own case as an example in this respect to his Philippian brethren,—a proof of the sincerity of his teachings and admonitions. He appeals to the fact that he himself, as a born Jew brought up in the strictest Pharisaism, had lived in the exactest observance of the Law and yet had become convinced that all this could contribute nothing towards his cleansing from sin, his justification, sanctification and salvation; on which account he had renounced all this, in order to find all in Christ alone. He says that as respects the righteousness of the Law, he was blameless. This is said not merely of the requirements of the ceremonial law, but also of moral action so far as it meets the eye of man; both being comprehended under the term law. In all this Paul had been blameless. In the sight of men he was without blemish. What he says applies not less to what is called rectitude among men, than to a piety which consists in particular religious acts. Although Paul satisfied the claims which men could rightfully make on him, yet it availed him nothing. When, through the light of the Spirit, the true nature of the divine law and true self-knowledge dawned upon his mind, he seemed to himself, with all this blamelessness before men, not less a sinner on that account, wanting that true divine righteousness in which all flows out from God, and all has reference to Him. He is the true end and aim of the whole life; while all that men call rectitude does not rise above the world. Hence he says, implying the insufficiency of all this: "But what things were gain to me, those I counted loss for Christ. Yea, and I count all things but loss for the excellency of the knowledge of Christ Jesus my Lord: for whom I have suffered the loss of all things, and do count them but dregs that I may win Christ." He would say here, that everything which formerly was in his view a distinction,—as descent from the theocratic nation, legal piety, blamelessness in a legal view,—all this now appears to him a disadvantage, so far as he should rest his confidence thereon and be thereby drawn away from Christ. Christ having now become all to him, all else must give place to Christ. All else, high as it may be in itself, must appear loss if it occasion the loss of Christ, whom none can gain but those who seek and desire Him alone; for that very knowledge of Christ, itself sufficing for all, in itself comprehending all, outshines and eclipses all beside.

And hence Paul says, that for the sake of Christ he has willingly suffered the loss of all; that he casts all else away as worthless in order that he may win Christ, who supplies to him the place of all. It is his whole concern to be found in Christ,* to stand in fellowship with him. And he thus contrasts that divine righteousness, founded in this relation and proceeding from inward faith, with a righteousness which comes from without, proceeding from the works of the law, a merely human attainment secured by human efforts. In his view, all here depends ON KNOWING CHRIST. This knowledge is, in the Pauline sense, not something merely intellectual, not a mere matter of speculation, not certain specific articles of faith respecting Christ as they are speculatively developed and handed down; but, on the contrary, as shown in the following words, it is a knowledge which takes root in the life, a matter of personal experience, the believer's inward perception of Christ as the Son of God and his Redeemer. Paul then brings forward into special prominence the power of his resurrection, which of course presupposes the announcement of him as the Crucified, his sufferings

* Verse 9.

for the redemption of man from sin. This prominence he gives to the power of Christ's resurrection, as being the factual proof of the redemption effected by him;—as furnishing the evidence, in a glorified personality, of that imperishable divine life imparted to humanity, by virtue of the redemption from sin and consequent death; a life passing over from him to all who through faith stand in fellowship with him,—the beginning in them of a new divine life, to penetrate more and more their entire being, till they shall become wholly assimilated to it in soul and body. And hence he adds, "to know the fellowship of his sufferings;"—that is, how we are to follow him in sufferings, in order that we may more and more become partakers of the divine life in fellowship with the Risen One. He then sums up all in this, "to be made like unto him in his death;" to apply to one's self the image of his death, in order to attain to the fellowship of his resurrection. We must here refer back to what we have already said on this point, in another connection.* Thus we have here, in one view, all which pertains to the Christian life, all which constitutes the righteous-

* See p. 90.

ness of the Christian, in opposition to the requirements of legal piety or mere human rectitude.

The same class of persons is probably meant when, in a subsequent passage,* after having proposed his own conduct as an example to the Philippians, he warns them with deep sorrow against many who walk far otherwise, and whom he designates as enemies of the cross of Christ. Here, however, the reference to this class of persons cannot be proved with equal certainty. The words "enemies of the cross of Christ" may be applied to many classes of persons. They may be understood of such as, indeed, acknowledge Jesus the Crucified as their Saviour; but who still show by their manner of thinking and acting, even though themselves unconscious of it, that they are enemies of the cross of Christ. It might be of such as take their stand, consciously, as open enemies of the cross of Christ. This might at that period proceed from two different points of view, which indeed are found recurring in every age; viz. from the position of the wisdom-seeking Greeks, of whom Paul says that Jesus the Crucified was to them foolishness, and from that of the sign-

* Verse 18.

seeking Jews, of whom he says that to them Jesus the Crucified was an offence. It may be the unbelief which comes from the pride of wisdom, from the pride of reason, from the pride of culture, or the unbelief of the earthly sensual man. But this open and conscious opposition cannot, as appears from the connection, be the one here meant. It is inconsistent with the manner in which Paul contrasts these enemies of the cross of Christ with himself. Against such open opposers it was not necessary thus to warn his brethren. The class first mentioned must therefore be the one intended. Still the words admit of several applications. This not open but rather unconscious enmity to the cross of Christ, may be conceived as taking either a practical or more theoretical form; as manifesting itself only in action, or in doctrine as well as in action. As respects the first, this again may be understood in a two-fold manner. It may mean such as are wanting in that humility, which must spring from the belief that we owe all to the cross of Christ, to Jesus who was crucified for us; in whose life the conceit of self-righteousness, by which the cross of Christ is disowned and disallowed, predominates even though this may not betray itself in the doctrines which they preach. But it may also mean those who are far from taking upon them their cross, and thus following Jesus the Crucified; whose life, still devoted to flesh and sin, stands in direct contradiction with the cross of Christ, with faith in that Jesus who for this cause was crucified that he might free humanity from sin, so that all who attach themselves to him should now be crucified to sin, to the world, to themselves. The whole carnal, sinful life of such persons, who, as far as in them lay, made void the very object for which Jesus was crucified, might be called enmity to the cross of Christ. We grant that what follows might also be understood, as directed against men of this carnal course of life. Still we are led by the connection, when compared with the preceding context, to refer it rather to an opposition manifesting itself in the doctrines taught as well as in the life, to that very class of Judaizing adversaries indeed, against whom Paul has previously spoken. These he calls enemies of the cross of Christ, because their standpoint is one to which Christ the Crucified is an offence, a stone of stumbling—though in them this manifests itself not openly and consciously, but rather in an unconscious and covert manner; because nothing was more offensive to them than that preaching which required them to ascribe salvation to the Crucified Jesus alone as their Saviour,—to ascribe all to Him alone; because they held to a legal self-righteousness in opposition to the cross of Christ. It follows from what has already been said, that the views and conduct of such persons were in direct contrast to the worship of God in the spirit; their religious service consisting only in external things, their tendency being wholly to the earthly and sensual. Such a religion brought with it no moral transformation, might co-exist with sin, nay, might form a union with it, giving to the service of sin a false security; as often, in the history of Christianity, we have seen these same tendencies gain a footing under cover of its name. He describes them as those whose god is their belly, those who in all things act merely from earthly impulses, to satisfy their sensual wants; a reproach which Paul often casts upon the judaizing proselytists, that they turned their preaching into a means of gain, seeking to extort by it what might serve for their own advantage. He describes them as earthly-minded, which is explained by the foregoing; and all their hopes were such as corresponded to this earthly disposition. They expected in the future world, as they did in the thousand years' reign promised by them, not that divine life of which the true Christian even here partakes under the veil of the earthly; but, on the contrary, they dreamed of an increased enjoyment of mere earthly pleasures. "Whose glory," he says, "is in their shame," i. e. who seek their honor in that which redounds rather to their shame; as indeed everything, which might seem to distinguish them above others, was in fact a derogation of the Christian life, a renunciation of true Christian excellence.

In contrast with these, Paul now presents the wholly heavenward mind of the genuine Christian, his wholly heavenward hope purified from every stain of sense. This divine life, already freed from earth, forms in its aim and tendency the opposite of that world-ensnared religiosity, cleaving wholly to the earthly. This earthly mind, Paul would say, must be far from us who are Christians; "for our conversation is in Heaven." His meaning is, that Christians, as to their life, their walk, belong even now to Heaven;

in the whole direction of their life existing there already. This he deduces from their relation to Christ, their fellowship with him to whom they are inseparably united, so that where he is there are they also. While here, they are sustained by the consciousness that Christ now lives in Heaven, manifested to believers, though hidden from the world. Thither is their gaze directed, as their longings rise towards a Saviour, who will come again from thence to make them wholly like himself, to fashion them wholly after his own glorious pattern, to transform them wholly into the heavenly. Hence Paul says: "From whence also we look for the Saviour, the Lord Jesus Christ; who shall change our vile body, that it may be fashioned like unto his glorious body, according to the working whereby he is able even to subdue all things unto himself." There is not presented here a resurrection, as a restoration merely of the same earthly body in the same earthly form; but, on the contrary, a glorious transformation, proceeding from the divine, the all-subduing power of Christ; so that believers, free from all the defects of the earthly existence, released from all its barriers, may reflect the full image of the heavenly Christ in their whole glorified personality, in the soul pervaded by the divine life and its now perfectly assimilated glorified organ. This heavenly form of the Christian hope, the fruit of faith in the risen and ascended Jesus, stands opposed not only to that comfortless unbelief, which makes man a perishable creature like to the brutes, and cuts off all hope of what is beyond the earth; but also, as intended in this passage, to that mere carnal hope which transfers the forms of earthly existence into the future life. Both are scions from one root, the tendency of the natural man; who, whether in the form of sensual grossness or of refined culture, can never escape beyond the narrow limits of time and sense; who has no organ whereby to perceive and comprehend the divine and heavenly. It matters not, therefore, in which of these two forms this tendency of the natural man develops itself; whether it entirely denies and rejects what it cannot perceive and comprehend, denies all personal duration beyond the earthly state, because able itself to conceive nothing beyond this earthly form of personality; or whether it degrades to its own sensual standard what it is either unable or indisposed to deny, and wholly carnalizes the hope which it does not reject. In every form of superstition there is something of unbelief, since that upward impulse of the spirit is wanting by which alone it is possible to rise to the superhuman and divine; hence the divine, as such, is in reality denied and the earthly set in its place. And in all the forms of unbelief there is something of superstition. Every form of unbelief has its idols. It seeks in the powers and outward phenomena of the world, what can only be found in God and in powers which are of God. What Paul says of the idolizing of worldly objects is true also of this, that it makes itself subject to the elements of the world. It clings with all the greater force to the earthly, because it is an utter stranger to all which can give true satisfaction to the spirit formed in the image of God. It strives all the more eagerly for earthly interests, because it has renounced the higher interests pertaining to the spirit, which are connected with its true home; and hence the earthly interest has swallowed up all other love, and all other desire, by which the God-related spirit is impelled. Christ, risen from the dead and ascended to heaven, whose life is hid in God and with whom in God our life is hidden (Col. iii. 3), to whom as our life we shall be like in glory when He, now hidden from the world, shall reveal himself in glory,—this, the believer's hope, stands in contrast with both these tendencies of the natural man.

We have spoken of the judaistic tendency existing at this stage of the development of Christianity, so far as this stood directly opposed to the pure Gospel and excluded all reconciliation. But there were also in the churches, such as were in a process of progressive development from Judaism, or some kindred stand-point, to the pure Gospel. These, far from being enemies of the cross of Christ, were filled with love to the Crucified Jesus as their Saviour; but they were still subject to many weaknesses in their faith, not being able to release themselves as yet from much which still clung to them of their former, not wholly extirpated Jewish views. Such persons, whom Paul is accustomed to contrast as "the weak" with the strong mature Christian, are often mentioned in his Epistles; those who still had scrupulous fears about partaking of meats offered to idols, and who, in regard to food and to the observance of certain days as holy, were still in bondage to the Jewish ritual. In these points they were unable to break loose at once from the yoke of Judaism. But did these persons then stand in the same relation as those first-mentioned? Should such as had come over to Christianity from another stand-point, the pagan; and who, though exposed to other dangers, could from that point make their way more easily to Christian freedom; or such as had advanced farther in the development of faith, had more nearly reached the maturity of manhood in Christ; should such withdraw fellowship from, and harshly repel these weaker, in many points less enlightened brethren? This would have been contrary to what Paul requires of Christian love, which bears patiently the infirmities of brethren. It would be to set bounds with impatient presumption to the operations of the Holy Spirit, who is able to lead on farther and farther those in whom He has begun to work; to sever at once the thread of development ordained by the wisdom of God, and alone conducting to Christ as from him it proceeded. How we are to regard and treat these subordinate stages of development, these minor differences, is taught by Paul in this epistle,—in few words indeed, but full of instruction. We must now endeavor to obtain a clear conception of their import.

After having, in a passage already explained, presented as the standard for all, that stage of Christian attainment which forgets everything hitherto accomplished; which, beginning with Christian faith, in entire devotedness to Christ strives ever towards the mark of the heavenly calling; he adds, "As many of us now as are perfect, let us be thus minded." This is the stage of the mature believer who has attained to full Christian freedom, who presses forward without hindrance in an ever-progressive development. "And if in anything ye are otherwise minded,"—otherwise, i. e. not in harmony with this principle,—"God will reveal also this unto you;" will also in that, wherein ye still think otherwise, reveal to you the right, and thus lead you to unity in adherence to this principle and in its application. Paul refers therefore to the great truth, that the Spirit of God which has revealed to them the light of the Gospel, will also carry on and complete this his revelation in them, even to that point of Christian maturity; that He will continually advance them in Christian knowledge; and where they are still in error and divided in opinion, there too will He yet make known to them the one true way. They should therefore not contend with overhasty zeal; as by this course one is easily estranged more and more widely from another, easily hardened in opposing views through obstinate adherence to what has been once adopted. Still less should they mutually condemn one another, but rather seek to preserve that unity of the Christian spirit which is above all these minor differences; while all submitting to the common guide, the Holy Spirit, should entrust themselves and one another mutually to Him, the best Teacher, to be led on continually under his guidance. As this work has in all the same divinely laid foundation, so should the farther development and the progressive purification of the divine work in each, be left to the operation of the Holy Spirit by whom it is first begun in each. There should be no attempt to do violence, by any external influence, to the peculiar development of another, which must follow its own laws grounded in his peculiar personality; or to substitute something forced on him from without, for the free development proceeding from within. This would be nothing else than attempting, by human arts of persuasion, (which yet have no power to penetrate to the inmost spirit, unless they find a point of connection in the existing attainments of the individual man) to accomplish that which can be wrought only by the Holy Spirit, that inward Teacher, whom all follow without constraint and in perfect harmony with their own freedom. It is only the action of the same leaven of divine truth, that can produce the same results in all; of that leaven which by degrees shall penetrate the whole spiritual life, purifying it from every foreign element. And if there is reference here to a REVELATION by the Holy Spirit, through which the believer is advanced in knowledge, it is based on the truth everywhere expressed or pre-supposed in the Holy Scriptures, that all divine things can become known only in the light of the Holy Spirit: as Paul elsewhere says, "No man can say that Jesus is the Lord, but by the Holy Ghost." But the idea of revelation in this passage nowise excludes the activity of human thought, which still farther develops and works out, according to the laws of human reason, what has been received by divine illumination. This activity of the human spirit is, however, pre-supposed to be one animated and guided by the Holy Spirit, who is the vital principle in the whole spiritual life; and hence all is here referred back to the Holy Spirit as the primary source, inasmuch as all is here the fruit of its illuminating, guiding and quickening influence; and all progressive Christian insight, whether immediately or mediately proceeding from the Holy Spirit, is comprehended in the idea of revelation.

We must now more particularly consider that which Paul makes the necessary condition of this result, viz. that all should yield themselves to the guidance of the Holy Spirit, and thus be led on by him in progressive Christian knowledge. But here it is necessary to inquire into the original form of Paul's words. The passage has been corrupted, by introducing into the text marginal explanations erroneously supposed to be the words of Paul. Divine Wisdom has not seen fit to guard against such corruptions in the course of ages, by a series of miracles, or by the authority of a visible church enjoying infallible guidance. But while free course was here given to natural causes, and thus such corruptions might occur through misapprehension, this was to become the stimulus to an independent spirit of inquiry, and to the cultivation also of all those mental faculties whereby we test and discriminate. By such exercise, under the guidance of the Holy Spirit, by the culture and application of that capacity to which we give the name of CRITICISM, and which is one of the natural endowments of the human mind, we were to learn to distinguish the true from the false, and by comparison to ascertain the original form of the Apostolic words. Even criticism, under the guiding and quickening influence of the Holy Spirit, belongs to the spiritual gifts of the church. By it we shall be able here to restore the true form of Paul's words; as by continued investigations, under the guidance of the Holy Spirit, a harmony of views in this respect may at length be attained throughout the church.

If like Luther we follow the later reading, we shall translate with him,—"At least so far as we walk after one rule whereto we have attained, and are like-minded." According to this, unity is here pointed out as that condition of which we have just spoken; it is an exhortation to unity. Such a thought, however, is quite remote from this connection. Unity is not the condition which the connection would lead us to expect; but, on the contrary, is that which results from the course of conduct required of the church by Paul. When all conduct, in reference to minor differences, as Paul according to our explanation has directed, unity will be maintained unimpaired in the church. Moreover, what is said of "the one rule" and of "the walking together in accordance therewith," of "being like-minded," does not suit well with the words "whereto we have attained." All had not as yet attained to the same grade of spiritual discernment. We find here, therefore, a combination of words unsuited to each other; and it is easy to perceive, how from false glosses appended in explanation of the obscure words (obscure when not rightly apprehended in their connection) "if we do but walk after that whereto we have attained" falsely regarded as an exhortation to unity, all the rest may have originated. We shall, therefore, following the oldest manuscripts that have come down to us, regard these as the genuine words of Paul: "if we but walk according to that whereunto we have attained;" i. e. if each one but faithfully applies to his own life the measure of spiritual discernment bestowed upon him. This then is Paul's meaning: the Holy Spirit will reveal to all whatever is still wanting to them in true Christian knowledge, and thus continually promote the union of their spirits, by purging away whatever foreign elements may still impair it; will from still existing differences develop a higher unity, if first of all that Christian fellowship, which rests upon the one common ground of faith, is firmly adhered to, and each one is careful to put in practice with strict fidelity his own measure of Christian knowledge, without contending with others about matters wherein they differ from himself. All progressive revelation of the Spirit, all new light of which man is made partaker, presupposes a faithful application of what has previously been given. Here too apply the words of the Lord, "He that hath, to him shall be given." How many schisms might have been avoided in the church, how many differences might, much for its interest, have been overcome and adjusted, if all had felt the obligation rightly to understand and apply the principle here laid down by Paul!

In Paul's Epistles, as everywhere in the Holy Scriptures, precepts, exhortations, and promises go hand in hand. This must be so, from the peculiar nature of the Gospel as distinguished from the Law. For as all promises are connected with some condition without which they cannot be fulfilled, and this leads to precepts and admonitions; so would these be of no avail were not the promise to the believer presupposed, that promise which ensures the power to fulfil what is required of him. Thus Paul begins with the words, "Rejoice in the Lord always; and again I say rejoice." He, the prisoner of the Lord, looking it may be to a near approaching death, finds reason to promise and to require an ever-abiding joy in the consciousness of fellowship with the Lord; to make joy indeed the ground-tone of the Christian life, to make the whole Christian life a jubilee of redemption. But with this connects itself the requisition for a Christian walk; since that joy in the Lord cannot exist, if the life of the Christian does not correspond to the law of the Lord, does not testify of fellowship with him. And since the Philippians, as we have already seen,* were placed in circumstances in which they might most easily be tempted to anger and retaliation, if the natural man were not held in check

* See p. 24.

by a higher power, Paul especially urges the admonition, "Let your moderation be known unto all men;" and adds, "The Lord is at hand," appealing to the consciousness that He is ever near.* This consciousness furnishes the motive to such gentleness under provocation. They walk in the sight of the Lord, and dare not give way to passion in the near presence of Him, who endured every wrong with heavenly patience and long-suffering. This consciousness that the Lord is near, will also restrain them from wishing to anticipate his justice, to take the work of retribution into their own hands.—But these words also form the transition to what follows,—to the requirement "Be careful for nothing." Here too we must take into account the miserable state of the oppressed Christians; and yet they were to be careful for nothing, in the consciousness that the Lord is near. Not all human care is forbidden by Paul, who himself, as we have already seen,† in this very Epistle lays claim to earnest human efforts. But

* This might indeed be understood as referring to time, viz. the nearness of his coming, towards which the Apostles and the apostolic age, overlooking all that intervened, directed their longing desire. But this idea, though appropriate in some points of view, is obviously less suited to the whole connection than the one which we have exhibited in the text.

† See p. 77.

such entanglement in cares as stands in contradiction with that requirement, "to rejoice always in the Lord,"—this is forbidden by him, from this should the conscious nearness of the Lord restrain the believer. Instead of indulging such care, he directs them rather to raise the soul to God, and all shall become light. The true meaning of these words appears from the contrast which follows: "But, in all things, make your requests known to God in prayer and supplication with thanksgiving." There is a carefulness which is inconsistent with confiding prayer to God, which excludes the spirit of filial supplication. Such a carefulness Paul forbids. As he had made the whole Christian life a joy in the Lord, so now he makes it also a perpetual prayer. The two stand in intimate connection. Neither can exist without the other. He does not require the suppression of those wants, the sense of which begets anxiety, but that the sense of want should take the form of prayer. Thus will the burdened spirit become lightened, and care of itself will fall away. Yet, although the Christian has wants to spread out before God in prayer, and much to ask of Him for the future, he still finds in every situation enough that calls for thankfulness to God, since all things work together for good to those who love Him. Paul had already enjoined on the Philippians, afflicted as they were, to rejoice always in the Lord; and in this it is assumed that there is nothing unreasonable in the requirement, that they should give thanks to God. The whole Christian life should be a prayer, the prayer of thanksgiving and of supplication, in the consciousness of grace received and the conscious need of renewed grace. Assuming that the Philippians followed these directions, he could impart to them the precious promise which assured their safety in all conflicts: "And the peace of God which passes all understanding, shall keep your hearts and minds through Christ Jesus."—What does Paul here say? What is the sense, so far as we can indicate it in brief, of his deep and sublime words? If the Philippians so conduct, then will that peace with God, which they have received from Christ, remain with them; that peace which is the fountain of all other peace; which can exist in the midst of conflict with the world, and can be disturbed by no other power; that peace of which Jesus spake (John xiv. 27), "Peace I leave with you, my peace I give unto you; not as the world giveth give I unto you." And hence he adds, for those whom he left behind amidst the conflicts of the world, the consoling promise, "Let not your heart be troubled, nor let it be afraid." This peace, as it has God for its author, Paul accordingly describes as a peace which is above all human conception. He who has this peace has more than he himself knows, more than he is able to set forth in thoughts and words. It is an overflowing heavenly repose, with which nothing earthly can be compared; which fills the spirit of him, who, having been reclaimed from disunion with the Infinite and the Holy One, is now conscious of being in harmony with Him. The power of this peace, says Paul, will conduct the souls that live in fellowship with Christ, safe and unharmed through all conflicts and assaults from within and from without. From this proceeds the groundtone of their thoughts and feelings, this is their protection, which avails against all human care. With this may be compared the words of Paul in the Epistle to the Colossians:* "And the peace of God rule in your hearts!" The peace with God

* Chap. iii. 15.

procured to the believer through Christ, the peace which has its life in God, of which they are assured in union with him,—that peace, amid all fluctuation, is the controlling, the determining element in the Christian life.

THE

EPISTLE OF JAMES,

PRACTICALLY EXPLAINED,

BY

DR. AUGUSTUS NEANDER.

TRANSLATED FROM THE GERMAN

BY

MRS. H. C. CONANT.

"Why call ye me Lord, Lord, and do not the things which I say?"

NEW YORK:
LEWIS COLBY & CO.,
122 NASSAU STREET.
1853.

It is with great pleasure that the translator offers to the Christian public, the second number of Neander's Practical Expositions, believing that it will be found no less interesting than the preceding volume on the Epistle to the Philippians. It is characterized by the same masterly power of development, the same depth and fulness of Christian experience. Seed-thoughts crowd every page; and many single passages, in sublimity of moral sentiment and beauty of illustration, equal anything which Neander has written. As being more strictly practical in its character, and elucidating a portion of the Divine word less understood, it may be even more generally acceptable and useful than the former Exposition. It restores to us, so to speak, one of the lost treasures of the church; for no part of the New Testament has been more misunderstood and perverted, or suffered more general neglect, than this Epistle. Luther rejected it without ceremony, calling it "an epistle of straw;" and many more timid minds have been greatly perplexed by its apparent contrariety to the doctrines of grace. The discussion of its character and claims, hitherto confined to scholars, is here presented in a form intelligible and practically useful to common Christians.

By the light of Neander's comprehensive mind, we see in James not the opponent of Paul, or of the great doctrine of justification by faith alone; but the earnest expounder of that "Law of Liberty," of which justification by faith is the chief corner-stone. Paul develops the principle; James depicts its results in the life. Paul unfolds the great love of God towards us; James points out the tests, whether this love has been received into our hearts and become there the vitalizing, reigning principle. It is the tree known by its fruit, the enkindled light by the light which it imparts, the life within by the outward signs of life. In the personality of James, and the character of the churches whom he addressed, we find the true key to this Epistle. Placed side by side with the Sermon on the Mount, it is seen to be a faithful reflection of that divine original; its whole essence and intent being comprised in those words of our Saviour, which we have prefixed to this volume as its most appropriate motto: "Why call ye me Lord, Lord, and do not the things which I say!"

One opinion advanced in the author's introductory remarks, viz., that James was not an Apostle, may not gain the assent of all his readers. Neander himself formerly held,* with many other distinguished critics, that this epistle was written by the Apostle James, the son of Alpheus and of Mary the sister of our Lord's mother; who, as being the near kinsman of the Lord, was in accordance with Jewish usage called his brother. The writer may be permitted to suggest that the practical inferences, here so skilfully traced, might be drawn, though not indeed with equal force, from the author's earlier view. James, as the Lord's own brother, or as a near kinsman, must in either case have been subject to very similar influences, arising from near earthly relationship to Christ. In the exposition itself, there is nothing at variance with

* Paulus und Jacobus, 1822.

either supposition. Nor does either view affect what Neander so truthfully says of the relations of the mother of Jesus, and of the contrast between the earthly and the spiritual; since there were, as we have every reason to believe, "brothers of the Lord" in the strictest sense.

To facilitate the use of the translation, the first part has been divided into sections with a brief statement of the contents of each, for which the translator is responsible. The quotations from the Epistle are given in the words of the English version, with the author's variations in brackets wherever they are made the basis of his view.

The third and last number of this series, the Exposition of the First Epistle of John, was prepared for the press by the author, and has been given to the public since his decease. A translation of it will follow as soon as practicable.

H. C. C.

ROCHESTER, N. Y., Jan. 1852.

THE EPISTLE OF JAMES.

INTRODUCTION.

§ 1. Diversities in modes of religious development, and in the consequent forms of faith.

It is the remark of one of the early Church Fathers, that what Paul says of himself,—viz. that he became all things to all men, that he might win all to the Gospel,—is true in a still higher degree of Him who was in this the Apostle's pattern, of Christ himself. We see it in that manifold variety of manner, adapted to all the varieties in human character and relations, by which, both in his personal labors on earth, and in his spiritual revelations among all nations since his ascension, he has drawn men to a saving knowledge of himself. His manner, while laboring upon earth, is indeed an image of that invisible divine agency extending through all times, in which he evermore reveals himself as the same yesterday, to-day, and forever. This diversity Christ himself indicates, in those parables in which he describes how the kingdom of God is found; showing at the same time the one thing, in which all must finally agree who would become partakers of the kingdom of God, and the varieties of way and manner in which they are conducted thither. Only those attain to the kingdom of God who enter it by violence. Only those find the treasure hidden in the field, who are ready to sell all they have that they may become possessors of that field. Only those secure possession of that precious pearl, outshining in beauty and splendor all beside, who prize it above all else, and shun no pains, no cost to win it for themselves,—esteeming all other good as nothing, for the sake of that one highest good, the kingdom of God.

But in order to bring men to this decision of purpose, without which none can enter the kingdom of God, they must be acted on in various ways suited to their various characters and circumstances. Some are like the merchant, who having spared no pains or cost to find precious pearls, at length, through this earnest and laborious search, secures possession of that richest of all jewels. Such are those, who, impelled by longing after some satisfying good, already have sought it long in vain. They have found many things which satisfy in part; but in the end have learned, that of all these not one can give the spirit full and lasting satisfaction. Thus they are ever beginning the search anew, till at length, through this ever-renewed effort they attain to that one highest good, and find in it the full satisfaction which their souls require. Others again, seeking no treasure, come unawares upon the field containing it, and find it as it were by accident. Such are those, in whom the longing after the highest good, the kingdom of God, has not yet been awakened; who are surprised by an unsought gift, which imparts to their souls a satisfaction never imagined and never sought. The one class, by a gradual progressive development out of a life, in which preparative grace had from the first given tokens of its active presence, quickening and unfolding by various means the life-germ in the higher nature,—had thus been finally drawn into full fellowship with the Lord. The other, willing slaves of passions that long withstood the divine call, had been drawn at length, as by a power that constrained their resisting will, to him whose love seeks the deliverance of all.

Since now the mode of development is so different in the two cases, so also will be the form which faith assumes in each. To the one, the new state to which he has attained will seem but as the aim and completion of that earlier one, which by many progressive steps conducted to and ended in it; and that earlier form of life, out of which he passed into this new state, will always remain to him a dear and familiar one. To the view of the other, the new state will present itself as in direct opposition to the old. These two forms of conception are both founded in truth; each will, in its peculiar manner, contribute to the glory and furtherance of Christianity. The first is especially adapted to show, how all that preceded this new state was designed to prepare the way for it; and here the change will manifest itself in a less striking form. The second is certainly the more thorough and profound,—presenting a more complete development of the new life in its essential nature, in which it is exalted above all else.

This diversity and variety, observable in the whole process of development through which

Christianity has passed, in the entire history of the Church, appears also in the earliest stage of that process belonging to the apostolic age. But in its later history, we often find these differences,—which, as already indicated, should be mutually supplemental, serving each to complete the other,—separating the one from the other, and assuming the attitude of irreconcilable antagonism. The perception of the higher unity is wanting; although he who can recognize the One Christ in all his manifestations, partial as they may be and obscured by human narrowness of view, will be able even from this antagonism to deduce that higher unity. From this source have sprung those controversies, which have done so much to destroy rather than to edify. On the contrary, the relation of the great Teachers of the New Testament to one another, as exhibited to us in their lives and writings, enables us to view these manifold forms of conception as mutually completive; not excluding one another, but belonging together as parts of the same whole,—the One Christ in the broken rays of his manifold revelation through various organs.

It is in this light we are to regard James, the

brother of the Lord, as forming the counterpart to the great Apostle of the Gentiles. That we may be able rightly to understand and apply his Epistle, according to the plan adopted in our explanation of Paul's Epistle to the Philippians, we must first endeavor to form a distinct idea of his whole PERSONALITY, as exhibited in the circumstances of his personal development and in his labors, as well as in this Epistle.

§ 2. Personal relations and religious development of James.

In reference to the personality of James, the fact is an important one that he did not belong to the number of the Apostles. The Apostles were formed out of those disciples, who had attached themselves to the Redeemer with minds still undeveloped, and yielding with childlike susceptibility wholly to his influence. They had not been previously formed in another school, before coming into connection with him. Their whole development they had received in intercourse with him; and hence they were fitted, in a peculiar manner, to become vessels of his all-transforming grace, to receive in themselves a faithful impress of his image, and to serve as instruments for the diffusion of his word and his spirit through all ages. With Paul it was far otherwise. He had, indeed, this in common with the rest of the Apostles, viz. that he could bear testimony as an eye-witness to the Risen Christ, and had received an immediate, personal impression of him. But he had come to Christ, with a well-defined system formed in a wholly different school; and hence, in his case, the new man in Christ must present in its development the strongest possible contrast with his earlier character.

Unlike to both of these cases was that of James. He was a brother of the Lord according to the flesh. All those passages of the Gospels in which "brothers of the Lord" are mentioned, together with Matt. i. 25, are most naturally explained on the supposition, that after the birth of Jesus Mary bore still other sons. These were the "brothers of the Lord," of whom James was one. Inasmuch as marriage and the production of offspring, like everything belonging to our nature, was to be sanctified through Christ, there is nothing in such a supposition which is at all questionable, nothing derogatory to the dignity of the mother of Christ, or to his own. If anything offensive is found in it, it is owing solely to a mistaken veneration of Mary, and to that false ascetic tendency, whose views of the unholiness of the married state, and of the superiority of celibacy, are entirely at variance with the spirit of Christianity. On the contrary, it is only when thus seen in contrast with the usual course of nature, that the birth of Jesus, as effected by supernatural agency, appears in its true light and its true significance. Christ, as the miraculously begotten son of Mary, then appears in contrast with the offspring of Mary according to the laws of natural descent; the contrast between the natural and the supernatural (as Paul designates it, Gal. iv. 23 and 29), between him that is born after the spirit and him that is born after the flesh; the contrast which pervades the whole process of development in the kingdom of God.

James was therefore, in his religious development, distinguished from the other preachers of the Gospel, in that it neither proceeded so entirely and from its first beginnings from Christ himself as was the case with the other Apostles,—nor formed itself out of such a contrast between the earlier and the later, as appears in the case of Paul. His path of development, originating elsewhere, moved on for a time independently beside that circle of influences, which had formed itself from and around Christ, and not till a later period became wholly united with it.

Now it might seem, indeed, that one so closely connected with the Lord as his own brother, the daily witness of his life and actions, was the one fitted above all others to become his disciple; that one so pre-eminently favored from the first, must have been in many respects in advance of the Apostles themselves. On this view was founded the judgment of the common Jewish Christians, that they were bound to exalt James above all other preachers of the Gospel, and to pay special respect to his authority.

In the estimation thus formed of him, by the standard of the merely external natural relation to Christ, we perceive the intermingling of the Jewish spirit in the conception of Christianity,—its opposite constituting the true Christian standpoint; as, in general, the disposition to the outward and formal in religious things is Jewish, while the tendency to the inward and spiritual belongs to the nature of Christianity. The internal and external stand not seldom in inverse proportion to each other. He who stood in the nearest external relations to the revelation of the kingdom of God, to the manifestation of the divine in humanity, to the appearance of the Son of God,—might inwardly be farthest from it, and so remain if he stopped at the external manifestation, if he accustomed himself to see only with the bodily eye, and through this habit was hindered from penetrating with the eye of the spirit to that which was within. This we see in the whole relation of the Jews to the kingdom of God, and to the Messiah who proceeded from the midst of this people, destined to prepare the way for his manifestation. Christ himself testifies, in opposition to this outward Jewish tendency, that the external natural relation is of no account; that all depends rather on the inward relation, formed by the direction of the mind and heart; that not natural relationship, but submission of the soul, can alone bring one into union with him. So on one occasion, when he was occupied with his life-work, the preaching of the Gospel, among those who listened to his words with eager and receptive hearts; he repelled those who would interrupt him on the plea that his nearest kindred, his mother and brethren, desired to see him. Pointing to the circle of disciples, in whom the seed of the divine word was received into the good soil of receptive and retentive hearts, he said: "My mother and my brethren are THESE, who hear the word of God and do it." (Luke viii. 21, Mark iii. 34, 35.) Thus the essential point is not, how one is related to him by natural descent, but how he is in spirit related to the divine will revealed by him. Here also belongs the incident related Luke xi. 27, 28. A woman, powerfully affected by the divine impression of his words, cried out from the midst of the listening multitude: "Blessed is the womb that bare thee, and the breasts which thou hast sucked!" "Yea rather," he replied, implying the vanity of this supposed advantage, "blessed are they who hear the word of God and keep it!" Prophetic warnings! Not only against that externalizing tendency, as shown in the admixture of the old Jewish spirit with Christianity,—but against that same spirit as it has often, in later times and under other forms, reappeared in the Christian Church!

Thus the very thing, which might seem most favorable to the religious development of James, turned to his disadvantage. The saying which Christ used in reference to his fellow-townsmen among whom the greater part of his life had been spent, and who had been eye-witnesses of his progressive development from childhood,—"A prophet is of no honor in his own country,"—applies with equal force to the case of James and his brothers. For the very reason, that they had from the first been eye-witnesses of the human earthly development of the Son of Man, they were not able to penetrate beyond the outward human veil. It became to them a stone of stumbling. True they afterwards witnessed the revelation of the Son of God, both in the inward power of the divine life perceptible only to the inwardly awakened sense for the divine, and in those proofs of power exhibited in his miracles. Still the faith, thus at times awakened, gave way continually to that skepticism proceeding from the prejudices of the natural man, who judges only after the flesh and by the outward appearance; and thus, during the whole earthly life of Christ, they remained in this state of vacillation, wavering between faith and unbelief. But when that stone of stumbling was taken out of their way, and the Son of God no longer stood before their eyes in the earthly veil of the Son of Man; when He, who was believed dead, showed himself victorious over death and living in divine power, to those whose weak faith required such confirmation; it was then, that the decisive and final direction was given to the development of the religious life of James (1 Cor. xv. 7). From this time forward we see in him the decided, unwavering, zealous witness of the faith in that Jesus, as his Messiah, Lord and Saviour, who had been his own brother according to the flesh. (James i. 1.)

§ 3. Stand-point of James as an inspired teacher, and his relation to Paul.

The manner, however, in which he testified of Christ, took its character from his previous training and course of life. He, above all others, stood on the ground of Jewish piety in the Old Testament forms; and had already completely developed himself within this sphere, when he was led to that decisive faith in Jesus, as the Messiah promised in the Old Testament. From this new point of view, his previous Judaism unfolded itself in its true and full import. Christianity now appears to him as the true Judaism. The spirit which proceeds from Christ explains the forms of the Old Testament, and leads them to their proper fulfilment. The position of James is precisely that taken by Christ in the Sermon on the Mount; which contains the germ of all that is peculiar to the Gospel, without expressly declaring the abrogation of the Law; where all is presented under the idea of the kingdom of God, and the reference of each particular to the person of Christ, though everywhere implied and forming the central point of all, is nowhere asserted in words. Hence in the development of the divine kingdom,—where as in all the works of God, the works of grace as well as of nature, no chasms are allowed but all proceeds by progressive steps,—James forms a very important transition-point from the Old to the New Testament. Something would be wanting to us, if we had not James in the New Testament. And that narrowness of view, which disdains to follow patiently this gradual development,—demanding everywhere and at once the perfected form,—may find its punishment in the consequent incompleteness of its own Christian knowledge. As a means of leading pious Jews to faith in the Gospel, this position of James was of special use. Just in proportion as it would have been detrimental to a Paul, whose mission was the conversion of the heathen nations, was it advantageous to James in the sphere of labor assigned to him in Palestine, and particularly in Jerusalem among unmixed Jews. Thus divine wisdom manifests itself in assigning to each his sphere, his peculiar mission in the development of the kingdom of God, adapted to his peculiar qualifications. The sole concern is that each rightly fulfil his appointed mission, understand and faithfully adhere to his prescribed limits; while at the same time he recognizes the divine call in him also, to whom as the possessor of other gifts another sphere of labor has been assigned,—and is willing to regard their several spheres as each the complement of the other. Such was the relation of James to Paul.

James did indeed know, from the first, what the voice of prophecy had indicated, of the coming extension of Jehovah's worship among the heathen nations, and of their participation in the blessings of the divine kingdom,—a glory which belonged to Messianic times,—and also that this was to be fulfilled through Christ as the Messiah. But the possibility of a worship of Jehovah except in the old legal forms, or of a participation in the kingdom of God in any other way, remained hidden from him at first, even after he had attained to a settled faith in Jesus as the Messiah. The intimations in the discourses of Christ that his word should become the leaven, which, by an indwelling power alone and independently of all else, should penetrate the life of humanity; in Jews and Gentiles alike leavening all and forming it anew; that the new spirit of Christianity should burst asunder and break through the forms of legal Judaism; these intimations he did not yet understand. This belonged to those things of which Christ said, in his parting words to his disciples, that what they could not yet comprehend should afterwards be revealed to them by the Holy Spirit. But this revelation of the Holy Spirit was not imparted to all at the same time, nor in the same way. This too was determined by the different stand-points from which they had attained to faith in the Gospel. Accordingly, more or less of preparation might be required for leading them to that more perfect knowledge; it might be effected more by a process of thought inspired and guided by the Holy Spirit, and thus enabled to develop and apprehend the whole sum of revealed truth,—or it might be more the effect of immediate illumination by the Divine Spirit. In the history of the church, we meet with many melancholy examples of opposition and estrangement, when the spiritual insight attained by one is still withheld from another, and the one thus becomes free from the narrow limits in which the other is still confined. Even in the apostolic church, this was the source of much disunion and division.

But James was far from that narrow obstinacy of temper, which would not allow any stand-point but his own; would permit no opposing facts to influence his convictions,—promptly rejecting the truth revealed to others because it was not imparted through him, and thus setting bounds to the farther development of the kingdom of God. When, at the apostolic conference (Acts xv.), the controverted point respecting the observance of the Mosaic law was for the first time discussed, and Peter and Paul bore testimony to the effects of the Gospel among believing Gentiles, who had not submitted to circumcision, nor in any other respect to the observance of the Law; these undeniable facts were proof enough for James, that through faith in the Saviour, the same divine results were produced among the heathen as among believing Jews. In this he saw a fulfilment of the Old Testament predictions; and he now learned their true aim and import, as he had never understood it before. The mild conciliating spirit of James is shown, by the manner in which he sought to reconcile the differences between the Jewish and Gentile Christians. He could do justice to a stand-point wholly different from his own. Believing Gentiles, on the ground of their faith merely, were to be admitted to equality with believing Jews in the fellowship of the divine kingdom; only, for the furtherance of harmony with believers from among the Jews, they were to conform in certain external points, which might also serve to withhold them from participation in everything connected with heathen worship. But while James recognized the equality of churches consisting of uncircumcised Gentiles, and allowed to the preaching of the Gospel among the Gentiles its own rights as an independent calling; he at the same time remained true to his own peculiar stand-point, according to which the old forms were to be continued as depositories of the new spirit, and the Jews were to retain their religious nationality unchanged. Still, as we see from the Acts of the Apostles, he was ever the mediator between Paul and the zealots among the Jewish Christians, who were prejudiced against him. Here too he always conducted in the same spirit of mildness and conciliation.

§ 4. Character and condition of the Churches to whom the Epistle was addressed, and nature of the errors against which it was directed.

In order now to understand and rightly apply the Epistle of James, we must endeavor to form a distinct conception of those to whom it was addressed, and whose peculiar circumstances he had especially in view.

We can, indeed, say nothing definite in regard to the region where these churches are to be sought. The Epistle itself furnishes only general information, sufficient, however, for the practical purposes we have now in view. The essential points are these: There were churches consisting exclusively of Christians of Jewish origin, in which all the practical errors of Judaism were associated with faith in Jesus as the Messiah; and in which there were many, who gave little or no evidence of the new creation which is the necessary product of that faith.

That wholly earthly direction of mind, which was often connected with false zeal for the honor of God; the insatiable love of gain, and consequent divisions from the clashing of selfish interests; these were the faults which they had brought with them from their earlier Jewish state, into their new Christian relation. The aristocracy of wealth held in check the pervading spirit of Christian love, whose office it is to repress and triumph over all earthly distinctions. Instead of being obliterated by that spirit of love, the distinctions caused by the unequal distribution of wealth, were recognized and maintained at the expense of that fraternal relation, which should characterize a community of Christians. Furthermore, it belonged to the defects of this false Jewish spirit, that, instead of regarding piety as a whole, proceeding from the inward temper of the heart and embracing the entire life; it held only to particular observances of the outward life, in which piety should manifest itself,—that tendency to the external in religion of which we have spoken. This manifested itself in the great value attached to external descent from the theocratic people, to circumcision and the works of the Law, making justification dependent thereon. This same spirit now passed over to the Jewish Christians; and became especially prominent, wherever they had the ascendency in opposition to Gentiles and Gentile Christians.

This tendency was one which, from its very nature, belongs exclusively to no age; it was no mere thing of the past, extinguished with Judaism once for all, and never to reappear in the Christian church. The declaration of the preacher of wisdom is applicable here,—that "what has been will be, and there is nothing new under the sun." What we here term the Jewish spirit, had not its origin in anything inherent in Judaism as a divine institution; but is to be referred rather to the nature of the unrenewed man, drawing down the divine to his own level, and seeking to appropriate it to himself without renouncing his own peculiar nature. Now as the nature of the unrenewed man remains ever the same, there must at all times proceed from it this same erroneous tendency, which we may characterize as in its spirit and nature Jewish.

This Jewish spirit shows itself equally, when the unrenewed nature of man mingles its disturbing influence with the conception of Christianity. It is seen in the disposition to value one's self on the ground of descent from a Christian people, or from some particular nation distinguished in earlier times for its piety, and on this account assigned a more conspicuous place in the history of God's kingdom; without considering that if his own life does not correspond to the peculiar character and position of such a people, this connection, instead of being his glory, will become his condemnation. So is it also with pretensions based on a father's pious deeds, without any effort to imitate his example. So is it when connection with a particular church is made one's only boast, his sole ground of hope, and no importance is attached to the practice of genuine Christianity; when, in short, in the outward organization of the church, the essence of Christianity itself is forgotten. In each and all of these cases, we perceive the same practical error of the Jewish spirit. So if we base our confidence on a zealous devotion to the external observances of Christian worship, attendance upon divine service, the celebration of the sacraments, without going beyond the outward form; this is in spirit precisely the same, as that Jewish reliance upon circumcision and the works of the Law. The name alone is changed; the thing itself remains the same. Hence all the arguments and warnings against such a tendency, which we find in Paul's Epistles, may be applied with equal propriety to these same practical errors in every age of the church, although the particular forms of it with which he contended may exist no longer.

It does not appear indeed, in the Epistle of James, that he combats this tendency in precisely these forms, as is the case in Paul's writings. Yet is the root, the essential tendency, the same. He is obliged to instruct his readers in the nature of true religion,—wherein that form of religion, of which they made so much account, must therefore have been deficient. It is only a different form of development which is here treated of; the same radical tendency is too obvious to be mistaken. There were two leading forms of this tendency. One of these consisted in an undue estimation of outward works of the Law. The other exalted the mere knowledge of the Law, of the true God and of what pertains to his worship, into the principal thing; and on the ground of knowledge merely,—of the mere profession of belief, of faith simply as an act of the understanding,—claimed superiority over the Gentiles, although the course of life by no means corresponded to this knowledge and outward profession. Paul likewise combats, in the second chapter of the Epistle to the Romans, this false reliance on mere knowledge of the Law. Of the same character was that dead learning in the Scriptures, such as Christ condemned in the Pharisees, who thought that in them they had eternal life, and yet would not be directed by them to him who alone could bestow eternal life. The consequence was, that each one was anxious to gain currency for his own religious views, to set himself up as a teacher for others, without first taking care to mould his own character in conformity with divine truth. Hence arose the contests between these would-be teachers; another form of that bias to the external and the literal, but springing from the same root as those before described,—no less capable of co-existing with an ungodly life, and of serving as a support for it.

The question now arises,—does the false idea of

faith and the over-estimation of mere faith, which James opposes in this Epistle, belong also to this same radical tendency; or are we to regard it as something different, and derived from another source? Do we find here so clear a reference to the Pauline idea of faith, as to make the conclusion necessary, that the doctrine of justification by faith, as taught by Paul, had been misunderstood and misapplied in these churches? Some might have imagined, that they could glory in justification solely by faith in the Redeemer, while they continued to live in the practice of sin. Against such misunderstanding and perversion, Paul himself seeks to guard his doctrine, in many passages of the Epistle to the Romans. In later times,—when the doctrine which Paul made it his especial object to maintain in opposition to Judaism and judaizing teachers, had been re-established in its rights by Luther, in opposition to a Jewish spirit which had once more crept into the church; there then followed a new service of the letter, a new phase of this tendency to outward forms, and again the connection between faith and life was rent asunder. Much which James says of this tendency in his day, might be applied to this case with equal propriety.

This question, whether James is here contending against a misapprehension of the Pauline doctrine, or has no reference whatever to it,—is by no means necessarily connected with the question of the relation of Paul's teaching to that of James. James might have intended to oppose a misunderstanding of Paul's doctrine,—nay, even the doctrine itself, if he had first met with it in this erroneous form, without previous understanding with Paul in regard to his object; and yet a perfect harmony might be shown to exist between the two methods of exhibiting truth, each serving as the complement of the other. For it may easily happen, when one man has formed,—in accordance with his peculiar course of training, and the bearing of the counter-view which is before his mind,—his own peculiar mode of conceiving and stating a truth; that the very opposition made to it by another, conceiving the same truth from a different point of view, may show their essential agreement,—what was intended to counteract serving only to explain and complete. Thus a representation of Christian truths, even if called forth by opposition to the peculiarly Pauline form of doctrine, might have found place as a completing link, in that collection of writings containing the original pure revelation of Christian truth. Both these forms of conception and teaching might constitute parts of the same whole, as being mutually completive, in the one revelation of the Holy Spirit through different human organs inspired by him. Their relation to each other must therefore be especially considered hereafter.*

Now although it is possible that such a form of externalizing, as the one we have mentioned, might attach itself to the Pauline doctrine, and though, as we have seen, this was afterwards actually the case; the question still remains, whether we are justified in assuming this in regard to the particular churches brought to our knowledge in this Epistle. It was in churches like these, formed among Jews and exclusively of Jewish converts, that a perversion of the Pauline doctrine was most unlikely to arise; inasmuch as the Pauline standpoint was one with which they had nothing in common. The Pauline view of faith presupposes the strongly marked distinction between Law and

* Page 36.

Gospel, a doctrinal position opposed to legal righteousness, to the merit of one's own works. Opposition to the Jewish tendency to externals was the precise ground on which it planted itself; and where that tendency prevailed, a perverted form of this view could as little gain admission as the view itself.

But to resume our question: may not this particular error,—the false idea of faith and over-estimation of mere faith,—which James opposes, be also traced back to the same radical tendency? Let us only compare what precedes and what follows the discussion of this topic in the second chapter. It is preceded (chap. i.) by a rebuke of those who founded an imaginary claim on the mere hearing of the word, on the mere knowledge of it, without holding themselves bound to practise it; to which is added the rebuke of a mere fancied and seeming service of God. What now is this but that very same spirit of reliance on the external, which manifests itself in a mere adherence to certain articles of faith,—faith in the one true God, the Messiah,—and on this ground alone claims to be righteous, without recognizing the demands of this faith upon the life? As knowledge and practice are at war with each other, so are faith and life. A merely theoretical faith corresponds exactly to a merely theoretical knowledge. The same man, who satisfies himself with being able to discourse much of the law without obeying it, is also the one who makes a boast of his faith, without holding himself bound to the practice of that which faith requires. The same man who finds the essence of religion in certain external works, and claims to be a true worshiper of God merely on the ground of professing the true religion, is the one also who claims to be accounted righteous through a faith which produces no works. If we turn now to what follows (chap. iii.), we find that James is here rebuking those who were ever ready to exalt themselves into teachers of others; but who, by teaching what they did not practise, made themselves the more liable to condemnation. What then is this but that same radical tendency over again? And on what ground should we be justified in rending the intermediate passage from its connection, and making it refer to something else, the explanation of which must be sought elsewhere than in this one radical tendency?

It is true, that in the manner of meeting these errors, which we will now further consider, James is distinguished in a peculiar way from Paul. It is the more practical man in contrast with the more systematic; the man to whose wholly Jewish development, faith in Christ was superadded as the crown and completion,—in contrast with him, whose faith in Christ took the form of direct opposition to his earlier Jewish views, as the centre of a wholly new creation. Hence with James, opposition to error takes more the form of single propositions and exhortations; with Paul it is a connected view, in which all proceeds from one central point. With James the reference to Christ appears only as one particular among others, a peculiarity especially objected to this Epistle, as if Christ were not to be found in it; while with Paul, on the contrary, the chief object is to exalt Christ, who is everywhere placed foremost, and is everywhere represented as the centre of the whole life, from whom all is derived, to whom all is referred. But yet, in these single propositions and admonitions of James, we are able to trace the higher unity lying at the basis; and can show that all have reference to Christ as the living centre, even though he is not expressly named. There may be a form of moral development, which receives its true light and its true significance through reference to Him as its centre and source, although he is not expressly recognized by name; and his name may be often on the lips, while yet the whole inward character has formed itself without reference to Him. In this light we must now endeavor to understand the controversial and admonitory passages of this Epistle.

The churches to whom it was addressed consisted of rich and poor; and undoubtedly the latter were the more numerous class among the Christians. We know that the Gospel everywhere, and especially among the Jews, found freer entrance with the poor and lowly than among the rich and powerful. Not that riches in themselves exclude from the kingdom of God, or necessarily form a hindrance to faith in the Gospel. When Christ says, that it is easier for a camel to go through a needle's eye, than for a rich man to enter into the kingdom of God, he means such as he who gave occasion to these words; those to whom,—though perhaps unconsciously,—the earthly is the highest good; whose treasure being on earth cannot, therefore, be in heaven; whose heart belongs to the earth where their treasure is, and is therefore far from that direction towards heaven, without which no one can ever share in its blessedness. Indeed he himself adds in the same connection, that although the salvation of a rich man is impossible with men, i. e. by mere human means, yet with God all is possible. He would say by this, that divine help is needful, in order that riches may not prove a hindrance to the attainment of the kingdom of God. This then is the import of the words; not that riches in themselves are a hindrance to this object, but that misdirection of the affections into which the rich man more than others is liable to fall. The rich should be awakened to a consciousness of this, and should be incited by a sense of the difficulties inherent in his case, to apply to God for the strength which he needs; that even while in possession of all earthly riches, he may still keep his treasure in heaven and his heart directed thither. In this Epistle itself we learn what is necessary to the rich for this purpose. Yet though riches are not, in themselves, a hindrance to participation in the kingdom of God, still it was often the case among the Jews, that the rich and mighty forgot in worldly enjoyments the higher wants of the inner man; lost the fixed consciousness of dependence on Him, whose power confers and disposes all; imagining that they possessed all things, they had no room left for the feeling of want and of the necessity of deliverance from it. Thus too in the Old Testament, the rich, the proud, and the ungodly are often ranked together as of one class.

But every external situation may become, according to one's temper of mind, either a help or a hindrance to salvation; and nothing can here injure or promote his interests independently of his own will. Thus may poverty also,—that physical want which depresses the spiritual nature, which prevents the inner man from awaking to self-consciousness, and to the feeling of his higher spiritual wants,—prove an obstacle to the attainment of the kingdom of God. Poverty, too, has its peculiar dangers, and this is not overlooked in this Epistle. In general, however, it was the poor and lowly, pining under the oppressions of the rich and powerful, and under the pressure of physical want, who most readily felt the need of deliverance from spiritual want, from inward poverty of soul. On this feeling of physical need, could more easily be engrafted that consciousness of the soul's necessities, through which they might be conducted to the Saviour. As in their case, there was nothing to deceive the soul into a seeming satisfaction of its wants, they could the more easily be drawn to that which furnished the true satisfaction for all its higher necessities. Moreover, the poor in this world could more readily than the rich attain to that poverty of spirit, to which, as Christ says, belongs the kingdom of Heaven. Thus the Gospel found, among the Jews, a readier reception from the poor than from the rich; and on this account, Christians were reproachfully called The Poor. We do not mean by this, that all these poor who received the Gospel, had been led to it by true poverty of spirit, and had thus been prepared to receive, as poor and needy, the true riches of the Gospel. Among them too was to be found the influence of that carnal mind which prevailed among the Jews,—begetting, not the true hope of the heavenward directed spirit, but rather the expectation of a recompense for bodily privations in the imagined carnal enjoyments of the kingdom of Christ. Now the faith of such, if we choose to call it by that name, had its source in the carnal mind of the natural man; and hence, the earlier form of this natural man was transferred with them out of Judaism into a professed Christianity,—where it was, as we shall see, opposed and rebuked by James.

As the poorer and lower class, the Christians had, as we have intimated, much to suffer from the persecution and oppression of the powerful and rich; partly on account of their religion, partly for the promotion of selfish interests, their religion serving as the pretext. The rich who called themselves Christians without being so in truth, were infected with the common vice of the rich among the Jews, and failed in the exercise of love and even justice towards their poorer brethren in the faith. Accordingly, we find in this Epistle words of consolation and encouragement for the oppressed and suffering, and of rebuke for the rich both within and without the church.

EXPOSITION

OF THE EPISTLE.

Its opening words are addressed to the Suffering,—exhorting them to steadfastness and submission. "My brethren, count it all joy when ye fall into divers temptations." [Ch. i. 2, 3. The idea of temptation is a comprehensive one in the Scriptures. By it is designated, whatever may become an obstacle or impediment to Christian faith and Christian virtue,—prosperity and adversity, the world without and the world within ; everything which, though it may indeed occasion the overthrow of faith and virtue in the conflict, thus puts them to the test, and may therefore serve also to confirm and strengthen them. In this more general sense it might, in itself considered, be understood here. But it is evident from the connection that here, as in many other passages, are meant the sufferings by which the Christian life is tried. Now to those who sigh under sufferings such as we have described, he addresses not merely the exhortation, to bear them patiently in the prospect of future glory. Far more than this. The feeling of suffering should lose itself in joy. They should do nothing but rejoice. How could James say this? It was because with him all has reference to what is noblest in man, what constitutes his true being, the imperishable, the inner man as it is termed by Paul. And knowing that these temptations, rightly used, must serve for the improvement of the inner man, and for this purpose were ordained of God; he therefore calls upon Christians not to be disquieted, but to rejoice in these sufferings, bearing in mind the end which they must promote for the children of God. The right improvement of suffering, on Christian grounds, is therefore presupposed, as indicated by James in the succeeding words: "Knowing that the trial of your faith worketh patience." It is here implied, that faith has its appointed process of development and purification in this life,—a process consisting in an unceasing conflict. Faith is in his view something radically different from, and elevated above, every other governing principle in man; something endued with an inward divine power; which must, however, approve itself in conflict with this opposing power, with all which proceeds from the flesh, from the natural man. There are indeed manifold trials of faith, and to all these the words of James apply. But it is the conflict with external circumstances, which is here especially meant. Here then is it to be tested, whether the faith is genuine, deep-rooted in the inner life; such an one as, through indwelling divine power, is able to overcome the world. The opposite case is presented by Christ, in what he says of the stony ground; where indeed the seed of the word springs up quickly, but soon withers because it has no sap (Luke viii. 6); a conviction which is not a firm and deeply rooted one, and in time of temptation vanishes away (v. 13). But so long as faith approves itself in this warfare, holds out in the conflict with the world, it demonstrates thereby its divine power. The test becomes an attestation. From the victorious contest faith comes forth with a confirmed constancy, and constancy manifests itself as a fruit of faith. It is by this means that the Christian first learns what he himself possesses.

But James well understood the character of the churches whom he addressed; and that Ch. i. 4, 5.] among them the idea of faith was liable to the perversion of which we have spoken. It is everywhere his aim to counteract this one-sided tendency to the particular and the external. Hence he adds, that even if faith had thus approved itself as steadfast, in these outward conflicts with the world, yet this one thing alone would not constitute the Christian life. In manifold directions, must faith pervade the entire life, and manifest its power. "Let steadfastness," he adds (or as Luther translates it, patience), "have its perfect work." Luther understood this of time; it was to approve itself as perfect by persevering even to the end. But from the connection with what follows, and from the whole connection and course of thought in the Epistle, we should rather understand it thus: To the faith which has approved itself as steadfast, must correspond all the works pertaining to faith, the entire sum of the acts in which faith expresses its inward character. But James, in reference to the unity of the whole Christian life, designates the entire Christian course, all Christian action, as one perfect work,—as must be the case in order to correspond to true faith. Thus we can rightly understand what he immediately adds: "that ye may be perfect and entire, wanting nothing;" implying that with persevering faith connects itself the whole sum of the true Christian walk. By completeness is not meant an absolute perfection, nowhere to be found in the Christian life on earth; but, as often elsewhere in the Scriptures, all which belongs to Christian maturity, to what Paul terms Christian manhood,—as by wholeness ("entire") is meant the exclusion of whatever would mar the Christian life. When he desires that they may be wanting in nothing, he has in mind the aggregate of all qualities, powers, and capacities which Christianity develops, when its efficacy is fully proved as a leaven for the entire nature of man. Hence he subjoins a direction, intended to encourage them under the consciousness of any deficiency in this respect. He shows them what they must themselves do, if they would attain to that also, in which they are still deficient. What he might have expressed in wholly general terms, applicable to everything in which they might be conscious of deficiency, he applies (with his usual preference for the specific over the general idea) to that point especially wherein these particular churches might feel, or ought to feel, their need. Above all things was needed true wisdom, to give to the whole life its proper reference to the kingdom of God. Wisdom, or prudence (for which in the original the same word is used,—the prudence grounded in wisdom and subservient to it, the prudence of wisdom, of Christian love, being alone regarded as genuine) is by our Lord himself often held up as the chief object of attainment. But, as already remarked, there prevailed in these churches, as a fruit of the Jewish spirit, a proneness to a vain show of wisdom, to the over-estimation of mere knowledge, the conceit of knowledge and wisdom. So much the more did they need to be admonished, that true wisdom is based upon humility; that it is not to be learned in the schools from Doctors of the Law; that it can be obtained only from the fountain of eternal light. Hence James adds to what he has already said, "If any of you lack wisdom, let him ask of God, that giveth to all men liberally [with simplicity], and upbraideth not: and it shall be given him." Thus he counsels them, when they feel the consciousness of their deficiencies, to turn to God in prayer. God is designated as he who gives with simplicity, i. e. out of pure love, for the mere sake of giving,—simplicity being here contrasted with a liberality apportioned and limited by self-interest. He is represented as he who reproaches no one with his benefits, but who is ever ready still to give, if there only exists a susceptibility for his gifts. They should not turn then to such teachers as hold back from them a part of the truth, impart to them grudgingly, and reproach them with their indebtedness; but to the love of a Heavenly Father, who gives without measure and is ever ready to give.

It is prayer, therefore, which James represents as the condition required of the believer, in order that he may share in the communication from that heavenly fountain. This is the necessary relation between imparting and receiving in divine things. God alone being the Creator and Bestower, the human spirit can here only hold the attitude of a recipient. And this direction of the spirit, in order to receive what God is ready to impart, consists in prayer. The direction of the soul towards God in the feeling of personal need, and in the conviction that God alone can and will satisfy it, the longing towards God of the spirit hungering and thirsting after wisdom,—this is prayer. To seek the truth from God, and to pray, are one and the same thing. The whole life of the spirit, filled with this longing and impelled by it towards God, is prayer. So in those words of Christ,—to seek, to knock, in order to find the hid treasure, and to pray, are all classed together: "Ask and it shall be given you, seek and ye shall find, knock and it shall be opened unto you." (Matt. vii. 7.)

But in addressing churches so ensnared by tendencies to the outward in religion, it was
Ch. i. 6–8.] all the more necessary to warn them against this in respect to prayer; which only then deserves the name, when it is the voice of the spirit itself, breathed from its inmost depths; lest they should suppose prayer in words, without that direction of the soul to God, to be all that was required. This warning is contained in the following words: "But let him ask in faith, nothing wavering." Trust in God is here represented as that direction of the spirit, from which prayer must proceed. To the eye of faith God must be present, as He to whom the prayer is directed. There must be the assurance, that he can and will supply the wants uttered before him, in order that it may be

true prayer, prayer of the heart and not merely of the lips. The reason is immediately added, why prayer of the opposite character will not be heard. "For he that wavereth is like a wave of the sea, driven with the wind and tossed." Thus the steadfast direction of the soul to God is essential to prayer. But where there is doubt, there this ruling bias of the soul towards God is wanting. When, on the one side, the soul feels itself drawn towards God, and trust in Him begins to awaken; then on the other, the worldly tendency asserts itself, and strives to check the budding emotions of faith and trust. Hence the man, who is drawn hither and thither by conflicting inclinations, is compared to the wave, driven to and fro by storm and flood. James represents such a man as one who is at variance with himself, one in whom there exist, as it were, two souls;* who is unstable in all his ways, fickle-minded, unreliable in all his actions. Such is the character of his whole life, and his prayer answers to his life. In this it is implied, therefore, that prayer must be in consonance with the steadfast direction of the whole

* Eng. version, double-minded.—Tr.

life towards God; all must originate in one and the same temper of heart.

But here the question may be asked: How is this faith which is essential to prayer, to be obtained? Is one to abstain from prayer, because he lacks this measure of faith? But as in the words of our Lord above quoted, it is the necessary condition on which every gift of God is bestowed, that we knock, that we seek, that we ask of God; most surely faith is to be included, which is the gift of God, and always represented as something divinely wrought in man. He who is conscious of his lack of faith, who desires to believe more, to become stronger in faith, must in this also seek of God that wherein he is wanting. As that unhappy father in the Gospel narrative, of whom believing confidence was required in order to the healing of his son, cried out under a sense of the weakness of his faith, "Lord, help my unbelief!"; so will the feeling of that want of which we are speaking, of that lack of faith which stands opposed to true prayer, itself impel to prayer for strength to believe. He who is assaulted by doubts will turn his back upon doubt,—upon the world which threatens to ensnare his soul in unbelief, and will look to God; turning away from doubt, he will give himself to prayer. Thus through prayer will faith increase, and the strengthened faith will in its turn lend new power, new wings to prayer.

Thus have we seen how James, beginning with the exhortation to steadfastness under sufferings, was led on from one suggestion to another. [Ch. i. 9–11. Turning now his thoughts to the poor, who constituted a majority of these Christians, and who had much to suffer from the oppression of the rich, he addresses to them the consoling words: "Let the brother of low degree rejoice [glory] in that he is exalted." Instead of being cast down by the sense of his poverty, his low estate in respect to earthly relations, the Christian should rather feel himself raised above them, by the consciousness of an exaltation transcending all height of worldly honor; of that divine exaltation which is founded in the divine life, in the dignity of the Sons of God. This glorying he enjoins, with no occasion to apprehend self-exaltation; for the glory here spoken of is not one which man owes to his own powers and efforts; it is a dignity bestowed on him by God alone. This glorying is, therefore, the very opposite of all pride and self-exaltation, and can exist only in connection with true humility. But as this dignity is not adjudged to the poor on account of their poverty, so are the rich by no means excluded from it by their riches; although as we have already shown, these may to many become a hindrance in the way of their attaining it. To the rich, too, the way is pointed out, by which they may attain to that high dignity. "Let the rich," says James, "glory in that he is made low." That is: by humbling himself on account of that which passes with the world as great, he attains to the consciousness of that true dignity, which springs only from a sense of the nothingness of all earthly greatness. By this conviction of the worthlessness of his earthly riches, he is prepared to appropriate as his own the true riches, the only true dignity. Self-abasement is the path to true exaltation. So long as the rich man prides himself upon his wealth, and fancies that therein he possesses the true riches, the feeling of necessity for heavenly possessions, for true greatness, will not germinate in his heart. This very feeling of need, this desire, is the necessary condition of personal participation. Thus poor and rich among Christian brethren, must be united to each other by the same consciousness of equal dignity. James then goes on to picture the vanity of riches, by images drawn from the natural scenery of the East. Like the fresh grass, which at morning stands in all its flowery splendor, but under the scorching breath of the south wind suddenly withers and dies, so will the rich man perish in his ways. As he has his treasure only in earthly things, and has wholly merged himself in them, to him is transferred what is said of the vanity of those possessions, which he has made his all.

But the sufferings of the oppressed Christians are ever before the mind of James. Having spoken of these sufferings as trials for the verifying of their faith, he now extols as happy the righteous who endures temptation; since, by thus approving himself, he would win the victor's crown of eternal life, which the Lord has promised to all who love him. But how shall we reconcile with this the warning, not to ascribe temptations to God, which James immediately adds? Does he not regard God, as having himself ordained these sufferings as a means of testing faith? But there are different applications of this term, and we must

[Ch. i. 12–15.

distinguish between outward and inward temptation. The difficulties which beset one from without, may serve to awaken in him the latent power of the higher life. But they may also show his inward weakness,—may become the point of connection for that which stands opposed to the divine life. That which might otherwise have been the means of attesting his faith or Christian virtue, through his own fault becomes temptation to unbelief or to sin. Thus the outward temptation becomes an inward one, and thereby endangers the soul. When Christ bids us pray: Lead us not into temptation, this can certainly be no other than inward temptation; for his disciples were to be left behind, in the midst of those temptations of the world which should serve as tests of their faith. The object of the petition must have been, that the outward might not become an inward temptation. In like manner, James, in his use of the word, passes from one of these related ideas to the other.

But he must have found special reason for this warning in the peculiar state of these churches; and the explanation is to be sought in that same spirit of externalizing, of which we have already spoken. As this spirit shows itself in the conception of what is good, so does it also in the conception of sin. At no time have there been wanting grounds of excuse for sin; which men have regarded as something cleaving to them from without, and have sought its origin in merely external causes, instead of tracing it to its inward source in the faulty direction of the will. So it would seem that many in these churches excused themselves, on the plea that they were in subjection to a higher power, which hurried them away into sin. The Almighty, whom no one is able to withstand, has plunged them into these temptations. To this James replies: "Let no man say when he is tempted, I am tempted of God;" for as God cannot be tempted by aught that is evil, being elevated above all evil, so neither from him can temptation to sin proceed. The Holy One can tempt none to sin. He then lays open the fountain of temptation in man's own bosom, and describes the process by which the sinful tendency gains ground in progressive steps, till its final development in outward act. The source of temptation, he represents as lying in those desires inherent in every man, by which he is excited and led away; which lie in wait for him, as it were, but which he has power to withstand.

They gain strength only because they are not resisted; because he who might subject them to himself, submits himself to them. Thus prevailing, thus ripened into fruit, lust bringeth forth sin; and sin completed in act is followed by death.

We are by no means to infer, as is clear from the connection of thought in this passage, that these desires are not in their own nature sinful; or that the prevailing sinful tendency of the will would not involve death, even if it should find no expression in outward act, as though all turned on the outward act alone. The thought is this: Evil, from the first breaking forth of desire, proceeds on in ascending stages of development, until,—overpowering all the opposing influences of the higher life,—it is consummated in act. In this consummation in act is shown an increased strength of sin; and though man was previously able, by overcoming the enticements to sin, to maintain and to reestablish in himself the true life; yet now, through sin which has gained the victory over him, he falls a prey to death. James, therefore, warns them against indulging in such false and delusive ideas, as that God can be the author of evil.

Having thus directed them to look for the source

of temptation in themselves alone, and warned them against supposing that temptations could come from God; he now further opposes to this delusion the thought,—that only whatever is good, whatever is true, proceeds from Him. As he is the Father of all material light, so is he also the Father of all spiritual light. With him, therefore, can be no alternation of light and darkness. From him, the unchangeable fountain of light raised above all darkness, nothing which tempts to evil can proceed. As light and all that is good, so darkness and all that is evil, are uniformly classed together in the Holy Scriptures. [Ch. i. 16, 17.

From this general thought, James now passes again to its application to himself and his readers. To God alone were they indebted also for the dawning of the divine light on them, and for the new life thereby imparted. "Of his own will begat he us, with the word of truth, that we should be a kind of first fruits of his creatures." We here perceive in James, as in Paul, the opposite of the Jewish tendency to the outward. He presupposes in the Christian a moral transformation, wrought from within. The word of truth, the divine power of the Gospel, is that whereby [Ch. i. 18.

the new higher life has been produced. He too describes this as something not consequent upon any human desert; all are indebted for it to the will of Him from whom all good proceeds. He too characterizes this moral transformation as a new creation. Those in whom it was first effected, he describes as the first-born of this creation; since from them it should continue to spread, till its final completion in a world pervaded and transformed by the divine principle of life.

Ch. i. 19–21.]

But it is ever the manner of James to pass at once from the general to the particular; a trait originating partly in his own personal character, partly from the peculiar practical necessities of those to whom he was writing. He knew their disposition to content themselves with the general thought, without making an application of it to their own life. To incite them to this was his constant aim. He therefore proceeds at once to show how the divine word, received into the soul as the generative principle of the new creation, must manifest itself in the course of life. Neither does this take the form of a mere generality in his mind; but he passes directly to the special application most opposed to the practical errors of these churches. We have already remarked on the propensity among them to assume the office of teacher,—the inclination to talk much and to do little; how they were thus led to pass judgment lightly upon others, to revile them, and how every passion found herein its nourishment. Against this he warns them in the words: "Wherefore, my beloved brethren, let every man be swift to hear, slow to speak, slow to wrath." One extreme must be driven out by the other. There is a self-willed silence, and there is a self-willed forwardness to speak. He who is inclined to be too inert and passive, to hold his peace when he ought to speak out boldly, must be exhorted not to give himself thus wholly to silence, but to be willing to speak when duty requires. But James is dealing with those, among whom the very opposite fault prevailed; those who lacked the sobriety, patience, and humility, to hear before they spoke; and of course he must make use of the opposite exhortation. As a warning against the temptation to anger, easily furnished by over-hasty speaking, he tells them that passion is least of all adapted to effect the work of piety. "For the wrath of man worketh not the righteousness of God." From the particular instance he now returns to the general thought with which he started, placing the two in close connection with each other. As passion forces man towards the outward, withdrawing him from the calm, ever-deepening inner life of the spirit, and banishing again from the heart that generative principle of the new creation, the Word of God, instead of allowing it to penetrate more and more the inner spiritual nature: he therefore counsels them to purify themselves from all that is evil, all excrescences of the inward life which passion nourishes, and in meekness to suffer the word implanted in their hearts to take deeper and deeper root therein. So shall they attain to the salvation of the soul, through the power of this word thus penetrating more and more their entire life. "Wherefore" (namely, because anger is in contrariety to the divine righteousness, and is the rank soil of every evil thing)—"lay apart all filthiness and superfluity of naughtiness, and receive with meekness the engrafted word which is able to save your souls." James, it is true, is addressing those in whom the ground of salvation was already laid; but he presupposes also, that they can only become partakers of salvation, by continuing to build on that foundation, and to yield submission to the word which they have once received, that they may experience in themselves its purifying and transforming power.

Having constantly in mind the practical errors under which these churches were suffering, he comes back again and again to the [Ch. i. 22–24. warning against that delusive tendency to exalt the outward. He exhorts them, not to imagine that it is sufficient to have a mere knowledge of the word, to be intellectually conversant with it. He warns them against the self-deception, that by such a knowledge merely they had complied with what he has just said, had really received the word into their life, had thus become Christians. The essential point is, the practical application of the word to the life. Herein must it manifest its efficacy, as a principle which works from within upon the outward character, and takes possession of the entire life. He says to them: "But be ye doers of the word and not hearers only, deceiving your own selves." He sets this in a clear light by a familiar illustration. He compares him who receives the word with the understanding only, without applying it to the life, to one who, having seen his image in a mirror, goes away and immediately forgets how he looked. Thus he whe merely busies himself in a superficial way with the divine word, may have learned indeed what is the true aspect of his life in relation to the divine Law and its demands. A light has dawned upon his mind, as to what he is and should be. But turning away again from the divine word, hurried along by the current of life and by his own passions, he immediately forgets it all like him who just saw his image in the mirror, and all is of no avail. "For if any one be a hearer of the word and not a doer, he is like unto a man beholding his natural face in a glass; for he beholdeth himself, and goeth his way, and straightway forgetteth what manner of man he was."

With him who thus contents himself with a mere superficial study of the word of God, in whom knowledge and practice are at variance with each other, James now contrasts one who has looked into the depths of the divine Law, and lives in that contemplation. He here marks the distinction between the law of the letter, in its nature external, and that which Christianity has made the inner law, the law of the spirit, received

Ch. i. 25.]

into the inner life. This he calls the perfect law, in contrast with the law of Moses viewed only in its externality, which as such,—that is, as a law of the letter merely,—can bring nothing to perfection, but leaves everything as it found it. The former he calls the law of liberty, inasmuch as it makes him free who has received it into his inner life, in contrast with the bondage of the letter. To this law one cannot hold the relation of a mere external hearer. Whoever has actually received it into himself as the perfect law, the law of liberty, is constrained by an inward impulse to manifest it in the outward life. "But whoso looketh into the perfect law of liberty, and continueth therein, he being not a forgetful hearer, but a doer of the word, this man,"—he adds,—"shall be blessed in his deed."

But how does this accord with Paul's representation, of the characteristic difference between the relations established by the Law and the Gospel, when he gives as the watchword of the former, "Do this and thou shalt live" (who does it, he shall live therein); and of the latter, "The just shall live by faith?" There would indeed be a contradiction here, if James were speaking of the Law in the same sense as Paul,—if he meant that by works of law one could merit salvation. But this is far from James' purpose. He is speaking of the Law, as made by faith in Christ a living inward principle; of that Law as Christ unfolds it in the Sermon on the Mount, and which presupposes and includes in itself faith. In this view he may justly say, that one must feel himself blessed in the practice of this Law, and in this way alone can become a partaker of that blessedness which Christ imparts to the believer. It is precisely the same thing as Christ himself says, at the close of the Sermon on the Mount: "Whosoever heareth these sayings of mine and doeth them, I will liken him unto a wise man, which built his house upon a rock." Certainly, to this Paul also would have assented. To this certainly corresponded his own manner of teaching,—that only he can experience in himself the divine power of faith, can be blessed through faith, who furnishes the evidence of it in his life; faith being in his view that inward principle, which works from within the transformation of the whole life, that faith which works by love; as he himself says: "Though I had all faith, so that I could remove mountains, and have not charity, I am nothing." (1 Cor. xiii. 2.)

James now passes once more from the general to the particular, to the special application of what he has just said on this principle of active obedience. [Ch. i. 26, 27. The case which he presents, as requiring special notice, is selected with a view to the peculiar circumstances and faults of these churches. Writing to other churches he might have selected other examples. "If any man among you seem to be religious, and bridleth not his tongue, but deceiveth his own heart, this man's religion is vain." James takes for his starting-point the Christian principle, that religion must embrace the whole life. Hence he calls that religion merely imaginary, seeming, unreal, which allows the continuance of the moral defects originally predominant in the character; as, for example, in the application to these churches, that tendency to passionate anger, that want of control over the tongue. Of those who continued to live on thus as before, and yet made pretensions to religion, James says that they deceived themselves, that their religion was vain. Here again, in contrasting with this that religion which is genuine, showing itself in the life, he adduces the particular acts in which such a religion must manifest itself; in this, too, making the selection with special reference to the circumstances of these churches. To take the part of the orphan and the widow, to protect them against the pride and oppression of the rich,—this is pure and genuine religion. "Pure religion and undefiled before God and the Father, is this, to visit the fatherless and widows in their affliction, and to keep themselves unspotted from the world." He thus closes again with the general; the injunction, to keep one's self pure from all defilement by the world, having reference to the whole Christian life. He does not mean that external, often falsely conceived opposition to the world, which would hinder the Christian from serving as the true salt and the true leaven for the world. This would stand in direct contradiction with that course of active labors in the world, which James everywhere enjoins in this Epistle. He means that one should keep himself inwardly unspotted from the world; that while externally acting upon it, he should guard himself against the infection of its impurity; that he should remain superior to the world, pure from the world whilst acting upon it. There are two things, therefore, essential to true religion and inseparable in it: viz. conflict against the evil which is in the world, the practical exercise of love; and in connection therewith, the keeping oneself inwardly pure from all ungodliness that reigns in the world. The former, moreover, cannot truly subsist except in connection with the latter.

We have already spoken of the distinction between the large numbers of the poor, and
the much smaller number of the rich, in [Ch. ii. 1.
these churches. Diversities and inequalities of condition, originating in the natural organization and relations of society, were not to be done away by Christianity, but rendered less grievous; were to be equalized by the common bond of love, and made a ground for the exercise of this Christian love. If it be true, (a matter on which we cannot decide with certainty) that the first glow of Christian enthusiasm gave rise for the time to a proper community of goods; yet was this a state of things adapted only to that period, when the new feeling of fellowship with each other in the divine life burst forth with a power, which for a while swallowed up all individual distinctions. But this

could not be permanent. The inequalities founded in nature must at length re-appear, and the individual and personal be again allowed its just claims. Only the feeling should still remain, which united all as one heart and one soul; and through the love that cared for the wants of all, made as it were a common stock of the possessions of all. But this was now wanting in these churches; and the differences of rank and wealth were no longer repressed by the consciousness of that higher Christian equality. Hence, in opposition to such an unchristian aristocracy, James says: "My brethren, have not the faith of our Lord Jesus Christ the Lord of Glory, with respect of persons." He thus expresses the contradiction, between the disposition to estimate the worth of believers by such temporal advantages, and faith in Jesus as the Lord of Glory! To him who acknowledges Jesus as such, the one dignity of belonging to him must seem so great, that all personal advantages of an earthly nature must be less than nothing in comparison. His glory, in which all believers are called to participate, far outshines all earthly splendor.

He then proceeds with a more specific application

of this reproof. "For if there come unto your assembly a man with a gold ring, in goodly apparel, and there come in also a poor man, [Ch. ii. 2-4. in vile raiment: and ye have respect to him that weareth the gay clothing, and say unto him, Sit thou here in a good place; and say to the poor, Stand thou there, or sit here under my footstool: are ye not then partial in yourselves [at strife with yourselves], and are become judges of evil thoughts?"* The Greek word which we have translated "at strife with yourselves," indicates a state in which solicitude, doubt, conflicting thoughts, arise in the soul; as is the case where the simplicity of faith is disturbed, and discordant aims, worldly thoughts, take precedence of that one sole interest which should be all in all to the Christian. Here then are meant, in contrast with the Christian view of the equality of all who stand related in Christian fellowship, those worldly and foreign views, which give an undeserved deference to one, while they deny to another the respect due him as a member of the same community. These are the evil thoughts of which he speaks.

He now goes on to show them, from the history

* Those who judge from, or under the influence of, evil thoughts.—Tr.

of the spread of Christianity at this very time, from the living example of the present, how entirely such a way of judging is opposed to the Christian stand-point. He appeals to the fact, that on the poor pre-eminently have been bestowed the highest dignity of the Christian calling, the greatest riches in faith, the heirship of the kingdom of Heaven. And they despised the poor, whom God had so highly exalted! "Hearken, my beloved brethren; Hath not God chosen the poor of this world, rich in faith, and heirs of the kingdom which he hath promised to them that love him? But ye have despised the poor." We must here remark once more, that when James here speaks of the kingdom of God as promised to those that love him,—this love of God, in his sense of the words, is doubtless to be understood as connected with faith. He means Christian love; which presupposes the revelation of the redeeming love of God in Christ, and the consciousness of this love received through the Holy Spirit.

Ch. ii. 5, 6.]

In contrast with these poor, among whom the calling of God pre-eminently found access, he places the rich who oppress the Christians, who drag them before the judgment-

Ch. ii. 6, 7.]

seat,—if not on account of their faith, yet for the sake of extortion,—who blaspheme that holy name by which Christians are called. "Do not rich men oppress you, and draw you before the judgment-seats? Do they not blaspheme that worthy name by which ye are called?" We suppose that by the rich here are meant, such of the rich as were opposers of Christianity. James makes use of the well-known fact, that while the poor more readily received the Gospel, the proudly rich showed themselves the violent enemies of Christians and of Christianity. It is possible, indeed, though this would be less suited to the intended contrast, that rich men who called themselves Christians are meant; who might be said to blaspheme the name of Christ, through the scandal which they brought upon it by their course of life.

He calls on them to consider, how entirely such a course is at variance with the essential principle of the divine life,—viz. with [Ch. ii. 8–13.
Love. With him, too, Love is the fulfilling of the Law. "If ye fulfil the royal law, according to the Scriptures, Thou shalt love thy neighbor as thyself, ye do well. But if ye have respect to persons, ye commit sin, and are convinced of the Law

as transgressors." But he was dealing with persons ensnared on all sides in the outward and formal; who, therefore, among the transgressions of the Law (which they could not comprehend in its full majesty and strictness) made a difference in degree, as measured by an external standard; and who, judging by such a standard, might suppose it easy to satisfy the claims of the Law. To them such a predominance of the egoistic, as was shown in that preference of the rich, and that contempt of the poor, seemed no very grievous sin. It was therefore necessary to admonish them that the Law, as an expression, in one indivisible whole, of the divine will the divine holiness, demands absolute obedience; that only by such an obedience can one be justified, and that in every single act of transgression the whole Law is broken. "For whosoever shall keep the whole Law, and yet offend in one point, he is guilty of all. For He that said, Do not commit adultery; said also, Do not kill. Now if thou commit no adultery, yet if thou kill, thou art become a transgressor of the Law." Accordingly in applying this principle, in the sense of James, to the special case here spoken of, we must say: He who, in this one thing, permits his conduct to be determined by that selfishness which is in conflict with the law of love, has thereby violated the whole Law. He has violated it in reference to its substance, as the expression of the divine will wherein all is of equal dignity; and in reference to the ruling motive of his conduct, Self in opposition to Love.

Does James then mean, that in judging of sinful agents and acts no differences in degree can be admitted? By no means. It is only necessary to distinguish here between the abstract and the concrete, according as the question respects the principle itself in the unqualified strictness of its demands, or the varying relations which human agency bears to it; inasmuch as, while all must acknowledge themselves guilty before the Law, there may be gradations in guilt, according as the higher nature of man has more or less asserted its own freedom and superiority, or as the disturbing element of self may still show its predominance. Certainly James could not intend to say that any one, even among Christians, wholly meets the demands of the Law. The higher his conception of the dignity of the Law, as already shown, and the stronger his opposition to the usual standard of merit as consisting in particular external acts and observances,—the less could such a view be attributed to him. What immediately follows is to the same effect. It is assumed that, however different may be the actions of men, all appear as guilty in the sight of the Law. But as Christ teaches us to pray: Forgive us our debts as we forgive our debtors; so does James exhort, that by exercising gentleness and mercy, in the consciousness of still remaining sin, we should show ourselves meet subjects of the divine compassion. Christians should speak and act with the continual sense of their need of divine mercy; then will meekness in speech and action be its spontaneous expression, and mercy triumph over strict justice. In this view, therefore, he calls the law by which the Christian is judged, a law of liberty. For he is no longer under the yoke of a law requiring absolute obedience, which none can render, as the condition of salvation; but is connected with a law which is fulfilled by the free obedience of love, not of fear,—in the consciousness of sins forgiven and confiding reliance on the mercy of God. "So speak ye and so do, as they that shall be judged by the law of liberty. For he shall have judgment without mercy, that hath showed no mercy, and mercy rejoiceth against judgment."

As James everywhere marks the distinction between appearance and reality; and opposes those tendencies which make appearance pass for reality; as he declares himself against dependence on mere knowledge of the law without a corresponding course of life, against a pretended piety which does not show itself in works of love; so, from the same point of view and with the same connection of ideas, does he condemn a faith which fails to show itself in corresponding good works. [Ch. ii. 14–19. "What doth it profit, my brethren, though a man say he hath faith, and have not works? can faith save him?" It should be carefully noted, that James does not say; if one has faith,—but if he professes to have it. He speaks of a merely professed faith, not of that which is genuine. Of such a faith, which by its want of good works proves itself to be spurious, he declares that salvation is not to be attained by it. In the view of Paul also, good works are necessary fruits of true faith. One which professed to be such, and yet was wanting in these fruits, he would not have regarded as justifying faith, indeed would not have allowed it the name of faith. The meaning of James is clear from the illustration which follows. Faith without works, he compares to that love which never manifests itself in deeds, and is shown only in professions. "If a brother or sister be naked, and destitute of daily food, and one of you say unto them, Depart in peace, be ye warmed and filled: notwithstanding ye give them not those things which are needful to the body: What doth it profit? Even so faith, if it hath not works, is dead being alone [is in itself dead].

When James says that faith without works is dead, he certainly could not mean that works, the mere outward and phenomenal, constitute the living element of faith, that through them it becomes a living faith. On the contrary, he presupposes that true faith has life in itself, has in itself the living principle from which alone works can proceed, and that in works it makes itself known. The want of works was to him a proof that life was wanting in that faith, and hence he calls it a dead faith. He introduces a third person, speaking from James' own point of view with him who professes to have faith without works, and proving to him that the one cannot exist without the other. "Yea, a man may say, Thou hast faith, and I have works: show me thy faith without thy works, and I will show thee my faith by my works." In this James proposes,—for it is he who says this in the person of another,—to one who boasts of his faith though he has no works, that he should make the trial of showing to him the existence of his faith without the aid of works. To James it would be easy, by his works to show the faith which animates him, and in the strength of which those works were performed. As a proof that such a faith without works is of no value, he adduces the faith of evil spirits. Faith in God, in its true sense, can only there exist where he is consciously recognized as the highest good, where the whole life has reference to him; that faith which includes in itself a living fellowship with God,—a practical, not merely intellectual faith. With evil spirits, on the contrary, the consciousness of dependence on the Almighty and Supreme forces itself upon them against their will. They would gladly throw off this dependence, but they have not the power. It is something merely passive, with which their own free inclination, the self-moved submission of the spirit, has nothing to do. It is not a faith of the heart, but merely of the intellect; presenting God as in opposition to the spirit striving to escape from him,—God the Almighty, only as an object of fear to the spirit estranged from him, and unwilling to acknowledge him. "Thou believest there is one God; thou doest well: the devils also believe, and tremble."

By the Jews Abraham was claimed, as the representative of the faith in one God in the midst of nations devoted to idolatry; and therein was placed (as by others indeed in his circumcision) his great significance. James therefore proceeds to show, that the significance of this faith did not consist in a passive belief of the understanding in one God. It was a devotion of the whole life to God. It proved its genuineness by works of self-denial; by his readiness, in love to God and reliance upon him, in confiding resignation to his will, to deny all natural feelings and make of the object dearest to himself an offering to God. He, therefore, who would follow Abraham in his faith and by that faith be justified before God, must also attest his faith by like works of self-denial. "But wilt thou know, O vain man, that

Ch. ii. 20–24.]

faith without works is dead? Was not Abraham our father justified by works, when he had offered Isaac his son upon the altar?" Thus might he say, that faith and works must here have wrought together. How wrought together? For the justification of man before God? So that Abraham could not appear as one justified before Him, until after the works had been performed? Had James intended this, it must have been on the supposition, that God can know man only so far as he manifests himself in outward acts. He could not therefore have recognized him as the omniscient God, who looks into the heart, and discerns the inward feeling before it comes to light. Recognizing his omniscience, he must have known that to the eye of God, this faith, which afterwards showed itself in such works of self-denial, already appeared as genuine justifying faith. But speaking from the stand-point of human consciousness, taking into account only the outward manifestation, he might so express himself; viz. that faith and works wrought together for justification. So also when he says, that "by works was faith made perfect," he could not mean that works,—the mere outward phenomena of faith,—are that which perfects faith itself; but only that in them faith shows itself genuine and complete, the attestation of faith in the life and conduct. "Seest thou how faith wrought with his works, and by works was faith made perfect? And the Scripture was fulfilled which saith, Abraham believed God, and it was imputed unto him for righteousness; and he was called the friend of God." And in that sense he then says: "Ye see then, how that by works a man is justified, and not by faith only."

To the example of Abraham he now adds that of Rahab. Here, also, against the false Jewish position, that this heathen woman was justified on the ground of passive faith in the One God, he declares that this faith was required to approve itself in works, the fruits of an inward disposition, contemning for the honor of God all worldly considerations. "Likewise also, was not Rahab the harlot justified by works, when she received the messengers, and had sent them out another way?" He concludes the whole discussion with the words: "For as the body without the spirit is dead, so faith without works is dead also." In this comparison, faith without works answers to the dead body without the animating spirit. But

Ch. ii. 25, 26.]

it is only because the point of comparison is not fully brought out. We cannot suppose him to mean, that works answer to the spirit; for the spirit is certainly the inward, animating principle. Works, would answer to the activity of the living body. He means then: the want of works is proof that the faith is a dead one, destitute of the vital principle, and is therefore to be compared to a body which is dead.

James then passes to another, and at first view apparently quite different topic. But upon nearer inspection, it is found to be closely connected with the foregoing. For the very same tendency which made a merit of merely knowing and talking of the Law, of an empty show of faith without a corresponding life; would also lead men to set themselves up as teachers of others, and to have much to say in the assemblies of the church, without the inward call to this work. "My brethren, be not many masters [be not many of you teachers]." As the ground of this warning, he refers to the increased responsibility which one draws upon himself, by assuming to be the teacher of others; "knowing that we shall receive the greater condemnation." The ground of

[Ch. iii. 1, 2.

the tendency in these churches, to make so light a matter of teaching, was that very want of self-examination and self-knowledge, which had so much to do with all the faults rebuked by James. Under the influence of that superficial moral judgment, which took into account only the outward and apparent, they could not rightly estimate the importance of words. It was not considered, that speaking itself was an act, and was to be judged by a moral standard ; and that one may sin, not less by the immoral use of speech than by any other act. He bids them beware of this danger. He shows how hard it is, to observe the just measure, to exercise the proper self-control, in the use of speech ; what injury may proceed from a single word ; and by this he would admonish them, to be so much the more conscientious in taking upon themselves the office of speaking. He who considered well that responsibility and its danger, could not so lightly resolve upon assuming it. Accordingly he says : "If any man offend not in word, the same is a perfect man, and able also to bridle the whole body." That is : He who on all occasions, exercises self-control in the use of words, will also be able to exercise the same in all other respects.

He then proceeds to show, by many striking examples drawn from actual life, what power may reside in things seemingly trivial,—how much depends on the government of the tongue. "Behold we put bits in the horses' mouths, that they may obey us, and we turn about their whole body. Behold also the ships, which though they be so great, and are driven of fierce winds, yet are they turned about with a very small helm, whithersoever the governor listeth. Even so the tongue is a little member, and boasteth great things. Behold how great a matter [forest] a little fire kindleth! And the tongue is a fire,"—(that is, as a spark can set a whole forest on fire, so may a word spoken by the tongue be the occasion of great mischief)—"a world of iniquity: so is the tongue amongst our members, that it defileth the whole body, and setteth on fire the course of nature [life], and it is set on fire of hell." By this is meant, that as the tongue is set on fire by the flames of hellish passion, so from the tongue does the fire spread over the whole course of life. He then shows how vain a thing is man's dominion

[Ch. iii. 3–8.

over the natural world, if he, aspiring to rule the world, is himself through passion a slave of the world; what a reproach it is to man, claiming subjection from all animals, not to be able to bridle his own tongue. "For every kind of beasts, and of birds, and of serpents, and things in the sea, is tamed and hath been tamed of mankind. But the tongue can no man tame; it is an unruly evil, full of deadly poison."

The show of piety James opposes in all its forms. Such is that pious cant, in which, along with praise to God in words, are mingled a hateful censoriousness and bitter denunciation of men, in whom God's image is to be honored. James exposes the inherent inconsistency of such conduct, which to his view is mere hypocrisy. "Therewith bless we God, even the Father; and therewith curse we men, which are made after the similitude of God. Out of the same mouth proceedeth blessing and cursing. My brethren, these things ought not so to be. Doth a fountain send forth at the same place sweet water and bitter? Can the fig-tree, my brethren, bear olive berries, either a vine figs? So can no fountain both yield salt water and fresh." Thus does James express

Ch. iii. 9–12.]

the ground-thought of this whole Epistle, viz. that all turns on the inward temper from which the whole life takes its direction; and nothing could be more remote from that tendency, opposed by him at all points, which confines its regard to the merely external, to single acts and empty show.

As James has contended against a false faith, unaccompanied by works,—so does he, in like manner, against that knowledge and wisdom in divine things, which does not make itself known by a living activity in a corresponding course of life. He requires of all religious knowledge, that it approve itself, as a product of the divine life of the spirit, in a course of conduct proceeding from that inner life. "Who is a wise man, and endued with knowledge amongst you? Let him show out of a good conversation, &c." With this view, he gives special prominence to that which stood most opposed to the faults of these churches; contrasting with the unbridled passion of those who made such account of their knowledge, the spirit of meekness as being the mark of genuine wisdom and knowledge: "let him show... his works with meekness and wisdom."

[Ch. iii. 13.

"But if ye have bitter envying and strife in

your hearts, glory not, and lie not against the truth." It is the inward temper which,
Ch. iii. 14–16.]
in his view, marks genuine knowledge also, genuine wisdom. This must derive its being from above, must be the product of the divine life, and through its divine impress must make itself known also in the outward life. The opposite proceeds from a principle of the natural man, not from that which is divine. For the Holy Scriptures often designate, under the name of the Flesh, everything evil, all which stands opposed to the Spirit of God, to the divine life. When the term is used in this general sense, it includes also the spiritual nature of man,—the reason, the soul, in so far as it has not been made subject to the Divine Spirit, but claims an independent being, to be something in its own right,—independently of God and aside from God, and hence in opposition to him. All this is comprehended in the idea of the Flesh, in that Biblical sense. It is by no means limited to what we call Flesh, sensuality in the narrower sense of the term. From Flesh, understood in this more general sense, is distinguished in biblical usage that which in the nar-

rower sense is designated as natural,*—viz. the spiritual nature of man (the reason, the soul) as being unlike to God, and conformed to the world. Reason, however highly developed and cultivated, remains still within the bounds of the natural man. It is of this James speaks; and this with him is the same which actuates apostate spirits. "This wisdom descendeth not from above, but is earthly, sensual [natural], devilish. For where envying and strife is, there is confusion, and every evil work."

He then enters more fully into particulars, and describes the traits which characterize genuine wisdom. He does this with special reference indeed to the false conceit of wisdom among these churches, but yet in a manner practically useful for all times. As characteristic of the wisdom that comes from above, he names first, purity,—i. e. freedom from all worldly stain; then [Ch. iii. 17.

* This term is used here, as already familiar to the reader of the English Bible, the same word in the original being so translated in several passages, e. g. 1 Cor. ii. 14. The German word (*seelisch*, of the soul, psychical, pertaining to the higher rational nature of man) is used by Neander, as explained in the text, of the rational soul not under the influence of the Holy Spirit,—in other words, of the *natural* or unrenewed mind and affections. It is therefore the best expression of his meaning to the English reader, though not a translation of the German word, for which we have no representative suitable to be used here.—Tr.

love of peace,—the truly wise not being stubbornly attached to his own opinion and contentious in support of it; then, that it is gentle, is easily persuaded,—i. e. ready to listen to others, willing to be taught, to acknowledge what is wrong on its own part, and to adopt the better way. All this gives evidence of victory attained over the love of self. The wisdom which is from above he farther characterizes, as full of mercy and good fruits,—meaning that knowledge and action must go together. We have already explained, in connection with a previous passage,* what James means by being in conflict with oneself. This he now excludes from the idea of genuine wisdom. He demands an inward harmony of soul, the stability of conviction; that the soul shall not be distracted by the discordant views, the mental conflicts of this state of unbelief. It is difficult to indicate his meaning in a single word. Candor, simplicity, perhaps comes nearest to the idea. Finally, true wisdom is without hypocrisy.

In what James has thus far said, his main object
Ch. iii. 18.] has been to oppose the contentious spirit of this conceit of wisdom. He now

* Page 71.

brings the opposite trait more prominently forward, by asserting that it is only in peace, in unity, that every Christian interest can prosper. "And the fruit of righteousness is sown in peace, of them that make peace." "Fruit of righteousness" may, in biblical usage, be variously understood. It may denote either the blessing which righteousness brings with it,—fruit for life eternal; or the fruits of righteousness in the works which it produces. But though the words are true in both senses, the latter seems to be the one intended by James,—and his meaning is: the seeds of all that is truly good in action, proceeding from righteousness, can only prosper where there is peace, and with those whose conduct tends to peace. Where all is strife, nothing truly Christian can prosper.

This leads him to speak, in general, of the source of the many controversies in these churches. This he finds in those insatiable desires which allow no one to be at rest. [Ch. iv. 1, 2. "From whence come wars and fightings among you? Come they not hence, even of your lusts, that war in your members?" Like Paul, James here presupposes an inward conflict in man, the conflict between flesh and spirit. As the power of evil is by Paul termed the law in the members, because in the body is the outward manifestation of man, and there the dominion of sinful desire shows itself; so James, in like manner, speaks of the lusts that war in the members. In the case of the unrenewed, the power of the sinful desires is opposed only by the activity of man's higher spiritual nature, which is too weak, however, to gain the victory over the opposing force. This conflict, which leads to no decisive result, and leaves man in unreconciled disunion with himself, is described by Paul in the seventh chapter of his Epistle to the Romans. It is otherwise with the Christian, the regenerated man. In him also this conflict is continued, but with this difference,—that in him the higher spiritual nature has been strengthened through the divine life imparted to him, whereby he is enabled to overcome the opposing sinful desires. But he must maintain the conflict in order to gain the victory; otherwise, the evil principle gains upon him more and more, and may at length succeed in wholly extinguishing the higher life. James exhorts to the maintenance of this warfare, and gives warning of the danger which threatens him who intermits it, as was the case with many in these churches. For there were doubtless many here, as appears from the rebukes of James, who called themselves Christians, but were yet strangers to the new birth, and stood in just the same relation to these two opposite tendencies as those who still belonged wholly to the world. Hence James says to them: "Ye covet" (namely earthly goods which ye may use in the service of your lusts) "and have not; ye kill, and desire to have [ye hate and envy], and cannot obtain."

In the original of the above passage it is said, "Ye murder." Luther has translated it "Ye hate," not without reason so far as respects the meaning; for it is hardly possible that James should speak of murder, in the proper sense, as so prevalent. But James purposely, without doubt, selects the very strongest expressions, in order to designate with the utmost precision the nature of that evil, which, whatever may be the outward form of manifestation, is still the same. Thus murder stands as the climax in the expression of hate and envy. For in the very nature of hatred and envy lies the desire, to remove their object out of the way. The selfishness which here betrays itself, sees in the existence of that object an obstacle to its wishes, from which it would gladly be freed. Even if the overt act has not yet been committed, and the power of the higher tendency is still too great to allow it, yet does it lie in the very nature of the emotion; and the divine word reveals to us, in the concealed germ of the heart, the very same thing which afterward, when expressed in act, becomes an object of general abhorrence. Hence Christ declares in the Sermon on the Mount, in opposition to the mere external conception of the Mosaic Law, that whosoever is angry with his brother, is in danger of the judgment, i. e. of damnation. And the Apostle John says: "Whosoever hateth his brother is a murderer."

Ch. iv. 2, 3.] James now directs them, as he had done at the beginning of the Epistle, to the fountain of all good, whence alone they could obtain all that was wanting to them, the supply of all their necessities. The ground of their unceasing and fruitless efforts, only involving them in strife, through the collision of selfish interests, he finds in their disposition to do for themselves, that which they should seek from God alone in the spirit of humble submission. To their neglect of prayer, which alone can procure a blessing on labor, he ascribes their vain endeavors and contentions. Such were not wanting indeed in these churches, as connected a certain habit of prayer with all the other external practices of religion, and proceeding from the same temper of heart. But such prayer he characterizes as one which could bring no fruit, because it was not the true prayer of the heart, and did not proceed from the right disposition of the soul towards God. It was merely the expression of earthly desire, seeking to make God subservient to itself; for they sought from Him only what they might use for the gratification of their lusts. "Ye fight and war, yet ye have not, because ye ask not. Ye ask and receive not, because ye ask amiss, that ye may consume it upon your lusts."

He returns continually to the radical evil, the want in the soul of the one determining ground-tone in the reference of the life to God; the direction of the whole spirit to the world, in connection with many external practices of religion. As in the Old Testament, the union of the people with God is represented under the

[Ch. iv. 4, 5.

image of a marriage, their apostasy from God under that of adultery; so James addresses them as adulterers, inasmuch as they claimed to be worshipers of God, and yet served only the world. He admonishes them that God requires the whole heart, that it cannot be divided between God and the world; that either love to God or love to the world must be the animating principle; that devotion to the world, as the aim of effort, a love of the world which seeks in the world its highest good, cannot exist without hostility towards God,—as the Lord himself says: Ye cannot serve God and Mammon. "Ye adulterers, and adulteresses, know ye not that the friendship of the world is enmity with God? Whosoever therefore will be a friend of the world, is the enemy of God." James reminds them in general of the declarations of the Holy Scripture, which everywhere testifies of the incompatibility of these two radical tendencies. "Or," says he to them, "suppose ye that the Scripture saith in vain, The Spirit that dwelleth in us lusteth to envy [is a jealous spirit]?" This spirit, he would say, can suffer no other to share with itself; where it would take up its abode, it excludes the love of the world.

"But,"—to the above warning he immediately subjoins the consolation,—"He giveth more grace;" more, to wit, than that [Ch. iv. 6–8. already bestowed, provided only that the one radical condition is fulfilled, in the entire submission of the heart, in the humbly receptive spirit. He reminds them of the passage from the Proverbs: "God resisteth the proud, but giveth grace unto the humble." Even if those, to whom his Epistle was directed, were not chargeable with the pride of unbelief,—they were yet wanting in the ground-tone of humility, the abiding sense of dependence on God, the ever-present consciousness that they were nothing and could do nothing without God. This want betrayed itself in excessive reliance on earthly possessions and human means. The prevalence of a worldly spirit always originates in want of humility. For this reason James admonishes them, that God withholds his gifts and aid from the proud, since the necessary condition on the part of the creature for the reception of every communication on the part of God, is wanting to them. But where humility is found, there is a susceptibility for the communication of all divine grace. He says to those, who pleaded in excuse for sin the irresistible temptations of Satan, or the withholding of divine grace, that it was their own fault if they thus fell. All depended on the direction of their own will. In order to resist the Evil One, who has power over no one except by his own consent, they needed but to humble themselves before God, to turn to Him in the consciousness of dependence. Thus will God impart himself to them, and thus will the Evil One be compelled to flee. "Submit yourselves therefore to God: resist the Devil and he will flee from you. Draw nigh unto God and he will draw nigh unto you."

Ch. iv. 8–10.] The inward and the outward James comprehends as one. Purity of heart from all worldly stains, must show itself in purity of the outward conduct. This is expressed by James (who delights to embody truth in a specific form) as keeping the hand, the instrument of sin, pure from every sinful act; and purity of life, exhibited in the external walk, must lead back again to its source, inward purity of heart. "Cleanse your hands, ye sinners, and purify your hearts, ye double-minded" (divided between God and the world). The Greek term expresses the idea (which we have already explained*) of a man who has as it were two souls; to whom is wanting the true harmony of the inner life, which proceeds only from the all-controlling direction of the soul to God; of the man who is divided between opposite tendencies to God and to the world. Such a spiritual state is in direct contrariety with that sanctification of the heart, which James requires; it being the very ground of true sanctification, that but one soul should dwell in man, that in all things the single animating principle should be love to God. It was therefore necessary, first of all, to arouse those who were sunk in worldly pleasure to a sense of the vanity of such enjoyments, to the wretchedness of their condition. A godly sorrow must be awakened in them; the anguish of repentance as a ground of true joy,—the joy in God of those who are dead to the world and wholly devoted to Him. So Christ says in the Sermon on the Mount, with which we find so many points of harmony in this Epistle: Blessed are they that mourn, for they shall be comforted. "Be afflicted" (feel your wretchedness), "and mourn, and weep: let your laughter be turned to

* Page 51.

mourning, and your joy to heaviness. Humble yourselves in the sight of the Lord, and he shall lift you up."

Thus James comprehends all in self-abasement before God, as the condition of all true exaltation, which comes alone from God ; as the Saviour has said : Whoso exalteth himself shall be abased, and he that humbleth himself shall be exalted. James here speaks of an inward act of the spirit, not of one which can become an object of outward perception; although this inward act must make itself known in the outward form of the whole life. Hence he says,—abasement before God, in the eye of God, as that which can take place only between the soul and God. Here too the relation is such as man can sustain to God alone, not to any created being. He who is conscious to himself of such a relation to God, for that very reason will be far from placing himself in a similar relation to any human being. As his whole life thus has its root in conscious dependence on God, he will thereby be secured from every form of bondage to man.

The want of humility showed itself in that proneness to judge censoriously of others. Here was a twofold expression of the want of humility, in reference to the Law. He who judges thus censoriously of others, is far from humbling himself before that holy law; from comparing his whole life therewith, and discovering how great is the chasm between his life and its demands. [Ch. iv. 11, 12.

Hence James says, that such an one makes himself the judge of the Law, the lawgiver, instead of applying the Law to himself and acting in accordance therewith. Such an one, he says, in speaking against his brother speaks against the Law, since he gives the lie to the Law that accuses him for judging another. Furthermore, such an one betrays the want of self-abasement before God,—inasmuch as he forgets how he himself, with him whom he accuses, stands in like dependence on the One sole Judge and Arbiter of happiness and misery. He sets himself in the place of the Supreme Judge, inasmuch as he presumes to anticipate his verdict. "Speak not evil one of another, brethren: he that speaketh evil of his brother, and judgeth his brother, speaketh evil of the law, and judgeth the law; but if thou judge the law, thou art not a doer of the law, but a judge. There is one lawgiver, who is able to save and to destroy; who art thou that judgest another?"

Ch. iv. 13–17.] The pride of the worldly spirit, in contrast with the nature of genuine humility, was the starting-point with which James commenced, and from which he proceeded to reprove the various forms of evil in these churches. In like manner he now brings forward another specific case, connected however with the same radical tendency of which we have spoken. It was that false reliance upon the Human, which leads one to make calculations upon the future, without for a moment taking into account the insecurity of human life; to form prospective plans of earthly gain, as if one were entirely certain of the future. James thought it necessary to admonish those, who were thus absorbed in worldly pursuits, of the uncertainty of all human things; that every moment of life is dependent on the will of God and his providence. "Go to now ye that say, To-day or to-morrow we will go into such a city and continue there a year, and buy, and sell, and get gain: whereas ye know not what shall be on the morrow: for what is your life? It is even a vapor which appeareth for a little time and then vanisheth away. For that ye ought to say, if the Lord will, we shall live, and do this or that." It is plain that in saying this, James did not mean to insist, that such a condition should always be expressed in words. For such expressions might easily degenerate into a mere form; and the tendency of these churches was to turn everything into form. Here again James shows his preference of the specific over the general. Instead of the general truth, of the uncertainty and dependence of the whole earthly life, he uses language adapted to suggest this general thought by its application to a particular case. From the particular he now passes over again to the general, and assails that false worldly and self-reliance in its whole extent. "But now ye glory in your vain confidence; all such glorying is evil." In closing this admonition, he warns them, that it is not enough to have known the truth here expressed; it was necessary,—and herein they chiefly failed,—that the known truth should pervade the life and control the conduct. "To him that knoweth to do good, and doeth it not, to him it is sin."

James now addresses himself to the rich, wholly immersed in the spirit of the world.
Ch. v. 1-6.] "Go to now, ye rich men, weep and howl for your miseries that shall come upon you. Your riches are corrupted and your garments moth-eaten: Your gold and silver is cankered, and the rust of them shall be a witness against you, and shall eat your flesh, [as ye have treasured up fire] for the last days." He speaks of riches under three specific forms, viz. in the garnered fruits of the field, in garments, and in gold and silver. All these, he would say, the rich heap up without profit. Their treasures in gold and silver, allowed through disuse to consume with rust, will witness against them to their condemnation; showing their guilt in suffering to perish unemployed, that which they should have used for the benefit of others. The rust eats into their own flesh, inasmuch as it is a token of their own perishableness and of the judgment that overhangs them; as they, instead of gathering durable riches, have treasured up for themselves the fire of God's wrath in treasures accumulated for a prey to rust. He then describes the oppressions inflicted by the rich (not necessarily such as belonged to Christian churches)

on the pious poor in humble life. "Behold, the hire of the laborers which have reaped down your fields, which is of you kept back by fraud, crieth: and the cries of them which have reaped are entered into the ears of the Lord of Sabaoth. Ye have lived in pleasure on the earth and been wanton; ye have nourished your hearts as in [for] a day of slaughter." That is; as one pampers the beast destined for slaughter, so have ye, giving yourselves up to the service of your lusts, and revelling in careless unconcern, prepared yourselves for the judgment that is hastening on. "Ye have condemned and killed the just, and he doth not resist you:"—the pious sufferer's patient resignation to God's will, in contrast with the pride and presumption of the oppressor.

He then turns to the Christian brethren, who had so much to suffer from the rich and powerful. He exhorts them to bear with patience every wrong, to wait submissively for the coming of the Lord, who will redeem his own from all evil, and will show himself the righteous judge of all. We must bear in mind, that the time of the Lord's coming was then looked for as already near at hand. It was natural, in

[Ch. v. 7, 8.

the Apostolic age, so to regard it. Christ himself had not chosen to give any information respecting the time of his coming. Nay, he had expressly said, *that the Father* had reserved the decision to himself alone (Mark xiii. 32); that even the Son could determine nothing respecting it. But still, the longing desire of the Apostolic church was directed, with eager haste, to the appearing of the Lord. The whole Christian period seemed only as the transition-point to the eternal, and thus as something that must soon be passed. As the traveller, beholding from afar the object of all his wanderings, overlooks the windings of the intervening way, and believes himself already near his goal; so it seemed to them, as their eye was fixed on that consummation of the whole course of events on earth. It is from this point of view that James here speaks. "Be patient therefore, brethren, unto the coming of the Lord: behold the husbandman waiteth for the precious fruit of the earth, and hath long patience for it, until he receive the early and latter rain. Be ye also patient; stablish your hearts: for the coming of the Lord draweth nigh." James,—who, as already remarked, had all the oriental fondness for imagery drawn from natural objects,—here transfers to history the laws of gradual development in the phenomena of nature. As the fruits of the earth mature only by slow degrees, and the husbandman must wait patiently for the early and the latter rain; so there is needed the same constancy of patience, while anticipating the final consummation of earthly history, in its gradual course of development. Here, too, everything has its appointed time; and one must guard against that impatient haste, which is unwilling to wait for the successive stages of progress, and is eager to reach the end at once.

He now proceeds to speak of the deportment of Christians towards each other, and commends the mutual exercise of long-suffering and forbearance. [Ch. v. 9–11. They should not indulge in mutual accusations, appealing to God against one another, but leave all to the judgment of God. They should not desire, by thus mutually condemning one another, to anticipate the Judge who will soon appear. His words remind us of our Saviour's admonition in the Sermon on the Mount: Judge not, that ye be not judged. "Grudge not one against another, brethren, lest ye be condemned: behold the judge standeth before the door." He then sets before them the examples of the prophets as models of patience; especially the example of Job, in whom, after he had endured every *trial* of his patience, the mercy of God was so gloriously displayed. "Take, my brethren, the prophets, who have spoken in the name of the Lord, for an example of suffering affliction and of patience." The thought is doubtless this: They have spoken in the name of the Lord, and yet have suffered so much,—and that for the Lord's sake. If the prophets, so highly honored and speaking in the name of the Lord, have endured such suffering, how could we expect a different lot? "Behold we count them happy which endure. Ye have heard of the patience of Job, and have seen the end of the Lord" (i. e. the end brought about by him, the final issue which the Lord granted to all his trials); "that the Lord is very pitiful and of tender mercy."

Then follow particular admonitions and exhortations, all which, however, are opposed in spirit to such errors, as were the fruit of the leading evil tendencies in these churches. In the Sermon on the Mount, Christ has unfolded the

Ch. v. 12.]

whole Law in its spirituality and glory; everywhere converting the outward and particular to the inward, to the completeness and unity of the inward temper and disposition; at once abolishing and fulfilling the Law, abolishing it in the letter and fulfilling it in its spirit. Thus to the command: Thou shalt hallow the seventh day, is given its higher spiritual import,—Let every day be holy to thee. In like manner, the requirement to regard an oath as holy, becomes in its true spirit: Let every word be holy to thee, as being consecrated to the Lord,—as addressed to him, since he is ever before thine eyes. What an oath is to others, shall every word be to the Christian. Hence among true Christians, there will be no need of oaths; since to each his word is holy, and such is the mutual confidence of all, that the word of each is so received among them. So should it be in a truly Christian church, in which all are recognized as genuine Christians. But in these churches, where the proneness to much speaking had naturally led to a careless use of words, there now prevailed the Jewish habit of using many asseverations, in order to give their words a weight which they had not in themselves.

Even if they shunned so frequent a use of the name Jehovah, they had other more covert forms of oath in its place,—the violation of which, however, they made less a matter of conscience. Against this James says expressly: "But above all things, my brethren, swear not; neither by Heaven, neither by the earth, neither by any other oath. But let your yea be yea, and your nay be nay; lest ye fall into condemnation." That is, their Yea and Nay should suffice in place of every other form of confirmation; for if their word is not in itself sufficient, and requires the aid of protestations to procure belief, they bring themselves into condemnation.

Then follows the general direction, which most of all stands opposed to the spirit of worldliness in these churches, to that tendency to distinguish between certain acts of religious worship and all the rest of life as belonging to the world. Nothing can be more opposed to such a tendency than the requirement, that every feeling of the Christian, in sorrow and in joy, shall take the form of prayer. Thereby are sorrow and joy to be sanctified and ennobled. In suffering, the feeling of pain shall be changed to

Ch. v. 13.]

the tone of prayer; from God is help to be sought in prayer,—power to sustain suffering and to be submissive under it. And joy, too, shall attune the heart to the praise of God, to gratitude towards Him to whom we owe every good. Thus shall sorrow and joy have this in common,—the direction of the heart towards God. And as life is divided between joy and sorrow, the whole life will thus become prayer. "Is any among you afflicted, let him pray. Is any merry, let him sing psalms."

Having thus referred everything to prayer as the soul of the Christian life, he now makes a specific application of the principle to cases of sickness. [Ch. v. 14–18. Here there was need of mutual intercession in the name of the Lord. As the Presbyters acted in the name of the whole church, and each one as a member of the body felt that he needed its sympathy and intercession, and might count upon it; individuals should therefore, in cases of sickness, send for the Presbyters of the church. These were to offer prayer on their behalf. With this was connected a symbolical transaction,—practised indeed in many churches of the East, but never prescribed as a general usage,—the anointing with oil; of which Christ had sometimes made use in the healing of the sick, as an outward sign of healing and sanctifying power. If it was the will of the Lord, the sick should be restored to bodily health. But, however this might be, he should certainly receive spiritual refreshment, the renewed and strengthened consciousness of sin forgiven; and this could not but favorably affect his bodily state. "Is any sick among you? Let him call for the elders of the church, and let them pray over him, anointing him with oil in the name of the Lord; and the prayer of faith shall save the sick, and the Lord shall raise him up: and if he have committed sins, they shall be forgiven him." We see that James ascribes the healing power, not to the anointing with oil, but to the prayer of faith. As he regards the Presbyters in the light of organs of the church, acting in its name; so does he hold all other Christians in such a relation, as members of one body, that they should mutually pray for one another in bodily and spiritual need; should confess their sins to one another, and pray for the forgiveness of each other's sins. He ascribes great efficacy to the prayer of fraternal love. "Confess your faults one to another, and pray one for another, that ye may be healed,"—whether spiritual and bodily healing united is meant, as in the last quoted passage, or merely spiritual healing. "The effectual fervent prayer of the righteous man availeth much." Of this efficacy of prayer he adduces examples from the Old Testament. But the Jewish tendency to externalize everything, led them to contemplate these holy men of old only from a distance, and as objects of veneration and wonder, not as examples for imitation. James therefore reminds them, that these men were frail mortals like themselves, and that the power of God can still work through the weak. This application was all the more appropriate, inasmuch as Christianity, by virtue of the common relation of Priest and Prophet belonging to all believers, had made that common to all which under the old dispensation had been the gift and prerogative of a few. "Elias was man subject to like passions as we are, and he prayed earnestly that it might not rain: and it rained not on the earth by the space of three years and six months. And he prayed again, and the heaven gave rain, and the earth brought forth her fruit."

This exhortation to mutual intercession, in bodily and spiritual need, leads to this further admonition,—that they should not harshly spurn from them such as, in their religious and moral development, may have erred from the right way, but should interest themselves in their case and seek to lead them back to the truth: an admonition which they specially needed, who were so prone to defame and condemn. "Brethren, if any of you do err from the truth, and one convert him, let him know, that he which converteth the sinner from the error of his way, shall save a soul from death, and shall hide a multitude of sins." This, then, is in James' view the highest work of love,—to rescue the fallen brother from that spiritual death to which he is verging. More than to excite in one repentance for a single sin, and thereby prepare the way for attaining forgiveness of one sinful act,—more than this is the rescue of a soul from a life of sin, and the restoration of the new divine principle of life. By this the many sins are covered, in which his former course had plunged him. This explanation of the words seems most in harmony with the connection. But, by the sins here spoken of,

Ch. v. 19, 20.]

might be understood the sins of him who thus rescues a brother from death. The meaning would then be: The love thus shown in active zeal for the spiritual welfare of another, shall cover many sins into which one may have fallen through infirmity of the flesh; inasmuch as Love outweighs all else, and above all else is adapted to subdue the still remaining evil of the heart. So we are taught by the Saviour himself, that to him who loveth much, much shall be forgiven. Were this the true meaning of the passage (which, however, is contrary to our view), still the covering of one's own sins would not be dependent on the success of his efforts for another; for this is not placed in the power of man, and he can gain nothing for himself thereby, for the very reason that it is something independent of his own purpose. It is the zeal of love, laboring for the conversion of another,—it is this that hides the multitude of sins!

Thus closes this Epistle, in that spirit of love which breathes through it all, and which everywhere shows itself in the life and labors of James!

THE FIRST

EPISTLE OF JOHN,

PRACTICALLY EXPLAINED.

BY

DR. AUGUSTUS NEANDER.

TRANSLATED FROM THE GERMAN

BY

MRS. H. C. CONANT.

WHAT THINK YE OF CHRIST?

NEW YORK:
LEWIS COLBY & CO.,
122 NASSAU STREET.

1853.

PREFACE.

The present volume closes the series of Neander's Practical Commentaries. Of his original plan, embracing all the more important portions of the Bible, only the Exposition of Philippians, of James, and of the first Epistle of John had been completed, when their revered author was summoned to a higher sphere. All these are now before the American public. They form a worthy close of his earthly labors, and to many, will seem the crowning glory of his noble life-work. The treasures of genius and learning, which enrich his more scientific works, here seem vivified by a new element, and melt under the fervor of his inner spiritual life, into a glowing stream of eloquent practical instruction. Not that this element is wanting in any of his productions. It was the informing spirit of his life, and of all his labors. But here it is predominant; all else is but the servant and instrument of Christian love, seeking to edify the body of Christ.

Here, in the Epistle of John, Neander found a peculiarly congenial field. There is a noble freedom and assurance in his tread, a glow of feeling, an eloquence of utterance, such as even Neander exhibits nowhere else. He moves along the high track of revelation as in a familiar path; gazing into its deepest mysteries with reverent but open eye, and interpreting them to us, not as subjects for speculation, but as sources of vital influence to the human spirit.

This exposition derives a peculiar interest from the fact, that it was intended to meet the religious wants of the time. He found the tendencies of the age of John reproduced in our own; and threatening as then, not to subvert Christianity by open opposition, but to corrupt Christianity itself, distilling into the sources of belief the poison of human opinion, under the name of Biblical criticism, and Christian philosophy. In developing the Apostle's meaning, he takes his stand, with a spirit and tone worthy of John himself, in defence of positive revealed religion. The Gospel history is to him no Myth; it is a record of divine facts. The Christ therein revealed, is the Eternal Son of God in human nature. He truly lived, he truly died; he rose victorious over death, and now lives at the right hand of the Father. Through his Life and his Suffering, he won immortal life for man; that life which consists in restoration to the likeness and fellowship of God. Only through him, can the human soul obtain this life. There is here no liberality, so-called, in the theology of Neander, truly liberal as he is on all minor points of belief. The crucified, the risen, the perpetually mediating Christ, must be the all and in all, or the soul wanders in darkness, cut off from the only fountain of salvation. On knowing Christ depends even the knowledge of God, as the universal Father and Creator. To the Christianity which does not accept Christ in his whole revealed character, as the incarnate Eternal Word, the divine-human Redeemer, he refuses even the name of Christianity. In his own emphatic words: "Whoever denies or mutilates this fact, is to be at once rejected. No other mark for the designation of the undivine, the false, the anti-Christian, should be needed for the believer." This commentary, as well as the two preceding, exhibits in a striking light Neander's estimation of the Scriptures, as the inspired word of God. In what English interpreter, guiltless of German learning, can be found a more reverent reception of their teachings, a more devout and diligent seeking after what is revealed, a more child-like humility in pausing at the boundary where revelation ceases? The word of God is to him the supreme authority, the final appeal. His sole object is to develop its treasures, to penetrate through the letter to the spirit, and to bring this into contact with the living heart.

But Neander found also, in the present age, a dead orthodoxy; which, while professing the most tenacious adherence to the Scriptures as the revelation of divine truth, no less dishonored and endangered true Christianity. In unfolding John's treatment of this error in his own age, he furnishes lessons of the richest practical instruction for the evangelical church of our time, and of all times. Religious truth is to him food for the soul, that on which it must live, something demanded by an inward necessity of its nature. Its office is not to exercise the intellect, but to raise and purify the spirit. Belief is the reception of this truth into the living heart, not the cold assent of the understanding. Hence both the earnestness with which he demands the reception of essential truths, and his comparative indifference to all points of doctrine, which do not affect the interests of salvation. Thus the true view of the person of Christ, is to him an object of infinite moment. This is not, however, for the sake of the knowledge in and for itself; but because it is only through this knowledge, that Christ himself can be rightly received into the soul perishing for his help. Only by knowing him as he is, can the soul rightly submit to him, trust in him, draw from him what it needs for the restoration of its God-like nature in the divine image. The right recognition of truth presupposes moreover, on the part of the percipient, that sense of his own moral state and of his relations to God, which converts the outward to inward knowledge. The famishing, the sick, the dying, KNOWS that he has in this truth received refreshment, healing, life, in his inner being. The Christ revealed TO him, has become the Christ revealed IN him; and in this inward revelation, continually derived anew from its divine fountain, lies the highest source of spiritual knowledge. For it is the perception imparted by the Son of God himself, the new God-related sense, which he alone can give. This is the Christian consciousness, so often mentioned by Neander in this commentary;

to which he ascribes so high an office, both as the immediate ground of belief in Christ, and the test of whatever is presented to the Christian as divine truth.

According to this view, a man's creed cannot in the Scriptural sense be right while his life, his spirit, is wrong. The letter of his creed may be right; but wanting that which made it God's truth, God's revelation to the soul, it is essentially false. It no less misrepresents God, is no less ruinous to the soul, than the unbelief which openly rejects the truth, or the false philosophy which corrupts it. How much orthodoxy, so-called, and contended for as essential to salvation, would at this Ithuriel-touch stand revealed in its true form, as from beneath, not from above! The spontaneous inevitable expression of belief in the Gospel, of orthodoxy in the sense of John, is Brotherly Love; love which regards all men as brethren, but whose most immediate sphere, where it unfolds in its highest power and glory, is the church, the body of Christ. Hard test! Who then,—we might almost exclaim, as, looking over evangelical Christendom, we see rather an arena of deadly combatants than the peaceful, loving home of the family of God,—who then believes! Convinced we must be, both that the true knowledge of Christ is as yet greatly wanting among professing Christians, and that all attempts at outward union, whether among individuals, churches, or the various great divisions of the church, is labor thrown away. The inward union, which springs from living fellowship with God through Christ, will gradually melt away all outward differences which mar the symmetry of the church; but the outward union can never heal the inward discord. So also with the evils of the world at large. All reforms which proceed not from this divine principle, however fair their appearance, will prove unreal and of brief duration. The source of all evil, whether in the church or the world, is estrangement from God; the one great cure, the restoration of the soul to a loving union with God, effected through the mediation of the divine Redeemer.

Herein lies the peculiar characteristic of this whole Commentary, —the conception of Christianity in all its relations and manifestations, as a matter of the life. A believer, a Christian, is one who is in living fellowship with Christ. If this living fellowship is lost, he is, whatever may have been his former experiences, in precisely the same peril with one who has never known it. Neander knows of no dead state of grace. The human soul, created in the image of God, and redeemed by his well-beloved Son, is in his view too noble, and its price too costly, to be thus taken to heaven as a piece of purchased merchandise. The salvation won by Christ for man, is the life of God in the soul; a conscious life, a reaching forth of its warm living affections after him, a life manifested by free, unconstrained, joyful obedience to his commands, by the spirit of holiness and love pervading the whole character and conduct.

On this view of the Christian life, rests his noble conception of the Christian church. It is not a body of men bound into an external unity by the same creed; but a company of individual believers drawn together by an inward affinity, by a common participation in that living fellowship with God. Neither are there here any distinctions of rank. It is one family of God, in which each member stands in immediate communion with his Father, and receives immediate life and light from the same divine Spirit. There is here no infallible head of the church on earth; no constituted priesthood to mediate between him and God; no articles of faith shaped and stereotyped by the ingenuity of man, to which he is required to bow. Each has the Anointing of the Holy One; all are Priests and Prophets, through the indwelling divine Spirit.

It seems especially meet, that the illustration of these vital truths should be the closing labor of Neander's life. The spirit which pervades it, reveals a soul matured and mellowed under the influence of these truths, to the deepest and richest tone of Christian experience. From his own christian consciousness flowed these eloquent expositions, of the true character of religious knowledge and belief, of the nature of sin, of the efficacy of redemption, of fellowship with God. Only from personal intercourse with heaven, was caught the fire of his almost inspired delineation of the power of prayer! And beautifully fitting it seems also, that it should be the exposition of these truths as revealed through the Apostle John. With him, the man of "burning love and burning hate,"* the beloved disciple and the son of thunder, the man of immediate perception and intuition of the divine, Neander had always felt a peculiar affinity. The illustration of John's writings had been a favorite labor of his life; and now, as its close draws near, we find him again holding communion with the aged Apostle, and interpreting his latest counsels to the church. Standing on the threshold of the unseen world, he seems to listen with a deeper spiritual sense to the inspired utterances, and interprets them in words of kindred sublimity, earnestness, and love. Their sweetness had hardly died upon his lips, when he was called "to the home of the Good, to Christ;" to join in that new song, to which while yet on earth his spirit and his life were so fully attuned, "Worthy the Lamb that was slain!"

The brief sketch which has been given, of the leading features of the following work, will be pardoned by those who are conversant with Neander's peculiar modes of thought, for the sake of the many to whom they are still new.

The quotations from the Epistle are given in the words of the common English version. The author's variations are added in brackets, wherever they affect the view expressed in the commentary.

H. C. C.

ROCHESTER, Sept. 1852.

* That is, in his original character, unmodified by divine grace. "Feurige Liebe und feurige Hasse," was Neander's characterization of the natural temperament of John.

INTRODUCTION.

In order rightly to understand this Epistle, we must make ourselves acquainted with the Apostle's sphere of labor at the time of writing it, and with the peculiar circumstances to which he had reference, in the condition of the churches whom he addressed. From the true historical explanation will follow, moreover, its proper application to all succeeding times, and to our own age more especially, as bearing a more marked resemblance to that which we may designate as the Johannic period; an age which, in the disorganization and destruction of the old order of things, is preparing the way for a new epoch in the development of the kingdom of God. In the opposing influences with which John had to contend as a preacher of the Gospel, properly understood, we shall see prefigured the very same which obstruct the progress of evangelical truth in our own day.

After the martyrdom of Paul, the influences which had already begun to oppose themselves to the christian life in the churches of Asia Minor, broke forth with increased strength when no longer restrained by the personal character and authority of the great Apostle. John was now called to supply his place in the guidance of the bereaved churches, left exposed to the perils of so dangerous a conflict. He had already labored long among them, when he sent out this pastoral letter, with reference to the many forms of corruption which here menaced genuine Christianity. Of these corruptions, some were chiefly speculative, others practical in their character. They were, in part, errors arising from a narrow and defective conception of christian truth; in part, practical mistakes which had no such deeper origin. But these errors, of whatever kind, with which John had to contend, did not respect merely those single points of difference in the mode of dogmatic conception, to which in later times a greater weight has often been attached, than is warranted by a more just estimate of their importance both to the inward and the outward christian life. On the contrary, they all had reference to that one great truth on which all others turn, the central truth of Christianity. The Apostle's example furnishes a model of the discrimination, too much neglected in after times, between that which is of practical importance in differences of doctrine, and that which cannot be so regarded.

In the Pauline period, all had turned on the question between Law and Gospel; on the question whether faith in Jesus, as the Saviour, would alone suffice for the justification and sanctification of men, or whether obedience to the Mosaic law were also requisite. Now, on the contrary, the central point of the conflict between truth and error was the PERSON OF CHRIST; and it became more and more evident, that a full and complete conception of Christianity, in its relation to faith and life, must be based on a full conception of the Person of Christ himself. The question had already taken this turn at the time of Paul's first imprisonment at Rome, as appears from his own opposition to those errorists in the church at Colosse. Here, even then, the Person of Christ in its relation to God, to the universe, and to humanity, formed the central point of controversy; and this was nothing else than a farther development of the inherent contrariety between genuine Christianity, and that which only assumes its likeness in order to vitiate it in its own peculiar nature. We see the same thing repeated in our own time, —all essential questions of religious faith resolving themselves more and more into the one question: What are we to hold respecting the Person of Christ?

That the Word,—He who from the beginning was with God and was God, He by whom all things were created,—became Flesh; this, as John himself teaches, constitutes the peculiar nature of the Person of Christ. Herein is that grounded by which he is distinguished from all else that has ever appeared in the history of humanity,—the union of the Divine Essence with human nature in all its properties and peculiarities, the humanization of the Divine Essence in order to remodel human nature after this revealed form of the divine. And as it is this which constitutes the peculiar nature of the Person of Christ, so does it constitute the peculiar nature of entire Christianity; its grand purpose being, as befits the destiny of man created in the image of God, to raise whatever is human to the glorious dignity of the divine life, to transform it into the divine. Thus, on the right apprehension of Christ as the Incarnate Word, depends also the true conception of the whole moral change wrought in the life by Christianity, in other words, the peculiar nature of all christian morality. The true conception of this union of the divine and human, in the Person of Christ, being thus essential to a true understanding of what Christ was; there readily arose two opposite forms of error, exalting the one at the expense of the other, instead of grasping the full and entire unity of his divine-human person, both sides in perfect agreement and harmony with each other. Both these erroneous and mutilated conceptions of the Whole Christ, testify of that very truth from which they diverge in opposite directions. For such, and no other, must have been Christ's manifestation of himself on earth, in order that the contemplation of it might make such opposite impressions. Of this no other example can be found in human history. On the one class, so powerful was the impression of the purely human in that manifestation, that they would recognize in him nothing but the man, though gifted with extraordinary divine powers for the fulfilment of his human calling. The other class, contending against this narrow conception of the idea of Christ, ran into the opposite extreme. To their view, the divine glory shone in the appearance of Christ with an overpowering radiance, before which all that was human vanished from sight. They regarded it only as the visible form, in which the manifestation of a divine existence had made its abode, in order that it might become an object of human perception. Between these opposite forms of conception,—the Ebionitish and Docetish, with which John had to contend,—there arose a third, that of Cerinthus, which seemed to reconcile the two extremes, but which was at bottom a compound of what was erroneous in both, and allowed neither to the divine nor the human in Christ its just claims. According to this view, Jesus was a mere man, in all respects like other men. But at his solemn consecration to his Mes sianic calling by the baptism in Jordan, the celes tial redeeming Spirit, as something wholly distinct from him, had descended upon and united itself with him. Thus the purely human and the divine were indeed both recognized; not however in their proper unity, but on the contrary as entirely distinct the one from the other, and only united in an outward and accidental relation. Thus neither the divine was recognized in its humanization, nor the human in its exaltation through the divine. The true significance of the Person of Christ, and of the new creation which was to proceed from him,—the God-man as the Redeemer of humanity,—was necessarily obscured in this view no less than in the two others. In opposition to all these fragmentary conceptions of the person and work of Christ, the Apostle John felt himself constrained to give the testimony derived from his own direct perception and personal experience of the life of Christ, in which the glory of the only begotten of the Father had revealed itself to him, beaming forth in his whole manifestation.

But it will easily be perceived, that these same contrarieties are repeated at the present day under new forms; and hence the Apostle's words apply with no less force to the spiritual aspects of our own age. The one class recognize in Christ only the enlightened man, the most perfect teacher of religious truth who had then ever appeared on earth, and the most perfect model for the human life. Christianity is in their view only a system of moral instruction, moral precept and moral example. They deny the supernatural, the divine in the life of Christ, and consider him as differing only in degree from the nobler of the race; they explain away the Gospel history, till everything in it is brought down to the level of common experience. Hence too, they cannot recognize nor comprehend those moral potencies proceeding from Christ, such as could proceed from no other, which are working the moral transformation of the world, and by which Christianity is distinguished from all other spiritual forces at work in humanity. The glory of a divine life, whereby everything human is transformed into the heavenly, remains hidden from their view. Christianity, in its peculiar nature, is to them still an unrevealed mystery. Others there are, on the contrary, who fully recognize the violence thus done to the representation of the life of Christ in the Gospel, who catch from the Gospel narrative the gleam of higher ideas; but they are ideas floating in ether, having no contact with the earthly and actual. According to their view, the historical manifestation had no actual existence; it is but a sublimated myth, which has become a medium for the divine. The historical Christ becomes to them a mere form of mist, a phantom, an illusion, as to the Docetes of the ancient world. There still remains, therefore, the same disagreement between the heavenly archetype and the actual being, which it was the very purpose of Christ's coming to do away; and which was to disappear more and more by the progressive incorporation of his divine life into the life of humanity, in those who enter into fellowship with him as their Redeemer. As the former will allow no guide but actual and ordinary experience, which can never rise to the divine Idea; so the latter content themselves with the contemplation of mere ideals which have no part in life, never become flesh and blood, never incorporate themselves with the actual; and thus on this side also, with all its tendency to the ideal, nothing remains but the common and actual. The one class admit only an ideal Christ; the other only an every-day Christ level to their low and natural view of the historical. The first admit only the spirit, the other only the letter; and thus both are lost, being rightly apprehended only in their unity.

From both these forms of error are to be distinguished those practical mistakes, which have no such theoretical basis. Here too, as in the former case, we find directly opposite forms of error. The one class, in the consciousness of redemption already received, lost sight of the still remaining necessity of redemption, which should be ever present to the view of the believer; that ever present sense of still inhering sin, from which he can be purified only by a perpetually renewed surrender of himself to the Redeemer. The other class hoped for forgiveness of sin, without renunciation of sin in submission to the Redeemer. They supposed that forgiveness might be obtained, without a thorough work of sanctification in fellowship with Christ. To them, forgiveness of sin was something merely external; just as faith had become something external merely, having lost its true inward significance. A mechanical and worldly Christianity had arisen; a natural result where Christianity has become a thing of custom and habit, as in these churches founded in the time of Paul, in many of which Christianity had already been handed down from one generation to another. Both these forms of error must be met by holding up to view the Holy One; Him who appeared as Redeemer to establish a kingdom of holiness in man; who, as Redeemer and Sanctifier, continues to work in that humanity, which is more and more to be purified and ennobled by him, and which can never cease to have need of Him as its Redeemer in all the progressive stages of sanctification. We need not stop to point out the perpetual recurrence of these practical mistakes, as it must be obvious to all.

To these theoretical and practical mistakes stand opposed the counsels, instructions, and warnings of the Apostle in this pastoral letter. It will therefore easily be seen, how we are to apply what is here written as if intended expressly for our own time. We will now proceed to the consideration of them in detail.

EXPOSITION OF THE EPISTLE.

CHAPTER I.

John commences without any preliminary introduction. His first words burst forth from the fulness of that which was the soul, the centre of his whole Christian life, that which formed the sum and substance of his preaching and of all his instructions. Taking his readers at once into the midst of that subject, on which no doubt all he had ever had occasion to say to them had turned, he begins by pressing home upon their hearts what had already become familiar to them from his lips; which needed only to be recalled to their remembrance, to be quickened and animated anew, and to be made the centre and axis of their whole christian life. We all remember the old tradition, that when this Apostle, in extreme old age, was carried in the arms of his disciples to the assemblies of the church, he did nothing but repeat this one admonition: "Little children, love one another." When asked the reason, he replied: "Because it is the Lord's command; and this being done, all is done." In this single trait, handed down to us by tradition, is fully expressed the peculiar nature and personality of John. It is not the rich variety in the development and expression of ideas, and of their remote relations, which we find in Paul. Here, on the contrary, are a few essential truths, repeated over and over in simple words, which, as they fell from the lips of Christ himself, had stamped themselves deeply into the susceptible spirit of John, and had become as it were ingrown into his own peculiar nature. With him all proceeds from the direct contemplation of Christ, the God-man, whose living image is ever present to his soul, and to whom he is ever directing alike his hearers and readers. He ceases not to testify of that which he has learned in daily intercourse with him, the divine source of life, and which is to him of all things the most certain. He can find no words strong enough to express the assurance of his conviction, that this divine-human life was a reality. His very forms of expression stand forth in strong contrast with that sublimation of the image of Christ by the Docetes, of which we have already spoken.

In his historical representation of Christ's Messianic labors, he distinguishes himself from the other Evangelists in this respect,—that he does not commence with the immediately preceding historical preparation, the prophetic advent of the Baptizer, nor yet with the beginning of the earthly life of Christ; but rises above the manifestation in time, to that divine Original which revealed itself therein. This characteristic peculiarity of John meets us also here, at the very commencement of this Epistle. No otherwise could John have spoken. The fulness of the divine essence, leading back to the Eternal Source in the invisible God himself, and the human manifestation,—all this he contemplated inseparably and as one. He beholds in Christ the revelation in humanity of Him who is exalted above all time, who had no beginning in time; who, antecedent to all creation, was from the beginning; the Eternal Image of the unknown divine existence. This having now presented itself in human nature to human apprehension, it was necessary that John, in reproducing the image of Christ to the view of his readers, should first of all comprehend both these in one; viz. that which was from the beginning,—and that which had become, to those who witnessed his life on earth, an object of unquestionable physical perception. He begins, not with abstract ideas, but by referring to a FACT, the highest of all facts in human history, and to its attestation by personal experience.

"That which was from the beginning, which we have heard, which we have seen with our eyes, which we have looked upon, and our hands have handled." It is noteworthy, that John here expresses himself in the indeterminate form. We should naturally expect a personal designation of Him who was from the beginning; who in his temporal manifestation had permitted himself to be seen and heard and handled, thus subjecting his reality to the test of all the senses. Yet John expresses himself thus indefinitely: "THAT WHICH was from the beginning, THAT WHICH we have seen and heard;" and again afterwards he resumes the same form: "That which we have seen and heard, declare we unto you." In the intermediate clause also, he designates him not personally, but by

Ch. i. 1.]

something relating to him,—" of the word of life." These expressions,taken in connection, are the very clue which is needed, to introduce us into the peculiar spirit and manner of John. All which he has to say to men proceeds from Christ, and leads back to Christ; it is Christ himself that appears in all; the sole object is to gain Him entrance to the hearts of men, to bring within reach of man that fountain of all true life, the self-communication of Christ. Thus it naturally happens that, in John's mode of conception, the distinction between the impersonal and the personal is lost from view. THAT WHICH he has to announce, that which was from the beginning, that which he has seen and heard, is no other than the self-revelation and self-imparting of HIM, who was from the beginning.

John does not immediately carry out this thought, in the form of expression with [Ch. i. 2.
which he had begun; but interrupting himself, expresses in a new form what was already in his mind and filled his soul while writing the first words: "Of the Word of life (for the Life was manifested, and we have seen it, and bear witness, and show unto you that Eternal Life which was with the Father, and was manifested unto us)".

What now are we to understand by "the Word of Life"? Shall we, as elsewhere, understand "word" in the sense of announcement? We must then refer it to that original proclamation of the Life, which was made by Christ. Even thus the mind would still be directed to the appearing of Christ himself: as, in what immediately follows, not merely the proclamation of the Life is spoken of, but the manifestation of the life in its self-revelation among men; and also the expression "That which was from the beginning" refers, as we have seen, not merely to an indefinite something, but to HIM who was from the beginning. He it is, then, whom we here find represented as the "Word of life." The mind is thus directed to what John calls "The Word," at the beginning of his Gospel. Christ himself is the Word, in whom the hidden being of God has revealed itself. Since, in his temporal manifestation as the revelation of God in human nature, he is the perfect expression of the divine nature in human form; this his temporal manifestation is by John referred back to the Eternal Word, in which the hidden being of God originally imaged and revealed itself, became objective to itself,—in which the whole creation had its archetype. As the spirit of man, before it reveals itself outwardly in the spoken word, expresses itself to itself, unfolds and becomes objective to itself, in an inner word, the word of self-consciousness ; so in God, this Word of his eternal self-revelation is to be distinguished from his hidden, unfathomable being. It was this Word which was from the beginning. It is this Word which John calls "the Word of Life." By life here he understands the divine life originating in God, proceeding from him alone as the only true life. Since now all communication of life from God is through the medium of this Word, it is itself the fountain of true life, and John calls it absolutely the Word of Life. He then proceeds, under this form of conception, to express what he had in mind at his opening words, what he wished to testify to his readers as something made certain to him by personal observation and experience. Having designated Christ as himself the Word of Life, he adds, under the same form of thought, the declaration that the Life absolutely, He whose nature is life, the divine life-fountain, has revealed itself in a human manifestation. He claims to have been an eye-witness of this self-revelation of the Life.

The eternal Life itself, which as the Word was hidden with the Father, has appeared in a self-revelation in humanity;—such, and no other than this, was the appearing of Christ. John testifies of that eternal Life, which appeared in Christ in order to impart itself to men; to impart to them this life which constitutes His whole being, and whose fountain he himself is. This it was the object of John's testimony to make known.

Resuming accordingly what he had begun, he now proceeds in the same form: "That which we have seen and heard declare we unto you, that ye also may have fellowship with us." [Ch. i. 3.]

Having, therefore, been himself an eye and ear-witness of the self-revelation of that eternal Life which seeks to impart itself to man, John declares what he has seen and heard, that those who hear may be led by it into that divine fellowship of life in which all are to become one. By the "fellowship with us," which he represents as the object for which he declares this, he means fellowship with those who testified, as original eye-witnesses, of the eternal Life which had made its appearance in humanity; a fellowship therefore derived from that original fellowship with the divine life-fountain so revealed, a fellowship with the Apostles grounded in fellowship with Christ. All fellowship of believers with one another, in the Apostle's view, springs from that original fact of fellowship with Christ. Thus is formed his conception of the Church.

This is of special importance as a guard against the tendency, which is ever reappearing, to externalize the idea of the church, to attach an undue value to a certain visible organization; while it is forgotten that fellowship with Christ is the main point, the essential element of the whole true church,—which, issuing from this source, grounded in this fellowship, may appear in a variety of outward forms. We must ever bear in mind that where this fellowship exists, there, whatever defects may still cleave to it, is a true church; as indeed there is no form of divine manifestation in sinful human nature wholly free from defect.

In explanation of what he understands by this fellowship, the Apostle immediately adds; "And truly our fellowship is with the Father, and with his Son Jesus Christ."

Fellowship with the Father, who can be truly

known as Father only in this self-revelation through the Son, is here represented as effected
Ch. i. 4.]
through the medium of fellowship with the Son. And since in this fellowship is grounded that eternal divine life, in which alone true blessedness and joy can be found; John represents it as the object of his whole preaching, as likewise of this Letter (intended to revive in their hearts the contents of that preaching, in opposition to all the corruptions and impurities of which we have spoken) to promote that joy: "And these things write we unto you that your joy may be full." All impurities and corruptions of the christian's inward and outward life, must also introduce disturbance into the joy or blessedness grounded in the divine fellowship of life with Christ. In this pastoral Letter, designed to avert such a danger, what he seeks is this: that their joy may be full, that in fellowship with Christ they may find their full joy.

In this Epistle, promises and the stipulated condition of their fulfilment, that which is to
Ch. i. 5.]
be performed on the part of those to whom the promises are addressed, are presented in constant interchange. With religious truth there is

always connected a practical application to the moral conduct and course of life; and nothing is said in reference to the latter which is not deducible from the former. As in his opening words, where he speaks as an eye-witness of the appearing of Christ, John plainly has reference to that erroneous sublimation of the Idea of Christ; so here when he is speaking of the practical, we cannot fail to perceive an implied reprehension of that secularized Christianity of custom and habit. "This then is the message which we have heard of him, and declare unto you: That God is light, and in him is no darkness at all."

First of all, he represents God under an image which they had doubtless often heard from his own mouth, as he too had received it from the lips of Christ: "God is light, and in him is no darkness." His nature is light; from Him all darkness is excluded. He is the opposite of all darkness. Light, in the Holy Scriptures, and especially in the writings of John, is often used as the image of the Divine; darkness, on the other hand as the image of the Undivine. Truth, holiness, bliss, all these may be designated as light, since they all belong to the nature of the Divine;

as falsehood, wickedness, and misery form the characteristics of the Undivine. What is particularly represented by the image of light in this passage, will appear from the exhortation which is founded on it. It enjoins a course of life contrary to all that is unholy, and the ground-thought must therefore be, that the nature of God is holiness; all that is unholy is alien to him.

From this view of the divine nature, the Apostle now deduces what is required as the
Ch. i. 6, 7.] condition of standing in fellowship with God; the signs by which this fellowship will manifest itself in the life; and on the other hand, by what signs it is to be known that no such fellowship exists. "If we say that we have fellowship with him and walk in darkness, we lie, and do not the truth: but if we walk in the light, as he is in the light, we have fellowship one with another, and the blood of Jesus Christ his Son cleanseth us from all sin."

The thought here lying at the basis is this: that since all spiritual fellowship presupposes an affinity of nature, and this inward fellowship of nature must also have an outward manifestation in the life; so no fellowship with God can exist without a life conformed to God. Since then God is light, fellowship with him must manifest itself through a life which is full of light; fellowship with the God whose nature is holiness, through a holy course of life. John does not here mean a quality of the life-walk required for the first attainment of fellowship with God; but assuming this divine fellowship of life, received through faith in the Redeemer, as already existing, his object is to point out the tests, whether the claim to such a fellowship be true or false,—whether the Christianity which is professed be a true, or merely a seeming and pretended one. This thought is expressed, in John's peculiar manner, both in the negative and affirmative form. He first says, in opposition to that mere seeming Christianity, that he who leads an ungodly life, and yet claims to be in fellowship with God, thereby makes himself guilty of a lie. Full of significance is the expression, "We do not the truth"; an expression belonging to the depth of conception peculiar to John. With him truth is not limited in its application to speech merely; it embraces the entire life. The entire life has its root either in falsehood or in truth. Truthfulness in speech is but one index of that truth which embraces, fills, vitalizes the whole inner and outer life. Hence, of one who makes claim to something which is contradicted by his course of life it is said, that his whole life is alien from the truth, that he does not practice the truth, that his life is chargeable with falsehood. Speech appears also as an action;— "We DO not the truth."

In contrast with this, John designates "Walking in the Light," in holiness, as a mark of fellowship with God who is in the light, who reveals himself in holiness. "If we walk in the light as He is in the light, then have we fellowship one with another." He does not speak here directly of fellowship with God, but of the fellowship of believers with one another; but in this is necessarily presupposed fellowship with God through Christ, as that from which the fellowship of believers with one another first proceeds. John thus distinguishes between those who belong, as true members, to the fellowship of Christians (in other words to the church, a designation never used by John) and those who belong to it only in appearance and not in truth, those whose pretensions are contradicted by their ungodly life.

Fellowship with God, as effected through Christ, and the fellowship of believers with each other, is here one and the same thing.

If now the life of believers while here on earth were already a perfect fellowship with God, if their course of life were a walking in the light free from darkness of every kind, and unstained by any farther act of sin, then John would have had no occasion to add anything more. But he was well aware that even in believers, although their life is in its determining tendency a walking in the light, yet the dark, the sinful, still mingle with it their disturbing influence; the former stand-point of darkness and sin, from which redemption has set them free, still remains in its effects. Hence, this "walking in the light" must be developed in a continuous conflict with the former darkness; from the light already received, the whole life must be gradually transformed into light. And hence, in reference to that sinfulness which still cleaves to the believer and opposes itself to the light, he says, that where that walking in the light exists as the determining tendency, the mark of fellowship with God, there the blood of

Jesus Christ will make known its purifying efficacy, its power to cleanse from all still inhering sin.

In the purification through the blood of Christ, we are obviously not to understand the blood of Christ literally, nor an outward literal purification by it, any more than the sprinkling of the conscience with the blood of Christ, spoken of in the Epistle to the Hebrews, is to be so understood. Only a spiritual cleansing can here be meant, and consequently only a spiritual means of cleansing. It is necessary to refer back the sensible imagery to the thought imaged therein. It is the language of the Holy Scriptures, the language of life; according to which one characteristic of the whole is put for the whole itself; and especially is that which appears as the crowning point put for the whole with all its characteristics, so that the single characteristic must be conceived of in that connection, in union with the sum of all the others, in order to be rightly understood. The blood of Christ, then, must be conceived of in its full significance, as it was present to the view of the Apostle, viz. as both a Doing and a Suffering; it being on the one hand a suffering for the guilt of humanity, and presenting on the other, in the perfect holiness of the life of Christ, an offset to the sin of humanity, a thought which we shall hereafter find still further developed in other expressions of John. Since now this suffering of Christ, once for all, possesses this redeeming and purifying significance, it continues to perform its work in all those who through faith enter into fellowship with Christ, till all in them that is sinful shall be cleansed away, and all be transformed into light. In this idea of purification two distinct things are included; namely, first, that the sin which yet remains shall no longer form a hindrance to fellowship with God, it shall be as if already done away,—the forgiveness of sins; and secondly, that the still operating sinful element shall actually be more and more cleansed away,—the progressive purification of the whole life. All this is an ever progressing appropriation of the once perfected redemption.

So in what John here says, we find two different things expressed. It is assumed that there is sin yet cleaving to those who are walking in light; though in fellowship with Christ, they are still in constant need of redemption through him, in constant need of him as the Redeemer; that we who are walking in the light with Christ IN us, have also still need of Christ FOR us. To those who, while walking uprightly in the light, are yet daily conscious to themselves of the still remaining influence of sin; who cannot but perceive in their own life much whereby the light which is in them is darkened, and who might be disquieted in conscience, when told that only those who walk in the light can stand in fellowship with God who is Light; to them is offered the consoling assurance of entire purification from their yet inhering sin. But the Apostle guards also against the self-deception of those, who trust to purification through the blood of Christ without a course of life corresponding to such an expectation, without the outward signs of an inward divine fellowship of life through Christ. Only those are to expect this purification, who, through the determining tendency of their lives, make it manifest that they stand in that divine fellowship and are sanctified thereby. Thus the close connection between the Christ IN us and the Christ FOR us, is here indicated.

But it is the Apostle's aim to meet the mistake
on both sides; on the one hand, as held by
Ch. i. 8.] those who suppose they may trust to Christ

for us, without the Christ in us; and on the other, by those who think that with the Christ in us, there is no longer need of the Christ for us, and who look upon themselves as already free from sin. He therefore continues to urge, in opposition to the latter view, the still remaining need of redemption on the part of the sanctified: "If we say that we have no sin, we deceive ourselves, and the truth is not in us." If then those who are walking in the light, suppose themselves to be already entirely free from sin, feel not the perpetual consciousness of its still indwelling power; this to John is an indication of self-deception, a token that the truth has not yet become the ruling element in the inner and outer life. It is clear that he here makes no exception, that he includes himself also among those who are still defiled with sin.

The two succeeding verses have reference also to the believer's ever-continued need of redemption and purification. "If we confess our sins, he is faithful and just to forgive us our sins, and to cleanse us from all unrighteousness. If we say that we have not sinned, we make him a liar, and his word is not in us." [Ch. i. 9, 10.

The ground for the believer's confidence, under this consciousness of still inhering sin, is thus presented by the Apostle in the faithfulness and righteousness of God. For the faithfulness of God includes in itself his truthful fulfilment of the promises which he has given. It necessarily implies, that what he has promised he will certainly bestow, provided only that believers on their part meet the condition affixed to the fulfilment of the promise. By the faithfulness of God is meant, the harmony of his action with itself and with his own nature. It is implied therein, that He will certainly perform what his word, his promises, the wants implanted in the soul and waked into conscious life by his providence, have taught men to expect from Him; that his dealings with men will certainly be in accordance with the wants and expectations thus excited; that in his dealings all parts will correspond, beginning middle and end will be in harmony; no contradiction, no discord in any part. Since then God is truth, it must follow as a necessary consequence that, having through his word, through the sending of the Redeemer and his sufferings for humanity, through the influence of his spirit upon their hearts, promised forgiveness of sin to those who believe; he will assuredly suffer nothing of this to fail, he will fulfil the promise which he has given, if they will but conform to the conditions with which the promise is connected. But righteousness is here conjoined with faithfulness. This might at first seem strange. We should rather expect that forgiveness of sins would be represented as an act of divine love and mercy. But we must here seek for a relation, according to which forgiveness of sin can properly be ascribed to the divine righteousness. The true index to the Apostle's meaning is found in the union here of faithfulness with righteousness. Righteousness, then, must here be understood in a sense akin to faithfulness. Now we call him righteous who gives to each one his own, to each his due, what his position, the relation in which he stands to the other, give the right to expect. God's righteousness is manifested in the observance of the laws which he has himself established in the moral world. Its office is the administration of these laws. Redemption, the forgiveness of sin, is indeed primarily the work of divine love; yet, that provision being once brought about through his love and mercy, the divine righteousness now reveals itself in the observance of the laws, according to which redemption and forgiveness are to be bestowed on man,—in the administration of the order established in the work of redemption. God, the Righteous, gives to each what belongs to him; he truly performs what the redeemed, as such, have reason to expect of him under the given conditions. The original provision is the fruit of divine love; the administration of its established laws, the work of divine righteousness. Hence, in this view, the divine righteousness stands in close relation to the divine faithfulness; and is the pledge that if the redeemed fulfil the laws, the conditions, according to which and under which forgiveness is to be imparted, God will truly bestow on them the forgiveness promised, will complete what he has begun, that he will do his part if the redeemed do theirs.

The condition to be fulfilled on the part of the believer, is expressed in the words: "If we confess our sins." Of course it is not an outward confession of sin which is here spoken of, but an inward act, grounded in the whole inward direction of the spirit; as that which is thereby to be appropriated and received, that for which man is thereby to be made meet, is also something purely inward. It is therefore that inward confession of sin before God,—the consciousness of sin both in general, and in its manifestation in particular sinful acts,—whereby, in a spiritual sense, man draws near to God. In this it is necessarily implied, that he is deeply penetrated with the sense of still inhering sin; recognizes the sinful as such in all its single forms; and with a deep feeling of sorrow on account of it, begs of God forgiveness of sin and purification from all remaining sinful tendency. All communications of God to man,—man, to whom God imparts himself not after a law of natural necessity, not by a process of constraint, but as to a being gifted with freedom,—are conditioned on his own voluntary acceptance, the free surrender of himself to the divine communication. As in the words of our Lord, God is represented as giving only to those who pray (and prayer is nothing else than this direction of the spirit towards God in the feeling of personal want) so here, confession of sin is made the necessary condition of that gift of God, which consists in the forgiveness of sin, as evidence of the free appropriating acceptance of the blessing. With forgiveness of sin is here conjoined the cleansing from all unrighteousness. This would not have been added, unless something new, something additional, were to be designated by it; as indicated by the emphatic expression: "FROM ALL UNRIGHTEOUSNESS." We cannot but perceive that a distinction is here made between forgiveness of sin, and the progressive work of purification from all remaining sin. With the forgiveness of past sin, is necessarily connected purification from all the sin which still remains, as a security against relapse into like sins.

To that affirmative proposition, the negative is now added. With the confession of sin is contrasted the boastful declaration, and of course the inward view and feeling which dictates it: "We have no sin." This implies first, that he who says it is wholly unconscious of still inhering sin, that he regards himself as sinless. In this again two things are included, viz. first, that he has no understanding of what is implied in a sinless state, of the true nature of that holiness for which man was created, and for which he is to be new created, to be born again; and that he has not rightly compared himself with that standard which he is required to reach, has not examined and tested himself by the model of the divine word, in the mirror of the divine law, in the divine light. And secondly, it is implied that he does not recognize the sinful as such in its particular acts, but has learnt to palliate it to himself, to deceive his conscience in regard to it. The guilt and the perverseness of such a position is now represented by the Apostle as consisting in this, viz. that it makes God a liar; that is, by such a position we show that we regard God as a liar, we deny him as the God of truth. First, inasmuch as the word of God uniformly represents us as sinners, and seeks to awaken in us a consciousness of our sins; we, by declaring that we have no sin, accuse the word of God, and God himself speaking through it, of falsehood. Secondly, since God in sending to us Jesus as the Redeemer from sin, has thereby declared that we are ever in need of continued redemption; we make him guilty of a lie,—asserting by this position of ours, that although it is through Christ we have attained to our present state of religious development, yet as being now sinless, we are no longer in need of him as Redeemer. Hence the Apostle charges upon such, that the word of God is not in them; an expression equivalent to the former declaration, that the truth is not in them. By it is meant, that the word of God does not dwell in such as the animating principle of their inner life, or that they do not dwell in it; which is one with saying that the truth dwells not in them as their life-element, that their life is alienated from the truth. Though in their external profession they acknowledge the word of God, they have not given it an abode in their inner life and consciousness. Their judgment of themselves is in contradiction to it. The word of God is to them a merely external thing.

CHAPTER II.

THE Apostle now turns to those for whose sake he writes, as a father to his children. Ad- [Ch. ii. 1.
dressing them personally as his children, he presses home upon their hearts a spiritual father's admonitory words: "My little children, these things write I unto you, that ye sin not." The expression, "these things," glances back to that main topic which had been his starting-point, viz. that it is only while walking in the light, that we can be certain of that divine fellowship of life bestowed through Christ. But with this all that follows is connected, and to all this the expression has reference. All which he had said to them respecting the sin still cleaving to the christian, and of the progressive redemption from it for which they may hope, has had for its aim, not to make them lenient towards their own sins, but on the contrary to excite them to a continued and un-

wearied conflict with sin. In order to apprehend and apply the admonition to abstain from sin, as understood by the Apostle after the law of Christ, our conception of the nature of sin, of what sin is, must be very different from that derived from the superficial moral judgment of the world. For this it is requisite that, trying ourselves by that higher standard, we should learn to detect what is sinful in our own life in order that we may overcome and avoid it; and as the source of the needed resolution, confidence, and alacrity for this, is presupposed the sense of divine forgiveness, and reliance upon the divinely purifying power of the work of redemption. Thus we perceive how all that precedes, starting from that central thought, serves as a basis for the exhortation, "That we sin not."

That connection, which we have noticed, is always present to the Apostle in the light of his christian self-knowledge and his knowledge of man. Hence, to the unconditional exhortation to sin not, he is constrained to add a ground of consolation to those, who, while honestly striving against sin have yet fallen under temptation, and who might thereby become wholly unsettled in regard to the work of their salvation, and be driven to despair. Another would have given this the adversative form: But if any one sin. In the style, however, of the undialectic and unrhetorical John, there is no occasion to change the connective word; as in many cases where another, Paul for instance, would have made this change, with him the simple "and" suffices for all the relations of his several propositions to one another.

Accordingly he says: "And if any man sin, we have an advocate with the Father, Jesus Christ the righteous: and he is the propitiation for our sins: and not for ours only, but also for the sins of the whole world." [Ch. ii. 1, 2. To those who are weighed down by consciousness of the sin still cleaving to them, and of defeat in conflict with it, John thus extends the cheering assurance of a mediator with the Father in Heaven. This mediator is Jesus Christ the Righteous, that is, the Holy; righteousness here being taken in its highest and absolute sense, namely, as what is right, what is as it should be, what corresponds to the idea of moral perfectness. He bids them, after having once attained to repentance for that still inhering sin, not to abandon themselves to the fruitless anguish of despair, not to consume themselves in a perpetual brooding over their sins; but on the contrary, to turn with full confidence to Him who is their everlasting advocate with the Father, Jesus Christ the Holy.

When man, having become conscious of the chasm, between himself in his sin and imperfection and the holy and perfect God, sinks under the feeling of separation and estrangement from that Being towards whom his higher nature strives to rise; there then awakens in him the want of a mediation, by which this chasm may be filled. Hence, in all religions, the founding of a priesthood, the recognition of a mediating agency between God and man, to whom he may address his prayers when he ventures not to turn immediately to God. There is, however, in every such human priesthood this inherent inconsistency, that they who are themselves sinful and in need of redemption like all other men, should undertake for others the mediation which they themselves need in common with them. Thus, the undeniable want which lies at the foundation of the priesthood universally, in connection with its insufficiency to meet that want, becomes a prophetic indication of Him who alone can truly satisfy it; of Him through whom the idea of a priesthood, so deeply grounded in the nature of man, found its realization, and with it all previous forms of priesthood their final end. This relation of Christ, to God and to humanity, is the especial object of the Epistle to the Hebrews. As man, he is in all respects akin to those who seek his aid, has partaken of their nature with all its necessities, all its infirmities, sin excepted; has himself experienced all their conflicts and temptations, and in all has approved himself as The Holy. Only as the Holy, as the realization of the holy archetype of humanity, can he stand as the substitute of sinners before the Father in Heaven.

This is not to be so understood, as if the forgiveness of the sins of believers were something yet to be obtained by the intercession of Christ. There is presupposed here, as appears from the immediately following connection, that redemption, that reconciliation of man with God, which was effected once for all through the holy life and the sufferings of Christ. Jesus Christ, as The Holy, is here contemplated in connection with his whole work accomplished on earth, wherein he manifested himself especially as The Holy One,—in the connection of his present life with God and previous life on earth. There is also presupposed, as already existing, that entirely new relation to God into which those are brought who are reconciled to Him through Christ. It is not said: We have an advocate with God, but with the Father; indicating that filial relation of believers to God as their Father, whom they have first been taught through Christ to know and honor as such. In it is included the permanency of this once established relation, as something not again to be unsettled, so long as the believer abides in this fellowship with Christ, so long as his faith continues steadfast. Only where it has already suffered disturbance, must the direction of the eye to Christ, by whom it was established, revive again the living consciousness of this relation.

There is thus presupposed, in this perpetual advocacy of Christ, that which he has once for all wrought out for the human race. But this too, is represented as something which shall continue working in divine power, until it has accomplished its final aim, the complete redemption and purification of man already reconciled to God through

Christ,—until the consummation of the kingdom of God. It is clear that this divine agency in the ever-progressing work of redemption, is necessary even for those who have been thus reconciled to God through Christ, and who are conscious of a filial relation to Him as their Father. It is made necessary by the frequent disturbances of this relation, through the after-workings of that sin from which they have been made free. Their christian life can prosper, only when in a continued living connection with the original divine foundation on which it rests, that common foundation of all which belongs to the development of the kingdom of God on earth.

But when we speak of the still operative power of the work of redemption, we are not to understand by this, merely the influence exerted by some past transaction upon the development of humanity, and of individuals who yield themselves to it, irrespective of the personal influence of him by whom that work was wrought; as though the sacred writer, when speaking of Christ as the perpetual intercessor, ascribed to him by a figure of speech the influences belonging to his once completed work. So the still operating influence of any great work, once wrought in human history by some master spirit, might be ascribed to his continued personal agency; a lively and graphic form of conception representing such an one,—for a time at least, until the whole aim and purpose of the work shall reach its full completion,—as still working on in that which had its origin in him. Thus it might be said of Luther, that he still lives and works in that Reformation which bears the impress of his own spirit. We might indeed, in such a sense as this, speak of Christ the Holy as the intercessor of believers, without knowing anything farther of his personality; and even though this personality had been a mere transient phenomenon, as regarded by a Sabellius, and as it is presented by a certain school, which, though totally opposed to Christianity, sometimes assumes its likeness.

But such a view is entirely at variance with the Apostle's meaning. Before his believing eye stands the LIVING CHRIST; approved by his victorious resurrection from the dead, as the Holy One, over whom death could have no power; risen and ascended to an eternal divine life in heaven, forever living with the Father in a glorified, divine-human personality. This living Christ he contemplates as still carrying on his work in person, and with the same holy love with which he labored on earth for the reconciliation of sinful man, still continuing to work in that glorified state with the Father. In his divine-human personality he forms the medium by which the human race, redeemed and reconciled to God through him, is brought into union with God as a Father. This connection between the living Christ and what he once wrought on earth, must therefore never be lost sight of. Thus Christ himself, in those last discourses transmitted to us by John, says on the one hand, that he will pray the Father in behalf of his disciples, and that in answer to his prayers the Father will bestow upon them what they need (John xiv. 16); and on the other hand, that he need not pray for them, since, by virtue of their connection with him, they are themselves already the objects of God's paternal love, already stand in a filial relation to Him (John xvi. 26, 27).

With special emphasis it is here said that Jesus, as THE HOLY, is the advocate of the redeemed, who under the sense of still remaining sin direct to him the eye of faith. Christ being the Holy

One, having in his life on earth given once for all a complete realization of the perfect holiness required by the divine Law; this his holiness stands forever the offset for all that is still sinful in those who have been redeemed by him, and are in fellowship with him. It is in this connection with him, as one with him, that they are presented to the eye of God. Herein lies the pledge that they also, by virtue of this union with him, shall one day be wholly purified from sin; shall be like him in perfect holiness, to whom even now, turning away from sin, they direct the eye of faith; shall be made holy as he is holy.

What now is the practical significance of this truth, that Christ the Holy is our ever-abiding ad vocate with the Father? To this perpetual mediation through the living Christ, to his ever-abiding priesthood for those who are reconciled to God through him, corresponds the ever-remaining need of mediation in believers, their constant dependence upon the priesthood of Christ, in union with whom they are a generation consecrated to God. Under every feeling of sin and infirmity, in all their temptations and conflicts, they may securely trust in their indissoluble union with this divine-human Personage; who himself has felt all their necessities, and is near to them in the intimate sympathy of perfect love. Moreover, their whole inward and outward christian life, flowing as it does from this sense of continual need of redemption, will take its character from this ever-continuing mediation of Christ and their own conscious connection therewith.

The whole christian life, as ordained for the glory of God, must be governed by its relation to him; and this relation must everywhere show itself to be the fruit of Christ's abiding mediation. To the christian consciousness, this will be an ever-present reality. As Christ the Holy can alone be, in an absolute sense, the object of divine love and complacency; so no other of the human race can be its object, except in connection with Christ as the perpetual mediator. Only that wherein Christ is found, only that which appears under his glorified image, can truly promote the glory of God. The glory, beaming from this heavenly relation, will throw its radiance over all the darkness that yet remains. Christian piety and all its fruits, must have their root in this relation to Christ as mediator. Thus Christ, in that last discourse to his disciples of which John has given us the record, says that God will bestow upon them the Holy Spirit in answer to his prayer (John xiv. 16) ; that the Father will send the Spirit in his name (John xiv. 26); both pointing to this perpetual mediation through Christ. To this also refers the prayer in his name, which he so earnestly presses upon their hearts in this discourse; the expression "through Christ" being, in general, equivalent to "in Christ." All this is thus placed in its proper light. In many apostolic expressions, the whole life of the church, and of each individual Christian, is represented under the figure of a sacrifice well-pleasing to God; a sacrifice which Christ, the perpetual mediator, the eternal Priest, offers to his heavenly Father. From this connection of christian truth we can also deduce the inference, that since everything in the christian life is comprehended in this mediation by Christ, and through it receives its consecration ; so everything human is in like manner to be thereby consecrated and sanctified, to be brought into connection with the life of Christ. Hence the distinction between worldly and spiritual, holy and profane, no longer exists; all this is done away by the perpetual mediation of Christ.

History teaches us to estimate aright the deep significance of this christian truth, here developed from the words of the Apostle. The entire dependence of all Christians alike upon this one advocacy, to the exclusion of every other, being based upon this truth; we accordingly see that whenever it became obscured in the christian consciousness, that dependence was again, as in the ante-christian period, transferred to a human priesthood and to a multiplicity of mediations, and again the distinction between priests and laity, between spiritual and secular, found admission. And thus will it ever be, when this reference of the religious consciousness in all believers, to the one mediation through Christ, is cast into the background, is obscured or misunderstood.

The Apostle has thus shown, that at the basis of the ever-continuing mediation by Christ, there lies the reference to what he once wrought for the reconciliation of man with God, to that one all-sufficient offering of himself. He accordingly now directs attention specially to the fact, that He is "the reconciliation for our sins,"—referring to that once-accomplished and still abiding and operative work of redemption. For he it is through whom man has been made free from sin; through whom that sin which pressed down humanity, separating it from God and his fellowship, and intercepting the communications of divine love, has been taken away, has become as if it were not; so that henceforth, all mankind should appear before God as freed from sin by this self-offering of Christ,—as in him pure in the sight of God. This,—which according to the divine plan, the purposes of divine grace, the yearning love of Christ who bore all mankind upon his heart, should embrace all,—is realized in those who open their hearts to its reception, who believingly appropriate the redeeming grace thus offered. It is so realized when they first enter into christian fellowship, renouncing the former standpoint of a life of worldliness and sin; it is this which marks the boundary between the old and the new life. But as John here shows, although this boundary has been once fixed, yet in the conflict with the remaining influence of that former state, there is still need of the ever-renewed appropriation of this reconciliation, which is Christ himself. When this reconciliation, as the all-sufficient agency for the progressive and ultimately complete sanctification of the redeemed, and the constant appropriation of it as such, have ceased to be recognized in their connection and become obscured in the christian consciousness,—new methods of atonement and purification have then been resorted to, as necessary for sins committed after baptism.

But when John speaks of the reconciliation for OUR sins, he feels constrained to guard against every limitation of the universal reference of the work of redemption. He calls to mind such words of Christ as those respecting the one fold and the one shepherd, and his vision widens to embrace all humanity; to behold in Christ not alone the reconciliation for those who already believe, but for those also who as yet know nothing of Christ, who as yet belong to the world. The reconciliation of Christ has for its object all humanity in its estrangement from God; all which belongs to the world, as it stands opposed to the kingdom of God. Humanity as a whole is to be embraced in the reconciliation with Christ, is to be thereby separated from the world and incorporated into the kingdom of God. The reconciliation, once instituted by Christ, continues its uninterrupted work until it shall have achieved this its glorious consummation.*

The Apostle passes continually from one aspect of this truth to another. He exhorts them
Ch. ii. 3.] now to confidence in Christ; now warns them against discouragement and despair, and now against false confidence and carnal security. His admonitions always keep in view both directions in which they are liable to go astray. Accordingly he here comes back again, to warn them against the false confidence of a merely seeming christianity, and to fix attention upon the characteristic marks of the true. "And hereby we do know that we know him, if we keep his commandments."

In contrast with a professed "knowing of Christ" which is contradicted by the life, John represents this as the sign of a true knowledge of Christ, viz. that we obey his commandments. There is indeed a knowledge which belongs only to the understanding, and has nothing to do with the life; but such, in reference to divine things, could not be admitted by John as real; he did not

* Compare the statement on page 58.—*Tr.*

even allow it the name of knowledge. For as truth according to his modes of thought is not a mere abstraction, belonging solely to the understanding, but is something pertaining to the inner life, to the affections ; so to him knowledge, in reference to divine things, is not merely a matter of speculation and of the understanding, but is something proceeding from the inner life, and as such must manifest itself in the outward course of conduct. The sum and substance of the knowledge must be actually present in the inner life. It presupposes an inward fellowship of life with that which is known ; and this must stamp its own peculiar character upon the whole life. The knowledge of Christ, as the Holy One, can only exist where there is spiritual fellowship with him, the Holy One ; where the soul has received into itself his holy image, and has been pervaded by its influence. And where this is the case, it must show itself in the whole conduct by the test here pointed out, obedience to the commands of Christ ; for the commands of Christ are inseparable from his own nature, from himself. As in all which proceeds from him he but presents himself; so his commands are but single features of the new life proceeding from him. Thus each one, by subjecting his life to a comparison with the commands of Christ, may ascertain whether the knowledge of Christ, to which he makes claim, be truth or appearance merely. True indeed, John could not admit, as we have before shown, that the life of any believer could present an absolutely perfect fulfilment of the commands of Christ. He cannot, therefore, so understand this test of christian self-knowledge; otherwise the result must in every case be unfavorable. But with all the imperfections which still encumber the christian life, there yet remains a strongly marked distinction between those with whom obedience to Christ's commands is a matter of earnest purpose, the current of whose whole life sets in this direction; and those to whom the desire to obey him is in no sense the soul of their life. Moreover, as different degrees obtain in the true and living knowledge of Christ, there will be likewise corresponding grades of obedience to the commands of Christ. The touchstone of all true religious knowledge, according to this view of John, is the practice of it in the life. But as his manner is, he here merely contrasts opposites in respect to their essential nature, without taking into account any gradations in the outward manifestation. How entirely opposed is the standard of judgment here established by John, to a one-sided speculative orthodoxy, a conception of truth as something merely theoretical, an orthodoxy of the understanding, not of the life! Orthodoxy, in the sense of John, is something which belongs to the life. How different an aspect would it have given to doctrinal controversies, had this stand-point of the Apostle been rightly understood and firmly adhered to!

In order to impress the truth more strongly by exhibiting it on both sides, John now, in his own peculiar manner, expresses in a negative form what he had first presented affirmatively. [Ch. ii. 4. "He that saith, I know him, and keepeth not his commandments, is a liar, and the truth is not in him.

In John's view, therefore, there is an inherent inconsistency in professing to know Christ, and yet not obeying his commands. One who does this he regards as a liar; and declares, as the ground of the disposition from which such conduct proceeds, that the truth is not in him. We must here apply what we have previously remarked respecting

John's conception of truth. Plainly he here speaks of truth as something which has to do with the disposition, the moral feelings. Such an one is represented by John as, in the determining tendency of his spirit, in his affections, estranged from the truth; as one in whom falsehood is the inwardly ruling principle. He is wanting in honest self-examination in relation to divine truth; hence, he does not consider what is requisite in order to make such a profession in truth, what is involved in the claim of knowing Christ. Thus arises first, self-deception, unconscious hypocrisy; and from this proceeds the conscious falsehood of seeking to appear more than he really is.

From the proposition thus expressed in affirmative and negative form, John proceeds to
Ch. ii. 5.] draw the inference: "But whoso keepeth his word, in him verily is the love of God perfected: hereby know we that we are in him." The commands of Christ are here referred back to his word, his doctrine in general. For John is not here speaking of single isolated moral precepts, but of the word revealed through Christ, embracing faith and life in their whole extent; his commands being, as we have already remarked, only

single features in which his life-transforming word is developed. Of one who thus observes this word and applies it in practice, the Apostle says that in him the love of God has reached its completion; that is, love to God, such as it must be to correspond to the idea of love, is existing in him. It forms the opposite of such a love to God as cannot be called genuine love; a love to God professed in words alone, giving no evidence of itself in practice, and contradicted by the course of life. Here also it is obvious, that although John only presents these opposites in their generic form, yet we are necessarily led to the idea of gradational differences in the actual life. Whilst genuine love can manifest itself only by obedience to the word of Christ, yet there being differences as to the degree in which this love has penetrated the whole life with its vitalizing influence, and eradicated whatever is selfish; there will be corresponding differences as to the manifestation of its power, in obedience to the word of Christ, in the fulfilment of his commands. We must constantly bear in mind, that it is not love to God in a merely general and indeterminate sense which is here presented, but love to God in the christian sense, with all which is necessarily presupposed in it as such. It is love to God in connection with the knowledge of Christ, and having its source therein; love to God as the Father, enkindled by the revelation of the redeeming love of God in Christ. John knows indeed of no other love to God. He beholds in man a being estranged from God; over whom impends the divine wrath, till succored by the redeeming love of God in the sending and sacrifice of his Son. It is through this alone that man becomes capable of loving God as a Father, and is constrained so to love Him. This love is now the new principle of life; is that which, if genuine, must of itself impel him who feels it to fulfil the word of Christ, to obey his commands. Thus with John, true knowledge of Christ and true love to God are in every respect coincident; and the actual life must furnish the test of both.

Hence he says: "Hereby we know that we are in him." Here the Apostle brings to view a state of being, which has its foundation in Christ; just as Christ is by Paul represented, as himself the foundation on which the whole structure of the Christian life is built, whereon it rests. Thus each believer has his life in Christ; its root is spiritual fellowship with him. To be a christian and to be in Christ, to be in fellowship with him and to live, are in the view of John one and the same thing. Christ himself is here the vital principle from which all proceeds. Out of him unfolds itself the entire new life. To know Christ, to love God as self-revealed in Christ, to be in Christ, these are all indissolubly connected, are one and the same; one cannot be conceived separate from another. And thus also, as we see, obedience to the word, to the commands of Christ, is the test whether one is truly in a state of fellowship with Christ.

In the succeeding words, John now more particularly defines what is implied in obedience to the commands of Christ: "He that saith he abideth in him, ought himself also so to walk, even as he walked." To abide in Christ, designates something more than to be in Christ. It means, not merely to have entered through faith into fellowship with Christ, but also to persevere therein steadfastly; to hold fast, with a true heart, what has been once received. It is implied, that there are such as have already known Christ for a long time, in whom therefore fellowship with Christ must have received a fuller development

[Ch. ii. 6.

as the animating principle of life And how then is this to make itself known? This abiding spiritual fellowship can only manifest itself, through a life conformed to him with whom the believer has thus entered into fellowship. We find here the confirmation of our previous remark, that not a multiplicity of single moral precepts by which one is to regulate his outward life is here intended; but the single commands are to be understood only as the development and application of an inward law, which is to embrace and transform the whole life. There is not meant here a law of the letter, like that of the Old Testament, which made its claims on men in single commands: "Do this and thou shalt live!" But here all refers itself to that new view of the life of holiness, whose model is presented to the believer in Christ himself. All single moral demands which he makes on men (as for instance, those ground-traits of Christianity developed in the sermon on the Mount, that Magna Charta of his kingdom) are nothing else than single features in which the life of holiness, whose perfect form he first revealed and actualized, is presented in contrast with what had been the standard of the world. Christ himself is in his commands; and they, on the other hand, are but single items of his self-revelation. He utters only that, testifies only of that, which he has himself actualized in his life. And thus also here, the Apostle speaks not of commands whose constraining force is from without, but of the spontaneous result of the process by which the new life in Christ is developed. There is implied an inward germinating power, which cannot but make itself known by such outward signs. If a man truly abide in Christ, then must Christ with whom he stands in fellowship, who dwells within him, be also reflected in his life which through Christ is formed anew. From the contemplation of the life of Christ, there must form itself a new course of life in conformity with that holy pattern, an unconstrained fulfilment of the commands of Christ. The life of each believer should be only a peculiar aspect of the image of Christ, as the great archetype of renewed and glorified humanity. Christ himself, assuming as his own all that is human, will glorify it in believers who live in fellowship with Him; the One Christ presenting himself in manifold forms of manifestation. And thus, on the conformity of the life to the model of Christ, must depend the proof whether the claim of being in fellowship with Christ is founded in truth.

As we have before seen, it is not John's object to propound anything new to the churches, Ch. ii. 7.] but to awaken them to a living sense of that which had always constituted the burden of his instructions; to guide them in the right application of that which they already knew. What he had always held up before them as the one command of the Lord, the sum and substance of all other commands; as the foundation whereon rested the essential nature of practical Christianity; this is what he would have them lay to heart anew, and this he introduces with a new personal address: "Brethren, I write no new commandment unto you, but an old commandment which ye had from the beginning. The old commandment is the word which ye have heard from the beginning."

We here find confirmation of what we have before remarked, viz. that although John speaks of commandments in the plural, yet he does not mean a number of single commands; for he here refers them all back to that One, which is itself no new commandment, but has been known to them from the first proclamation of the Gospel, and is here designated as the Word which they have heard from the beginning. We are not to understand by it merely the word as preached by John himself in these churches, but also as made known to them by the Apostle Paul. It was still, although in different forms, the same word which had ever been preached to them and received by them; and this preached word had for its central point that one command.

We shall now be able, of ourselves, to perceive what John means by this one command. It is the command which Christ bequeathed as his last legacy to his disciples,—the token by which they should be recognized as such,—after he had instituted the holy supper as the pledge and the symbolic seal of his own ever-continued fellowship with them, and of their consequent mutual fellowship with one another; the command namely, that they should exercise towards each other the same self-sacrificing love which Christ had manifested for them, and would continue to manifest even unto the end. (John xiii. 34, 35). He himself (John xv. 10, ff.), sums up all single commands in this "new commandment," as he there terms it, in what sense we shall presently consider. From all this it is evident, that the Apostle cannot here be speaking of single isolated commands, in the sense in which they are so regarded from the standpoint of the Law. For this Love is not a thing to be enjoined by an outward law,—is not a thing to be placed as a single command side by side with others. Love is something which can be produced only from within, which manifests its presence in the living spirit as an inward necessity, which contains in itself the impulse to all good and makes all other commands superfluous. The aim of all others is embraced within the scope of this, and in it are they all fulfilled; in the words of Paul, "Love is the fulfilling of the Law." It springs unconstrained, from the inward experience of redemption, from fellowship with Christ, and from the new moral bent of life grounded therein.

Yet, after having designated it thus as the old command, he adds: "Again, a new commandment I write unto you." Thus, what he had just enjoined upon them as old, may now it seems to him, in another aspect, be presented as new. But in what sense both old and new? This might be explained from the relation of the new

Ch. ii. 8]

dispensation to the old, in which view Christ calls this the new command, the characteristic feature of the new dispensation, whose sealing was set forth in the Last Supper. It was the old command as standing already at the head of the ten commandments; it was the new command as actualized and made new by Christ's self-sacrificing love for his brethren, especially by the sacrifice of his life for them. Thus illustrated,—love after this pattern of Christ, ready to offer up all for a brother's sake,—as such it is the new command.

True, nothing was enjoined by it which might not have been found in the old command: "Love thy neighbor as thyself." For the expression "as thyself," properly understood, can have reference only to the true Self, which, from the nature of the case, cannot be made an offering for others; which must, on the contrary, be the gainer by all the deeds of self-sacrificing love,—only in them, indeed, can find its own completion. And hence, in this love of our neighbor as ourself, might be included that unreserved, all-sacrificing love for others. But it lay therein only as a MIGHT-BE, not yet expressed, not developed, not known as a living principle. Nor was this effected till Christ, by the devotion of his whole life crowned by that final act of his death, gave the example of such a love, and in anticipation of that closing act gave it expression in words. In such a sense it might be called new; new as having not before been so understood, and new in relation to the Old Testament. It might be called new, moreover, as being now freed from all which checked its development under the old dispensation, as being made henceforth the sum and centre of all. As belonging in the germ to the Old Testament, it could be designated as the old command; as developed into new glory by Christ, it might be called the new.

But though such a distinction is in itself admissible, yet had it been what John intended to express here, it would certainly have been more clearly and definitely stated. There is, on the contrary, in the whole connection, no hint of such a distinction based upon the relation of the New to the Old Testament. It could only be so understood, if in what precedes, the designation, 'old' were applied to what believers had already learned from the Old Testament. But, as we have seen, it is here applied to what is old in respect to themselves and their present christian stand-point; old to them as being the same which they have heard from the first announcement of the Gospel. When, therefore, this same command is urged upon them as new, we may infer that it is to be taken in the same reference, viz. to the state of the church itself. In respect to the whole period since it was first made known to them, it might be called old; in another respect, that of the change supposed since then to have taken place in them, in respect to their having themselves become new, it might be called the new command. In respect to the religious development of the church itself, it might in one aspect be called old, in the other, new. This conclusion is confirmed by what follows, in which the Apostle's view is brought out still more clearly.

The succeeding words refer to this fact, that the command can now be presented as something new: "Which thing is true in him and in you." He means to say: It is true in reference both to Christ and the church,—that is, in reference to their mutual relation to each other,—that the old command has become to them a new one, something new in their christian experience. In what respect this holds true, is explained by the words which follow: "For the darkness is past and the true light now shineth." John here makes a comparison between a present, new condition of the church and a former one; and from this we see how it is that the old command, the expression of what was peculiar in the nature of Christianity, should now be presented to them as new. It is a comparison of their present condition,—as they had already long been christians, and Christianity therefore should have become so much the more their life-element,—with that of their spiritual childhood when Christianity was as yet a new thing to them. Life, apart from Christianity, as it belongs to a world estranged from God, is in itself and with all its results regarded by the Apostle as the kingdom of darkness; its opposite being the divine light of Christianity, and all that flows from it. When he says "the true light," he means by "true," according to the import of the Greek term, what in the highest and fullest sense corresponds to the idea. With him "the true," when used with a word applicable both to what is divine and to objects of sense, means only and always the divine. It is implied, that the word is applicable to the physical only in a subordinate sense; and at that lower stage of being is but an imperfect symbol, a mere image of that, which, in the highest and fullest sense with reference to the spirit of man, can be predicated only of the divine. Thus, for example, the true food for man is only that which nourishes the spirit to divine life, bearing the same relation to the true life of the spirit, as food in the lower realm of sense to the life of the body. Thus too, John contemplates Christ as himself the true light, holding the same relation to the spiritual as the sun to the natural life. What he here says then is this: With those who have been so long attached to Christianity, the darkness proceeding from their former heathen state is passing away, and the true light is now breaking. "Now," he says,—meaning their present in contrast with their former state of heathenism, or while still affected by its remaining influence. The light derived from Christ, the true light, was already banishing the former darkness, they were becoming constantly more and more enlightened. So Paul says to his readers (Rom. xiii. 11 ff.) that now their salvation is nearer than when they believed, that the end of the night approaches, the day of the Lord draws near. It is therefore true,

—both with reference to Christ, the true light which has dawned upon their souls, and with reference to believers who have received this light and been illuminated thereby, that this fundamental law of Christianity now verifies its character as the new command. To those who live in the light of Christ, who have become at home in the new world of Christianity, the old command must now, in contrast with the former state of darkness, present itself in new glory as the new command. In new power must it be revealed to their hearts, that BROTHERLY LOVE constitutes the essence of the christian life, is the essential mark of fellowship with Christ.

That the injunction to christian brotherly love is here meant by the new command, is implied in the succeeding words, which indicate the close connection between that assumed state of the church, that living in the light, and the exercise of brotherly love; as, in like manner, by darkness is designated the opposite of this love, viz. selfishness, which excludes love, which begets hate,—the characteristic mark of the life of darkness. Ch. ii. 9.] "He that saith he is in the light, and hateth his brother, is in darkness even until now."

With John, as will readily be perceived, the expressions "being in the light," being in fellowship with Christ as the true light, being enlightened by him, and being a christian, all mean the same thing; just as, on the other hand, "being in darkness," being shut out from Christ the true light, and belonging to the ungodly world, all have the same meaning. He who claims to be a christian, and hates him whom he should love as a brother, proves thereby, that however long he may have professed Christianity, he is in truth as far from it as ever. That spirit of hatred towards his brother is a sure token, that he has never yet become a partaker of the divine light; that the darkness of the world, the same spirit which governs the God-estranged world, still reigns in him. Not inwardly, but only outwardly, seemingly, has he renounced the world. The light of Christ has not yet risen in his soul; for this cannot co-exist with such a temper of mind.

Now it is worthy of note, that John makes but this one distinction: He that hateth his brother, and he that loveth his brother. He recognizes no intermediate state, which, while it is indeed far from self-sacrificing love, is far also from hatred of the brethren. This is John's peculiar manner; viz. without regarding intermediate steps and gradations in opposite moral states, to seize upon the radical point of difference, and thus contrast them in their essential nature and principle. And with full reason. For either love, to the exclusion of the selfish element, is the animating principle; or self is made the centre of all, and selfishness governs. Now in this selfishness, the opposite of brotherly love, inheres the tendency which, when consistently carried out, allows place to nothing that interferes with self-interest, and regards every one who comes in conflict therewith as an enemy, to be removed out of the way. Accordingly, in these opposite dispositions, viewed strictly with reference to their radical elements, we find only Love to the brethren, or Hatred of the brethren; love, which is ready for every sacrifice, or selfishness, which may also pass into hate. So Christ recognizes but two distinctions,—serving God, and serving the world.

Hence John says on the other hand: "He that loveth his brother abideth in the light, [Ch. ii. 10.] and there is no occasion of stumbling in him." This characteristic token of brotherly love, must show whether we are abiding in the light.

He who manifests in his life such a self-sacrificing love, reveals therein the power of divine light, whereby he has been made free from the former darkness of selfishness. As the life of Christ was the essence of all-sacrificing love, so fellowship with him is reflected in a similar life of love. We learn from the testimony of the Church Fathers, the Apologists of Christianity in the first centuries, that even the heathen saw in this fellowship of brotherly love the unmistakeable characteristic of the new christian life. "They love one another, even before they know each other!" were the words applied to christians, distinguishing them from the heathen world as governed by hate. Of one in whom brotherly love thus prevails John says, that with him there is no stumbling. This might be understood as follows,—a view which sèems clearly to be at the basis of Luther's translation,—"he who is so heavenly-minded, gives to another no cause of stumbling, no offence." And this is without doubt true, that the love which has only the best good of others in view, and is willing to sacrifice all rather than subject another to what is hurtful, will avoid everything which might in any way offend his moral feeling as a religious being, and thus become a means of spiritual injury to him. We need only call to mind what Paul, in the first Epistle to the Corinthians, says of christian love towards the weak. But although the words, taken by themselves, might be so understood, yet the consistency of the figurative representation, and the contrast with the following verse, requires another sense. The image is that of a man walking in the light, who is therefore safe from all danger of stumbling or falling. Accordingly it means: There is with him no stumbling, he himself stumbles not. As one who walks in the light of day sees his path clearly, and avoids everything over which he might stumble and fall; so does he who walks in the light of the spirit, pass with secure step along life's way. In this divine light he beholds the goal of his course, and the path which leads thither, clearly before him; and he is able to avoid everything which might be prejudicial to the interests of his christian life, to his salvation. Love, in John's view, is that which gives this security to the believer; Love is the soul of this walking in the light. Love bestows that true clearness of spiritual vision, by which the believer pursues his way securely to the goal; the circumspection, the true wisdom, necessary to shun every obstacle and danger in the accomplishment of the life-task which God has set before him. Love bestows that ready instinct, which knows at every instant how to turn circumstances to their right use, to distinguish in all cases between right and wrong. Love imparts true repose, wards off the influence of passion which would disturb the calm judgment of the spirit, keeps the soul steadily towards its one object, and secures it from all distracting influences. Thus, in every respect, is verified the Apostle's assertion, that he who loves his brother cannot stumble.

From this follows the opposite conclusion, in reference to those in whom not love but hate is the governing principle. Of such [Ch. ii. 11. John says: "But he that hateth his brother is in darkness, and walketh in darkness, and knoweth not whither he goeth, because that darkness hath blinded his eyes."

John here makes a distinction, between being in darkness and walking in darkness. The one respects the cause, the other the effect; the one the disposition, the other the course of life resulting from it. He who is wanting in the animating principle of brotherly love, and in whom hatred is the ruling power, being in a state of spiritual darkness can therefore only walk in darkness; as he to whom the illuminating light of the sun is wanting, or who from disease of the eyes cannot perceive it, wanders about in darkness, unable to distinguish the goal which he is seeking or the path which conducts to it. Just so it is with him who is under the dominion of selfishness, and of hatred. He cannot perceive the heavenly goal towards which the christian life is tending, nor the way thither. In respect to these he is as one who is blind. He can form no definite plan of life. Destitute of that clearness and collectedness of spirit, necessary in order to direct his course with steady purpose towards a well-ascertained end, he is every moment losing his way; his selfish impulses hurry him hither and thither; his whole course is an aimless, confused, inconstant effort he knows not why or whither.

Love to christian brethren and its opposite is primarily intended here, as it is by Christ also in his last discourses. But while love is here conceived of at its highest point, and in its most immediate sphere where its full power and glory can best unfold; yet this by no means excludes the universal love of man, which from the very nature of the case is included in christian love. It need not be specially mentioned; since in christian Brotherly love itself is imparted the yearning desire to draw all men within this fraternal sphere, to convert them all into brethren. For to this they are destined by virtue of their common origin, of the common image of God in all, and of the redemption provided for all; and Christ himself, he who gave his life for his enemies that he might make them brethren and children of God, is in this self-sacrificing love their model. It is the nature of love, in the christian sense, to efface all limitations and distinctions.

As exhortation and promise always go hand in hand in this epistle, John now, after having shown what belongs to the nature of the [Ch. ii. 12. Christian life, addresses them again as their spiritual Father, in order to cheer their hearts under the sense of unlikeness to this life, under the sense of sin. He calls to them all as his children: "I write unto you little children, because [that] your sins are forgiven you for his name's sake." He comforts them with the assurance of sins forgiven through the mediation of Christ. For the name of Christ are their sins forgiven; that is, for the sake of what Christ is as the Son of God and the Son of Man, the divine-human Redeemer,—it being as such that they invoke Him as their Mediator. There is reference here to what he had before said of the reconciliation effected by Christ.

He now proceeds to remind them of what belongs to their high estate as Christians.
Ch. ii. 13.] What he would say applies indeed to the whole church collectively. But turning with affectionate familiarity to the various ages in the church, he addresses to each exactly what is most appropriate to it. Thus the fathers, the young men, and the children, are each particularly addressed in the words: "I write unto you, fathers, because ye have known him that is from the beginning. I write unto you, young men, because ye have overcome the wicked one. I write unto you, little children, because ye have known the Father."

The Gospel announcement, beginning with the appearance of Christ in time, proceeded on to the knowledge of the depths of his divine nature;

rising above the temporal manifestation to him who was from the beginning, to the eternal, divine Word who had appeared in the Son of Man. This knowledge presupposes a higher stage of christian development, a longer intimacy with christianity, and this therefore is especially ascribed to the fathers in the church. But we must not forget, moreover, in what sense John uses knowledge. He means by it, as we have seen, no mere theoretical knowledge proceeding from the understanding, but a knowledge which has its origin in the life, which presupposes a fellowship of life with the object of knowledge, and which again re-acts upon the life. It is that higher and deeper knowledge of Christ, as He who was from the beginning, proceeding from a more intimate living union with the person of Christ. This is something more than the statement of a certain dogmatic formula respecting the person of Christ.

Turning now to the young men of the church, John applies to them what is especially adapted to their age. Youth is formed for conflict; the bold champions are from its ranks. In childhood, the elements of inward conflict still lie hidden and undeveloped. It knows not, at that age of unconscious innocence, what germs of evil it carries in its bosom, slumbering yet in the depths of its undeveloped being, and the peace of a childish faith still rules in the heart. But in the transition from childhood to youth, these hidden contrarieties burst forth. Desires and passions awake in their might, and strive against the higher law of the spirit. The natural reason, now becoming conscious of itself, asserts its claims, and calls in question what at first had been received with simple, childlike faith. On every hand breaks forth the hitherto unconscious and concealed discord in the twofold law of man's nature. Here now is need of conflict, in order that the divine seed, implanted during a childhood developed under the influence of christianity, (for John here supposes a church long established in christian truth) may be preserved uncorrupt, may be individually appropriated, and matured to fruit. But the christian youth must maintain the conflict ; that through the conflict he may regain as a conscious personal possession that peace, which, in the period of early childhood, was imbibed unconsciously from the influence of christianity, in whose heavenly elements of life it had unfolded.

Youth, called in the freshness of its power to conflict, must not shun the strife. In that divine seed implanted in a christian childhood, youth has that which renders victory in all those conflicts certain, provided only it is faithfully applied. Hence John does not say: Ye will overcome the evil one, that power in the evil one, which in all those respects arrays itself in opposition to the divine; but he says: Ye have overcome. He has in view such as, from childhood up, have been developed in fellowship with the Redeemer; and as He has triumphed once for all over the power of evil, his victory has thus become their own. Not with their own weak powers, not in reliance upon their own strength, do they maintain the warfare. Through faith in the Redeemer, who has overcome the power of evil, have they already conquered. And, in faith towards him their Redeemer, in fellowship with him, to appropriate through his strength his victory to themselves,—this is to maintain the conflict. Christ, the victor over the power of Satan and of the world, strives and conquers in them; they strive and conquer as his instruments. The christian life, though in its nature always one and the same, yet develops itself in successive stages, each having its peculiar standpoint. John accordingly contemplates youth as especially the season of conflict. The entire christian life is, indeed, a copy of Christ's own unremitted and ever-deepening conflict till it closed in that last cry: "It is finished." It must therefore be an ever-renewed conflict, till its last death-struggle ends in eternal peace. Still he regarded youth as especially the season of conflict; a conflict, however, which to the christian is immediately transformed to victory.

Finally, he turns to the age of childhood. The relationship of parent and child is the one most familiar to children; and filial love, therefore, furnishes the most easy and natural point of attachment for love to the eternal Father in Heaven. Accordingly, to the children of christian families, who from the first had learned in faith toward the Redeemer to know God as their Father; who had been nurtured into the filial relation to him as Father; to such he says, that they have known the Father. The term KNOW, we remark again, must of course be understood here in the sense peculiar to John.

As we naturally repeat what we earnestly desire to impress upon others, John now reiterates what he has just said, with some additions serving to illustrate and enforce it, and to prepare the way for the exhortation which is to follow. He had already said,—I write unto you; and he now repeats, emphatically, what he had just written. "I have written unto you," he adds, as much as to say: There let it stand! That which I write unto you, is now written. It is final. Nothing other have I to say to you; this you must receive, as said to you once for all. "I have written unto you, fathers, because ye have known him that is from the beginning. I have written unto you, young men, because ye are strong, and the word of God abideth in you, and ye have overcome the wicked one." [Ch. ii. 14.

It must be for a special reason, that John satisfies himself with a single address to the children; while he feels it necessary to enforce by repetition what he has said to those of maturer age, with whom more is depending upon their own personal agency. To what he had first said to the youth, he here adds something more; as in their case it might be needful to show HOW they had overcome the Evil One. It is superior strength by which victory is attained; and consciousness of strength is natural to youth. But this is apt to be connected with self-confidence, now first developed into activity, with a conscious ability to meet all dangers, to overcome all hindrances, to triumph over all enemies in one's own strength. But this self-confidence and self-reliance, will, if unsustained by strength from a higher source, soon fail in the conflicts of life and be put to shame. The Apostle directs them to another ground of confidence, another source of strength. While he reminds the young that they are strong, he at the same time indicates whence this strength is to be derived, wherein it must have its root, viz. that divine word already received by them and faithfully adhered to and applied by them; that word, fast rooted in their hearts and abiding there as an ineradicable principle. In the divine word, therefore, whose vitalizing power is the life of their spirit, lies their strength. Already, through the might of this divine word, have they virtually overcome the power of evil; in this word, which no other power can withstand, is the victory given them. We may translate, "abideth among you," or "abideth in you." The sense is the same. It cannot abide among them collectively, unless it has been received individually into the heart.

Having thus indicated all which believers need, in order to maintain successfully the conflict with the world, the Apostle concludes with the following exhortation: "Love not the world, neither the things that are in the world." [Ch. ii. 15.

These words have been often misunderstood, as if requiring for the perfection of the Christian life a withdrawal from the world, and from all worldly concerns. Manifold errors have arisen from this misapprehension, which is far from the meaning of the apostolic injunction. The New Testament assumes in all its teachings, that the world and all that is in it, as proceeding from God's creative hand exists only for his service and glory, which is the aim and end of the whole creation. Man, as the image of God, should have it for his highest his single aim, to actualize this purpose of the whole creation with a free and conscious will; to so use the world that all things, each in its own way, shall subserve this purpose. Through the redemption, and the new creation proceeding therefrom, man was to become competent thus to use all things; as Christ did not withdraw himself from the world and worldly things, but by his mastery over them glorified God in the most perfect manner. The Apostle requires only this: that God should be the single object of man's unconditional love. No other love may take place beside it; but this unconditional love must wholly rule the soul and the life, must make all else subordinate to itself. As Christ says (Matt. vi. 21), "Where your treasure is, there will your heart be also." The object of man's unconditional love, whatever it may be, decides the whole direction and character of his life, and imparts its own peculiar stamp to all his actions. Now love to God must demonstrate its power, by giving to the world and all that is in it a reference to God, by using it to his glory. All other love is not thereby excluded, but on the contrary, is embraced in it. Every object of affection is to be regarded with a love, proportioned to the place assigned it by God in the creation,—a love developing itself out of love to God. It is the nature of true love to God, not to withdraw from the world and worldly things; but in accordance with the purpose assigned to them by God, to use all to his glory. It is only a love to the world for its own sake, a love not proceeding from God and referring all to him, which the Apostle here forbids. It is the world, as the object of such a love, of which the Apostle here speaks; and it is this which he represents as standing opposed to the love of God.

In this sense he says: "If any man love the world, the love of the Father is not in him." It is in this sense therefore we are to understand the assertion, that love to the world excludes the love of the Father. That God is truly known and loved as Father, can show itself only in this, viz. that our estimation and use of all worldly things is determined solely by this principle of filial love to God. Nothing can stand side by side with this love; all else must be subordinated to it, must be derived from it, must be grounded in it. Whatever claims to stand beside this love, must be opposed to it. It is of such an opposition the Apostle here speaks.

John now proceeds to exhibit that general contrariety, between the direction towards God and that towards the world, under [Ch. ii. 16. three separate forms in which the love of the world manifests itself; and this he does in such a manner, that the particular appears as the confirmation of the more general. "For all that is in the world, the lust of the flesh, and the lust of the eyes, and the pride of life, is not of the Father, but is of the world." When the Apostle here represents the world as opposed to the Father, that which is of the world to that which is of the Father; he does not mean the world in itself, which he regards as the work of God, but in a moral view, as connected in his mind with that tendency of the soul which cleaves to the world, seeking therein its own highest good and sundering it from connection with God. "The world" here designates the ruling tendency of the spirit towards the world, the entire amalgamation of the spirit with it. So also, in particular, it is not the things of the world in themselves of which he speaks, but only as that general direction of the spirit attaches itself to them, manifests itself in them, identifies itself with them. This, therefore, is his meaning: all those single forms of worldly-mindedness, with whatever objects of the world they may stand connected, proceed from the same radical tendency, the amalgamation of the spirit with the world, and are opposed to that tendency which proceeds from the heavenly Father.

He now adduces three such forms, in which at that time the worldly spirit chiefly manifested itself, and against which christians needed to be put on their guard. First, he mentions the fleshly appetites; then whatever is an object of sensual pleasure to the eye. By the latter, many such sinful pleasures might be understood; as, at that time, especially the prevailing passion for heathen spectacles, with which even christians by intercourse with the heathen world were liable to be infected, as shown by examples in the second and third centuries. Many interpreters have regarded it as referring to avarice, inasmuch as the avaricious feeds his eye on the mere sight of his gold. What the Apostle here says is true, indeed, of him who makes of mammon his highest good. But this particular reference is so little suited to the words, that we are by no means justified in assuming it as the Apostle's meaning. Thirdly he mentions vanity, ostentation as exhibited in the life, state and pomp in worldly things, show and splendor as a means of gaining consequence. He means therefore that union of the spirit with the world, as manifested in the three forms of sensual appetite, of pleasure-seeking and frivolity, a vain love of pomp and show. In the sense thus intended by the Apostle, we are to apply his language to all the appetites and passions which make this world their object, and of which he here gives only these three characteristic forms.

He then proceeds to contrast the opposite issues of the two radical tendencies, as illustrating
Ch. ii. 17.] the difference of their origin and nature. "And the world passeth away, and the lust thereof: but he that doeth the will of God abideth forever." All that is in the world being perishable, so likewise is all the pleasure connected with it. He therefore who seeks his highest good in the perishable, will see that for which he has striven the prey of destruction, nothing left to him but bitter disappointment. But he who does the will of God, and on that fixes his love, will with his love survive all that is earthly. When all that is earthly has passed away, he will have attained to an eternal divine life of blessedness; living forever, with that which was the object and end of all his strivings, in a state beyond the fear of decay or death.

From these practical admonitions John now passes, with a personal address to the mem-
Ch. ii. 18.] bers of these churches as his children, to a

warning against those false teachers of a corrupted christianity, of whom we have spoken in the Introduction. "Little children, it is the last time: and as ye have heard that antichrist shall come, even now are there many antichrists; whereby we know that it is the last time." The christian observer of the signs of the times, learns from the Apostle to apprehend these, not singly as mere isolated phenomena, but as links of a more extended chain. He learns to inquire what place the present holds, in relation to the whole progressive development of the kingdom of God, and from this to judge of each particular event. Thus Christ too requires us to watch the signs of the times, and to regulate our conduct accordingly. We should not, with a frivolous inattention, pass by the events of the present time; but should seek to recognize in them the finger of God, the leadings of divine wisdom, and apply them wisely for our own direction, and for our influence upon the age. We should hear in them the voice of God, calling us now in admonitory tones to repentance, to caution and watchfulness, and now cheering us on to the exercise of hope and trust. The word of God abounds with many such an index to the right understanding of the signs of the present time.

The Apostle speaks of the period in which he was writing as the last time. So he designates the christian period. And it may always be so regarded, as forming the epoch towards which all prior revelations of God tended, and in which they were consummated; the whole previous development of the kingdom of God being only preparative to that which is the aim and end of all, viz. the appearing of Jesus as the Redeemer of humanity. Henceforth all centres upon this one object,—that the new element introduced by Christ into human history, as the leaven which is to penetrate all things, should develop and extend itself more and more, till the end shall be fully accomplished. Henceforth all may be regarded as one great connected period in the history of humanity; reaching to the final decision, which is to follow the personal return of Christ, to that last sifting, the final consummation of the kingdom of God on earth. This period may therefore, without reference to the question whether it be longer or shorter, ever be regarded as THE LAST TIME in respect to the development of the kingdom of God.

It is certain, however, that the Apostles connected with this designation of their own age, as the last time, another and more limited idea. The signs which they observed were ushering in, as they believed, the last time in the strictest sense; that of the dissolution of all earthly things, and the second coming of the Lord. They were not able to survey and compute the extent of the intervening period yet to pass away. If in this respect the event did not answer to their expectation, we shall find in this no cause of stumbling, nothing inconsistent with the Spirit's promised illumination, by which they were to be guided into the whole truth made known by Christ, and perfectly understand it. Though Christ had indeed promised them, that this Spirit should show them also things to come, yet this doubtless is not to be understood in an absolutely unconditional sense. It was to extend just so far, as was required for understanding what he had taught them of the divine kingdom, and was by no means a prophetic certainty respecting its whole future development. An error therefore in chronology, regarding "the last time" (properly meaning, in that general sense, the whole time subsequent to the appearing of

Christ) as a period of brief duration, and the hour of final decision as near at hand; this is by no means inconsistent with that promised measure of illumination by the Holy Spirit. That they should "know the times or the seasons" (Acts i. 7) was not at all essential to their calling as divinely commissioned teachers. Christ has himself said, that the coming of that last period was something hidden from the angels, and from the Son of God himself. The Father had reserved it for his own decision. It is easy to see why this could not be otherwise. That closing period is to be ushered in by the whole preparatory development of human history, in connection with the series of concatenated free agencies, and its coming is dependent thereon. Hence the ability to fix its date, implies an entire survey of all the divine arrangements for the guidance of free beings in connection with their own free agency, from the beginning to the end of time. But this can be possible only to such a foreknowledge as is grounded in divine omniscience. Thus Christ also, to the inquiry of his disciples,—when the complete manifestation of his kingdom in the world should come,—replied: "It is not for you to know the times or the seasons, which the Father hath put in his own power." (Acts i. 7.) Christ himself here teaches, that the ability to compute the time in that respect does not belong to the office of his disciples, and was not necessary to it. Thus was impressed upon their minds the limits of the divine and human; what they were to learn through the light of the Holy Spirit, and how far they were still to be left to their own guidance.

Their longing desires hastened towards the reappearing of their Lord, the coming of His kingdom in its glory. It was with them as with the traveller, who beholds from afar the goal of his pilgrimage. His eye embraces at one glance the whole intermediate space; the windings of the intervening way are overlooked, and the distant boundary on which his gaze is fixed seems just at hand. It is only when he has traversed a part of the way, that he begins to perceive how widely he is still separated from the destined goal. So was it with the Prophets, when they looked forward to the appearing of the Messiah. So was it with the Apostles, when looking for the return of their Lord. As the traveller in space, looking away over the intervening distance, seems to behold the object of his wanderings close at hand; so is it with the travellers in time, as they glance over the intervening periods towards the object of their longing expectation. Christianity seemed only the transition, from the earthly and perishable order of things, to that which is heavenly. Hence, their gaze being fixed alone upon that heavenly state, they saw the earthly only as ready to vanish away,—as the point of transition to the heavenly and eternal, and therefore of very brief duration. True, Christ in his parables respecting the kingdom of God, as for example when he presents it under the figure of leaven, indicates a more slow, a gradual process of development. But these words, like many others spoken by him, could only then be comprehended in their whole scope and significance, when interpreted by the progressive developments of history. Not till then could it be understood, that what the first christian age supposed would be effected by Christ's personal intervention at his second appearing, required on the contrary a long preparatory process, in the gradual spread of the leaven of christianity among all races of men, whose extension could not then be known.

Christ had, moreover, in his last discourses specified many signs, which should precede that final decision to be brought about by his second coming. But even these could not determine the exact date of its occurrence. For as the same law governs the whole development-process of the kingdom of God upon earth, so do the great periods in that process correspond to one another; the same law repeats itself in a constantly ascending scale. We find the succeeding periods prefigured in the earlier, as the earlier serve to prepare the way for those which follow. That last personal coming of Christ, for the establishment of his kingdom, is preceded by numerous manifestations of his spiritual coming, of a new and mighty revelation of Christ in the life of humanity,—of a new coming of the kingdom of God with power. These form the great epochs in the development of the kingdom of God. By these we may distinguish the several grand divisions in the historical development of the church. So too the signs, which are to announce the last personal coming of Christ, are prefigured in those which announce and prepare the way for the successive manifestations of his spiritual coming. Each great division of a new coming of Christ, in the progress of historical development, points to that last personal coming, serves as a type and preparation of that closing epoch. The same law repeats itself in an ascending scale, till at length it is fulfilled for the last time. Thus in Christ's own discourses (Matt. xxiv., xxv.), the signs of his first mighty spiritual manifestation in judgment on the corrupted Theocracy, and in the first entrance of his kingdom with power, freed from what had previously fettered and obscured it,—these signs are so mingled with those of his last personal coming to judge the world and to consummate the kingdom of God, that the different references can with difficulty be distinguished from each other. Hence it might the more easily happen, that at the coming in of those several great epochs in the historical development of the church, and especially in the first apostolic times, the signs of the present, which were to be repeated yet many times, should be taken as the signs of that more remote period, which in a stricter sense is designated as "the last time."

Here then, in the last discourses of Christ, we find a law for the historical development of the kingdom of God, the same to which the words of John now under consideration are to be referred, as are also those of Paul in his second Epistle to the Thessalonians (Ch. ii. 4). This is an ever-recurring law, in accordance with which the kingdom of God develops itself in an ascending conflict with the kingdom of evil; new manifestations of the latter kingdom preceding and preparing the way for new and more glorious manifestations of the former. Evil, by a gradual process of development attains to its highest point; the kingdom of Christ then develops itself in conflict with it; and, at length, through a new mighty coming of Christ, the kingdom of evil is once more subdued. Of this law the highest exemplification will be given at the final coming of Christ, and this is prefigured in each of the great decisive epochs of the church; they are all ushered in by a similar conflict. This is a view rich in consolation; but should serve also as an incitement to vigilance, when in any period we see the kingdom of evil pushing its encroachments with unwonted vigor. This law, derived from the word of God, teaches us what we are then to look for as about to come, and to perceive in the present the germinating future. The Apostle John, observing such signs in the conflicts at the close of the apostolic age, wherein the succeeding stage of development was then preparing, seemed already to behold the signs of that last time. He applied with propriety the law laid down for him by Christ himself, in reference to the conflict of the two kingdoms. But, as we have shown, he could not and he need not know, that these signs should be often repeated, till at length they should announce that final epoch; that this law should again and again find its fulfilment, till it should be perfectly and decisively fulfilled for the last time.

John assumes it, as something already well known to those whom he addresses in this letter, that in the last time One should arise whom he calls Antichrist. He could assume this as known, partly from the instructions received by the churches from himself, partly from what they had previously learned through the preaching of Paul. Doubtless their attention had often been directed to the dangers and the significant signs of the last time, in order that they might be fully prepared, in all watchfulness of spirit, to meet the great impending conflict. But John speaks of many antichrists; and thence draws the conclusion that "the last time," which was to be known as such by the appearance of Antichrist, was now near at hand. Does he then mean, that by Antichrist is to be understood not some single personage, but only the collective sum of all antagonism to Christ; the name being merely a personification of that in its unity which was, in fact, distributed among many individuals? By no means. On the contrary, the many individuals rising up on every side, in whom opposition to Christ, the anti-christian principle, makes itself apparent,—these seem to him only precursors, prophetic omens of that One in whom this principle is to reach its culminating point; who is to appear as its peculiar representative, the incarnation as it were of the anti-christian principle. Here too we shall find the workings of one uniform law, in the development-process of the kingdom of God: viz. that in good and evil, there are certain personalities forming the central point, standing as representatives of the conflicting principles; in whom that which exists as scattered fragments in many individuals unites as one great whole. On the one hand, those fragmentary workings of good and evil prepare the way for that one great personality, in whom they severally reach their culminating point; on the other, it is through the agency of these great personalities, that the principles which they represent are diffused through a multitude of others. Hence the Apostle, from the numerous individuals whom he saw rising up as the organs of anti-christianity, could justly infer the speedy appearance of that great personality, in whom the anti-christian principle should reach its highest manifestation.

The question now arises,—what is to be understood by Antichrist and anti-christianity? Is it in general opposers of Christianity, of faith in Jesus as the Messiah; for example, such opposers from among the Jews and heathen? But were this the true meaning, John could not have spoken of the advent of these antichrists as something new; for the idea would then be entirely coincident with that of the world, as opposed to Christianity and in conflict with it; and in that case believers must have always lived among antichrists, and needed no such special warning against them. Just so certainly as they themselves believed in Jesus as the Messiah, must they be the opposers of those who resisted his recognition as such. There could be nothing in this open stand against the Messiahship of Jesus, to tempt them from their fidelity to him. We can, therefore, come to no other conclusion, than that these antichrists appeared under an assumed and deceitful garb, by means of which they might procure admission among christians; and if these were not firm in their faith and clear in their christian knowledge, might by degrees gain an influence over them. We must regard it as rather a disguised than an open opposition to genuine Christianity. And hence too, we must regard Antichrist himself as an adversary of Christianity different from its previous opposers; as one possessing a peculiar power of deception, whereby even christians might be seduced into apostacy; as one who wins dominion over the souls of men by blinding and deceptive arts, putting himself in communication with their religious necessities in order thereby to delude and subjugate them; as one who knows how to instate himself, unperceived, in that relation to the human spirit which it should hold only to Christ and to God. Christ too, in his last discourses, points to such a power of delusion, exercised by those who set themselves up as prophets and Messiahs. Here also belongs what Paul says of the adversary, who with self-deification should establish himself in the temple of God. Hence, according to the different forms assumed by the antichristian principle at different periods, (when a new spiritual coming of Christ, for a new glorification of the church, was about to be evolved from the conflict of his kingdom with the kingdom of evil) might those signs specified in the Holy Scriptures receive a different interpretation. And this not without reason; since under these different forms was first revealed the antichristian principle, whose culminating point was to be finally reached in that representative personality. Thus in the times preceding the Reformation, when the secularized church, guided by the secularized Papacy, served under the christian name as an efficient instrument for obscuring and thwarting genuine Christianity, —one might believe that he saw in this the visible manifestation of Antichrist. And Matthias von Jarnow, the Bohemian reformer before Huss, might suppose that he saw the craft of Satan in this, viz. that believers instead of recognizing Antichrist in the present,—in the domination of the secularized church, in the triumph of superstition even to the deification of the human,—were beguiled into seeking it in some distant period. In our age, on the contrary, one would be disposed to recognize the preparatory signs of Antichrist in the self-deification of the natural reason; which, after having developed itself under the influence of Christianity, now arrays itself in arrogant self-consciousness and vain self-worship against that very Christianity, without whose aid it could never have attained to this self-consciousness. The question, "What is Antichrist?" will be interpreted, now from the stand-point of superstition and now from that of scepticism, according as the anti-christian principle manifests itself in the one or the other of these forms. Each of these interpretations will have its share of the common truth, which the light of the divine word imparts in the delineation of those signs.

Before designating these antichrists more particularly, John speaks of their rise and of their relation to the churches from which [Ch. ii. 19. they had gone out. "They went out from us, but they were not of us; for if they had been of us, they would no doubt have continued with us; but they went out, that they might be made manifest that they were not all of us." From this we learn, that these antichrists were not such as had from the beginning stood in a hostile attitude to the church, but such as had gone out from the midst of the church itself. The church had therefore carried in her own bosom, that which now developed itself in conflict with the spirit which formed her vital principle. The propagators of these false doctrines, by which genuine christian truth was corrupted, and whom the Apostle was constrained to resist, had themselves once been numbered with those whom the church acknowledged as brethren. Now this was well adapted to unsettle christians in their faith; seeing as they did the very persons whom they had known as brethren in the faith, who had testified of the same christian consciousness, the same christian experiences, now turning against that which they had once acknowledged as truth, and inculcating as truth something entirely different. The thought might naturally arise: may not these persons have really found their former convictions to be erroneous, and attained to a clearer insight which they are now desirous to impart to others? The church needed, therefore, to be guarded against the prejudicial influence of such an example. What then does the Apostle say in explanation of this, and for the consolation of such of his readers as might be disturbed by it? He tells them that these persons, although they had once been connected with the church in an external relation, yet had never in heart and soul been really united with it in the exercise of genuine faith. He distinguishes between genuine and spurious members of the church; between a union merely with its outward and visible form,—apart from all share in that inward spiritual act which constitutes its vital essence, genuine faith in the Redeemer,—and that same outward union as connected also with a participation in its spiritual essence; a distinction between those in the visible church who belong also to the invisible, and those who by the governing direction of their hearts are excluded from the invisible church, and belong only to the outward form. And what does he adduce in proof that such is here the fact? The result,—that which has been made apparent by the apostacy of those persons from the genuine christian truth, on which rests the essential being of the church,—by their opposition to this truth.

But does this imply, as supposed by many, that apostacy from christian truth in the case of such as have once made it their principle of life, a falling from the state of regeneration, is a thing impossible? This can by no means be deduced from these words. A false interpretation is given to them by those who stretch the sense so far; who make of the Apostle's declaration in regard to a particular case, a principle of universal application. The word of God guards us against such a view, by enjoining watchfulness, even upon him who has made greatest advancement, so long as the conflict of the earthly life shall endure; and by warning him who is confident that he stands fast, to take heed lest he fall (1 Cor. x. 12). So too the Apostle Paul, that mature believer, speaks of his conflicts and strivings,—lest he, who had preached to others, should himself be found a castaway. Such an apostacy cannot, indeed, be supposed to take place suddenly. But it may happen, that through lack of true watchfulness over himself, or through false self-reliance, a lack of humility, he who has once attained to the christian state, may gradually fall again under the dominion of that sin, which though subdued by faith still cleaves to him; may sink down again from the height to which he had thus risen, and so lose the divine life once received, but not faithfully guarded and nurtured. The Apostle John by no means denies such a possibility; he is only asserting what was the fact in this particular case. He only states the grounds upon which this specific occurrence is to be explained; which by no means justifies us in deducing from it a universal law, for the development of the christian life. What he says is no more than this: no such radical change has ever been experienced by these persons of whom he is speaking. What now appears, openly and visibly, had always really existed though under concealment and disguise. Even while still attached to the church, they had been strangers to the christian truth which is its vital principle. Under the mask of a christian profession, they had concealed the same views and feelings, which now manifest themselves in open opposition to the pure christian truth.

By this explanation of the true grounds of an occurrence, which seemed likely to perplex the minds of many, the Apostle seeks to counteract its influence upon those whom he addresses in this Letter. He shows them that what so awakens their surprise is nothing new, but has already been long preparing. He teaches them, moreover, that although the causes from which it proceeded were indeed something to be deplored, yet that the occurrence is in itself a salutary necessity in the development-process of Christianity. It served to bring out in a clear and convincing manner the truth, that not all who seem to belong to the church, belong to it in reality; to separate the genuine and spurious members from one another; to discriminate between what is truly christian, and what under the christian name belongs strictly to another principle; to carry out a sifting process in the development of the church. With this is to be compared Paul's declaration, that there must be heresies, in order that it may be made manifest who are the genuine members of the church. (1 Cor. xi. 19.) That which produces heresies is indeed an evil, is something to be deplored. But that, being present, it should thus develop itself; that the hidden should be brought to light, and what is kindred in spirit coalesce in one; this is a wholesome necessity, and is founded in the course of development ordained by divine wisdom: as in the diseased body, it may be necessary that the morbid elements should break forth in specific crises, in order that they may be cast out and subdued by the principle of healthful life. What the divine word here teaches, is a law which can be traced through the whole history of the church. By that divine word we are raised to a stand-point, for the contemplation of history and of life, whence we perceive in evil at once freedom of action, personal guilt, and that higher law of divine all-directing wisdom, to which evil itself, when it comes forth to light, is made subservient.

What the Apostle here says, is susceptible of a manifold application to the moral phenomena of our own times, and may tranquillize us when disquieted and perplexed in view of them. We see the contrariety, between christian truth and the errors which oppose it, becoming more and more clearly defined; the Divine and the Undivine, Christianity and World-worship, encountering each other more and more openly in the avowed convictions of men. To many this seems to have broken forth suddenly; and they know not how to account for it, that darkness should be permitted to gain such an ascendency. But a deeper scrutiny shows us, 'that what the Apostle taught in regard to the moral phenomena of his own times is true also here ; viz. that the cause of these inauspicious symptoms could have no sudden origin, but had long existed in the hidden germ. It is not strange that it should fill us with disquietude and grief, when we see those who have appeared to us zealous advocates of the same christian truth which we profess, whom we had with reason believed to be truly of us, suddenly go over to the camp of the enemy. Whence this change ? How could they apostatize from the truth, after having received the same divine experiences of its power as we ? How could the grace of God suffer them to fall ? How could that faithfulness and truth of God deny itself ? Should not He complete the work which he had himself begun in them ? But the Apostle's words furnish the true solution of this difficulty, and relieve our perplexity. It is but bringing to light that which was concealed. Such, though seemingly of us, belonged not to us. Nor had they ever held the same ground of faith, the same divine truth with us, though making the same profession ; and whatever zeal they might have shown for it, it was still a dead form under which they concealed another meaning. Their views had been always the same radically, though cloaked as yet under the christian garb, unrevealed to others, perhaps even to themselves. Such persons, living in a less active period, when these contrarieties had not yet broken out openly, might have gone on quietly in their natural course of development. Their profession would indeed, as now, have been mere pretence; they would have had the shell only without the kernel; not the pure element of christian truth, but its opposite, would still have been the vital element of their belief; but this would have been unobserved and unknown. Now, however, in this period filled and agitated by so many and openly manifested anti-christian elements, the kindred element in them is attracted by this influence, and is impelled to throw off the disguise,—to become conscious to itself, and to seek for itself an open expression.

But there may be still another case. These persons who seemed to belong to us, may have been really affected by the influence of the same christian truth which we profess. They may have enjoyed experiences of its divine power. But with this, there co-existed in them the anti-christian principle predominant in the age; and hence a conflict of opposite tendencies. But that in them which was allied to the anti-christian spirit of the age, at length so gained the mastery as to overcome the genuine christian element. And thus they themselves became sceptical, in regard to their own former experiences of the higher life; and at length were carried so far, as to impugn that for which they had once been witnesses. They belong to that class, in the Saviour's parable of the sower, in whom the seed of the divine word springs up quickly,—all the more quickly because it takes no deep root,—and through the hostile agency of the adverse spirit is as soon destroyed. Of such also it may be said, "They went out from us, because they were not truly of us." Of this class Judas Iscariot stands as a fearful example. He, it may be, once experienced emotions of the higher life. He may, at times, have received divine impressions from intercourse with the Saviour. When Judas first numbered himself among the disciples, Christ had already perceived what was in him,—that carnal tendency which looked for a temporal Messiah. Yet he did not thrust him away, but drew him to himself with a love which sought to exert a saving influence upon him. The other disciples, surrendering themselves to the Lord, and to his purifying and sanctifying influence, were by degrees freed from the power of this carnal spirit of the age. With Judas, on the contrary, that false spirit gained more and more the preponderance, repressing more and more those higher impressions, till at length they were lost to him altogether. Thus it was that from a disciple of the Lord, he became his most malignant enemy and his betrayer.

Thus enlightened by the words of John, in respect to the cause and the necessity of such occurrences, we shall be enabled to regard them, though not without grief yet without perplexity, and even to derive profit from them for the furtherance of our faith and of our salvation. We see that it is a needful sifting. We live in an age of sifting. Those who have the reality and those who have only the show of Christianity, those who belong to God and those who belong to the world, must be more and more separated from each other. This time of sifting summons each one to decide for himself between these two contrary tendencies, no longer to be reconciled with each other, but standing out in a more and more sharply defined antagonism. Each one is summoned to put to himself the momentous and decisive question: Under which banner shall I fight? He will perceive the deep significance of the words of the Lord; "He that is not for me is against me." He will learn to watch vigilantly over himself, lest the bitter root in his own nature, furthered in its growth by the kindred but poisonous breath in the life of the age, shoot up and increase, and choke the good seed. It is plain that an encounter with the open manifestations of the antichristian spirit merely, will not here suffice; it is the hidden root from which they spring, against which above all we must turn the sword of the Spirit.

Having thus removed the occasion of stumbling, thrown in the way of the weaker brethren by the apostacy of these errorists, he now leads them back into the depths of their own inward life pervaded by the Spirit of Christ, in order to show them that they had means enough for resisting these deceptive appearances, for distinguishing between the Christian and the Antichristian. "But ye have an unction [anointing] from the Holy One, and ye know all things. I have not written unto you because ye know not

Ch. ii. 20, 21.]

the truth, but because ye know it, and that no lie is of the truth."

The Apostle here presents, in contrast with those apostates, the whole body of true and steadfast believers. Such should have no occasion to fear the threatened danger from those falsifiers of christian truth. They should carry in their own hearts the touchstone, whereby to distinguish the Christian from the Anti-christian, the preservative against the infectious influence of error. And as for you,—this is what he would say, the emphasis being on "you,"—YE have the anointing from the Holy One, the anointing which proceeds from the holy God, the Father. He is here called the Holy One, as he through whom those who belong to him are made holy, filled with his holiness, and are thereby separated from the unholy, ungodly world,—the chosen from the midst of the corrupt world. The name Holy One is indeed also a designation of Christ; and it might be referred to him, as he who imparts this spirit to believers. But the preposition here used in the original ("from") would naturally direct us rather to God, as the eternal source from which this spirit proceeds. (Comp. John xv. 26.) So might we judge, should we take this passage by itself; but since both views are possible, and both convey strict truth, a comparison of it with a subsequent passage is necessary to a reliable decision. In either case, the difference of conception makes no alteration in the sense. The anointing itself consists in that Holy Spirit which, proceeding from the holy God, is imparted to those only who are his. It places them in fellowship with him, and guards them from all the unholy influences inherent in the world, to which also belongs everything which threatens to falsify the pure christian truth.

The word "anointing" suggests to us the ordinances of the old dispensation, from which it was borrowed. Kings, priests, prophets, received their consecration to the office appointed them by God, through an anointing,—the symbol of the power imparted to them by God through his Spirit for the fulfilment of their calling. By the outward and visible was signified that which, in its fulness and completion, was to be wrought inwardly upon the spirit. Now that which was expressed outwardly under the old dispensation, and by a single act, is in the New Testament converted wholly into the inward and spiritual, and working from within embraces the entire life. That which under the old dispensation was restricted to individuals, entrusted in some manner with the guidance of God's people,—individuals who were thereby separated from the body of the people,—now under the new dispensation belongs to the people of God universally. The limitations of the Old Testament are burst asunder by the spirit of the New. First of all, its founder himself,—the sovereign in God's kingdom, the Saviour,—is called the Anointed, the Christ, as having been consecrated to his work through the fulness of the indwelling Spirit of God; as possessing in himself the fulness, the sum of all those divine powers, which were only imparted singly as special gifts to the prophets of the Old Testament. So, by virtue of their fellowship with him, are all who are redeemed by him made partakers of the Holy Spirit which he imparts. From the fulness of the divine nature, the divine power dwelling in him, he imparts to all. This is the inward anointing, the inward consecration whereby they are inwardly set apart from the world, as those who belong to God through Christ. All are admitted without distinction to the same fellowship with him, and receive from him the same inward consecration to their divine mission through the Holy Spirit. Henceforth there exists no more among the people of God any such distinction, as under the Old Testament between kings, priests, prophets, and people; but all collectively are in like manner consecrated to God, have an equal part in that inward consecration, in the illuminating and sanctifying influence of the Holy Spirit. It is one royal priestly generation, whose nobility and high office is alike the heritage of all; all are prophets, through that common illumination of the Holy Spirit. Such are the weighty thoughts contained in that single word, that honorable designation of believers.

Believing himself justified in assuming this inward anointing in the case of those to whom he writes, he goes on to infer from this, that they already know all that he has to say to them,—all which is requisite to an insight into the nature of christian truth, to preservation from error. In that inner fountain all can be found, if they will only surrender themselves to that inward, heavenly teacher. He disclaims teaching any new doctrine, unknown to them hitherto. It is not as a missionary to those who are yet without the pale of christianity, and in whom the sense of the nature of christian truth is yet to be awakened, that he speaks. This christian truth is already known; the christian consciousness grounded in it, and a fellowship of christian consciousness between him and his readers, already exist. But why then write to them if they already know all, if the truth which he would present is already familiar to them? It is to revivify the consciousness already rooted in their being; to awaken that which slumbers; to call forth new life, new activity; to unfold to their view what they carry in their own breasts; to bring them into a clear and conscious possession of what they already have. He says to them, what they should say to themselves. Often are we thus directed, through a word spoken by another, to something which has long had its dwelling in our inner life. It unlocks the depths of our own souls. We learn by it to understand ourselves, to perceive within ourselves the presence of God. All genuine instruction in the truth must aim only to direct to the One Teacher of truth, to God himself, and to serve as his organ. The genuine teacher of truth is himself fully aware that such is his appointed office, and he desires no other. It matters not whether the instruction have reference to those universal truths, which each must learn from the general revelation of God, of the Eternal Word as the light of the spiritual world; or to the peculiar truths of the kingdom of God, of the Gospel, the witness of the incarnate Word,—the very truths here brought to view, and experimentally known to all believers through that inward anointing of the Holy Spirit. Thus the Apostle is far from wishing to make believers dependent on himself as the teacher of truth, to assume that it was from him they were first to learn what is truth. On the contrary, he bases his appeal on the presence in them of the fountain of divine truth, not possessed by him as his peculiar property, but shared in common with those to whom his exhortation is addressed. He presents himself to them as a witness of that christian consciousness which they had in common. It is to this very consciousness, this inward knowledge of christian truth, that he makes his appeal when warning them against the errors which are spreading all around them. They need no other proof; these errors must show themselves to be lies, through their contrariety with that truth which is experimentally known to their own hearts. By the test of an immediate consciousness they will at once perceive, that what gives itself out for truth is but a falsification of the original christian truth, which is to them of all things the most certain. This is the proof which they carry in their own souls, the inner witness to which the Apostle makes his appeal. It is on this very ground that he addresses them, viz. BECAUSE they know the truth; and can therefore accept nothing which is not the fruit of this truth, nothing which denies it, which stands in hostility to it,—since nothing that is false is of the truth. This he can properly presuppose; and he needs only to arouse this inward perception of christian truth, for the rejection of the falsehoods which oppose the truth.

What now is the application to the present age, of the important truths thus deduced from these words of the Apostle? The Apostles stood in a peculiar relation to the churches of their own as of all succeeding ages, such a relation as no man could thereafter hold to christians. They were the instruments, through whom the true image of the Lord and of his word was to be transmitted to all. The christian consciousness of their own time and of all times has its source in their testimony, is developed by it and out of it. They form the necessary medium between Christ and all succeeding generations. If we would gain the knowledge of Christ and of the way of salvation, we must trust their testimony. In this respect the church must always remain dependent on them, always stand in need of their teachings. But although the Apostle John was fully aware of this relation to the church, he wished not to exercise any spiritual domination, to present himself to his brethren as the teacher by whom they were again to be instructed. The church, having been once established through the preaching of the divine word and its reception into the inward life, can and must hold fast and apply what has been thus received, as its own independent possession. Through that inward anointing from the Holy One, of which the Apostle has spoken, should all believers, independently of all other authority, stand in immediate fellowship with Christ as the only Master for all; and the christians of every age should be thereby united, both with that first apostolic church and with each other. It follows from this that no one, who claims to be a teacher in the church, is justified in making it dependent upon himself and his single teachings, but that all should regard themselves only as organs of this common inward anointing; that they should only lead the way to this inward fountain of illumination through the divine word which is its source,—should make this itself an object of conscious knowledge; that the only aim should be to conduct to that fountain in order to draw therefrom; that so all which they teach may approve itself as true by this inward witness. That all may be trained up, through this common inward anointing, to the maturity and independence of a personal christian consciousness —this only can be the aim of all instruction of others and all spiritual influence over them. It follows farther, that no believer is at liberty to forego this maturity and personal independence, bestowed in that inward anointing, or to place himself in a dependent relation, inconsistent with this birthright, to any teacher whatever among men. And should any one attempt, through the pretence of new divine revelations, to make the religious convictions of others dependent on himself, or to set the teachings of human wisdom in the place of the divine word; there will ever be found, in that inward anointing, an element of resistance to such arrogated authority.

Another conclusion from the Apostle's words is this: that the multifarious forms, in which the anti-christian spirit manifests itself, should not perplex and disquiet the believer. He has in his own soul; in that christian consciousness, which unites him with the truly Christian in every age, and with the apostolic church itself; in that inward anointing of the Holy Spirit; the infallible instinct, the certain touchstone, to distinguish between what is of Christ and what is of Antichrist. It is only needful that, watching over himself, he adhere prayerfully to that inward divine voice, give faithful heed to that sure oracle, which guides the simple and humble-minded through all adversities and conflicts; so will he be secured against all the delusions of pretended higher truth, taught by a false conceited philosophy. He is convinced beforehand, that whatever stands in contradiction to that inward anointing, whatever would rob him of his Christ, however lofty may be the words in which it speaks, cannot be true. Neither will he be persuaded to sacrifice that individual free consciousness, imparted in that inward anointing, to the plea that a higher church authority is needed, as guide and leader through these conflicts of the christian and anti-christian principles; or that, on this account, new prophets must arise to bring repose and confidence to wavering souls. He knows in himself, that he has in that inward anointing all he needs; and he will permit himself to be deceived by no promise of something more certain, more reliable, or to be drawn away from listening to that inward divine voice, through whose teachings he knows all things.

After these preparatory remarks, John proceeds to point out more particularly the errors which he is here opposing. [Ch. ii. 22, 23 "Who is a liar but he that denieth that Jesus is the Christ? HE is [the] Antichrist, that denieth the Father and the Son. Whosoever denieth the Son, the same hath not the Father; but he that acknowledgeth the Son, hath the Father also."

By the teachers of false doctrine then, whom John is here opposing, he means such as do not acknowledge Jesus as the Messiah. Now this might apply in general to all opponents of Chris tianity among the Jews, to all who indeed acknowledged God as the Father, God as revealed in the Old Testament, but not Jesus as the Messiah. But as we have already remarked in the Introduction, this would be too general a designation to correspond to the special characteristics given by John. We are necessarily led to look for new enemies of genuine Christianity of a peculiar stamp, such as might actually deceive those who did not hold fast to that inward anointing of the Spirit. But if such are meant, as actually denied that Jesus was the Messiah, how are we to understand this? The answer is at hand. One may profess himself in words a believer in Jesus as the Christ, and yet his conceptions of the person of Jesus, or of him as the Christ, may be at variance with this profession. Either he does not truly believe in Jesus of Nazareth, as he really was and has exhibited himself in his life and history,—does not receive the true historical image of this Jesus as a matter of personal conviction, but has dreamed out for himself another Jesus; or he does not acknowledge him as in the true sense the Christ, does not ascribe to him all which belongs to him as such, does not assume the befitting relation towards him as such. In either of these cases it might be said, that one who holds such views denies that Jesus is the Messiah. That which stood before the eye of John, was the divine incarnate Word,—in the perfect union of the divine and human, as the veritable Jesus, the Christ. He who held this Jesus for a mere man, an enlightened man like the prophets, not acknowledging him as the Eternal Life manifesting itself in time, the fountain of divine life; or he who recognized in him the Son of God but not the Son of Man, denying the reality of his human manifestation, and changing his divine-human history into a misty phantom; he who thus, with reckless self-will, separated the Son of God and the Son of Man, could not pass with John as one who truly acknowledged Jesus as the Christ, but must appear to him a denier of the truth. Hence, with reason, John accuses those falsifiers of evangelical truth, as described in our Introduction, with not acknowledging Jesus as the Messiah. And as these persons, under a pretended profession of belief in Jesus as the Christ, were yet inimical to him, and by their teachings might seduce believers from him; it was so much the more necessary to warn against such, as Antichrists.

Thus explained, we can readily apply what John here says to our own times. It applies to those who do not acknowledge Jesus of Nazareth as, in the true sense, the Christ; to whom he is not that which he should be as the Christ, the Messiah, the Redeemer from sin, the Fountain of eternal divine life, the only Mediator between God and man, the Founder and sovereign Ruler of the kingdom of God. It applies also to such, as do not acknowledge Jesus of Nazareth in his true historical significance and reality, as presented to us in the gospel record; turning that whole record into doubt and uncertainty, sublimating him also into a form of mist, and leaving a mere phantom in his place; who, rending asunder the connection between Christ,—Christ in himself,—and the human historical appearing of Jesus, convert the Christ into a mere idea, and allow it only an accidental connection with the historical Jesus thus unsubstantialized by their unbelief. Hence all such, in proportion as this may be affirmed, belong to those whom John designates as the representatives of the anti-christian spirit.

The preaching of Jesus as the Christ being the fundamental article of faith in the apostolic church, the foundation upon which the whole christian life was to be built up, the one doctrine which contained in itself all that was necessary to salvation; only those errors, consequently, were regarded by John and his fellow-apostles as radical, as belonging in their essence to Anti-christianity, which in one way or another mutilated this one cardinal doctrine. This furnishes the clue by which we are now also to judge of truth and falsehood, of what is requisite to christian fellowship and what is irreconcilable with it, and by which we must learn to estimate everything according to its own intrinsic value.

Not all erroneous conceptions of the person of Jesus, are included by John in what he terms antichristian; but, obviously, only such as do not admit a recognition of Jesus as the Christ in the true sense,—only such as involve a denial of this, though they may not directly avow it. This also teaches us to distinguish carefully between conceptions of Christ, and what is essential to the recognition of Jesus as the Christ,—what is requisite in order to present him in the true relation to the religious consciousness. These conceptions may correspond more or less to the truth; but the errors are not necessarily always such as to obscure or mutilate that which constitutes the essence of the preaching of Christ, viz. what Christ is in relation to the religious consciousness. In more recent times, christians have often erred through neglect of such discrimination; and have supposed themselves to differ in respect to faith in the one Jesus Christ, as the ground of salvation, from those with whom they were only at strife over such conceptions of his Person, as are of minor importance to the inward religious experience. Against this error also, we are guarded by the standard of christian judgment here followed by the Apostle.

John develops still farther the great importance to religious belief, in its widest sense, of this doctrine of Jesus as the Christ. He shows the danger to religious faith in general from the denial of Christ; the close connection between the doctrine of Jesus as the Christ, which constitutes the peculiarity of christian faith, and the religious sentiment in general; how they stand or fall together. It is by no means implied that the champions of anti-christianity, whom he is opposing, expressly connected with their denial of Jesus as the Christ the denial also of God the Father. At a later period indeed we find a class, the Gnostics of the second century, of whom this might be said; who did not acknowledge the God revealed through Christ as the Father of all spirits, the Creator of the Universe, the God already made known in the Old Testament. But it cannot be conclusively proved that John had any such in mind. The opposite is more naturally inferable from his words, viz. that those of whom he is speaking professed belief in the God of the Old Testament as the Father; and John's reproach is, that with them this profession has lost its full truth and significance. In renouncing their belief in Jesus as the Christ, they had renounced also their belief in God as the Father. The same relation holds good, in respect to belief, in either case. As John, upon the grounds already explained, declares of some who professed belief in Jesus as the Christ that they were, notwithstanding, deniers of Christ; so also he declares of those who in words acknowledge God as the Father, that by denying Jesus as the Christ they do thereby deny God as the Father. It is this, the necessary and inseparable connection of these two articles of faith, which is here meant.

How then is this to be understood? We must

not fail to notice in the first place, that God is not here designated merely in general as God, but as the Father. Now as the Father,—He who with inexpressible father-love draws to himself the beings estranged from him by sin,—as such he has first revealed himself in Christ; giving his only-begotten Son as the means of reconciling to himself, and of restoring to his fellowship which is the eternal fountain of bliss, the alienated family of man. In him and through him do they first recognize God as their Father; only through him are they re-established in the filial relation to God. The whole life of Christ is a revelation of divine Father-love, towards the race estranged from God by sin. In him is first presented that endearing relation, into which, by sending his Son to appear on earth, he has entered with man. He, the Holy One, could alone be absolutely the object of the divine Father-love. It is in the Son that the Father first reveals himself. In the contemplation of his life we first perceive what God is, as Father; first learn to understand his paternal love. It is from him alone, the only absolutely worthy object of the divine complacency and love, that this love can be extended to all who are in fellowship with him, and in whom Christ,—whose they are, who dwells in them, and from whom their whole life issues,—presents himself, yea his own self, to the eye of the divine Father.

But certainly it was not merely this John intended to express, viz. that the knowledge of God as the Father is dependent upon the knowledge of Jesus Christ his son,—faith in God as the Father upon faith in Jesus Christ as his son. He did not intend to say merely: that to deny the Son, is necessarily to deny the Father as such. In the Johannic sense, this has reference not merely to the special relation which God, as Father, holds to those who are justified in regarding themselves as his children; but to the knowledge of God as God, in its most general and unlimited sense. The knowledge of God is, in every view, based upon the knowledge of Christ. In proportion as Christ is known and understood, is known and understood the God who reveals himself in him; as John himself says (John i. 18): "No man hath seen God at any time; the only-begotten Son, who is in the bosom of the Father, he hath declared [revealed] him." By seeing cannot here be meant bodily sight; for the Son of God is here represented as he who alone can behold the God whom no one hath seen. But God could be seen through the outward sense by no one, not even by the Son. As Spirit, he is forever the Invisible. It is not therefore the bodily sight, but a spiritual perception which is here intended; the perfect intuitive knowledge of God as the Invisible, that is, the Incomprehensible. The only-begotten Son of God could alone, by virtue of his being one with God, truly know him by direct intuition; and from this knowledge could, as man, reveal him in a form comprehensible by man. Though dimly revealed in the inner consciousness of man, who felt himself drawn to him by a mysterious influence; yet was God,—in his infinite exaltation, his unfathomable nature, his boundless perfection,—a God concealed from man, a God afar off. The Spirit, soaring on bold wing in search of God, sunk down exhausted to the earth. Often, during the ante-christian period, we find nothing remaining save a vague feeling of the Divine; or the idea of God, having become wholly earthly, had given place to the deification of nature. God was not recognized in his exaltation over the world, as He to whom the world is subject; the

God of Heaven, who also fills the earth, who is at once near and afar off. His Being was brought down to a level with that of the world, and the conceptions of God and of the world were commingled into one. The consciousness of God was lost in the deification of the material world; or a mere empty notion, an abstract idea of perfection without actual existence, was substituted for the idea of the living God. The God who dwells in inaccessible light, into which no human spirit can penetrate, must, in order to be truly known by man, come down to the human and within its finite limits. First in the revelation of the incarnate God, could the God afar off come near to humanity. First in this image of God in human nature, could the idea of God enter as a living and substantial element into the moral and intellectual being of man. Man, created in the image of God, was through this image in himself to rise to the Spirit who is the Father of all spirits, the eternal archetype. As spirit he should thus recognize, in his essential being, that highest Spirit from whom all spirits emanate, and who images himself in them. But the image of God in man having been marred by sin, and the connection sundered between the archetypal Spirit and those who are formed in its image, man has thereby become incompetent for this knowledge. Hence the more he strives, while in this state of estrangement from God, to lift himself by the mere force of thought to him from whose living fellowship he is separated, the farther does he remove from him, the greater the errors into which he falls.

Now that which had hitherto been wanting to man, the perfect image of God in human form, this is supplied by Christ,—the perfect man as the image of the perfect God. God, in his love and his holiness, gives a perfect reflection of himself as such in the life of Christ; for it is only in the union of these two attributes that he can be truly known as God. Now we can rise from the image to the original. In the mirror of Christ we perceive God. Here we attain to the idea of God, thus brought near and placed within the grasp of our spirits. The chasm which parted us from God is closed. The deeper we penetrate into the nature of Christ, the more deeply do we penetrate into the knowledge of God, whose perfect image he is. Hence, in this view also, as the confession of the Son involves the confession of the Father, the knowledge of the Son the knowledge of the Father; so also in the denial of the Son is involved the denial of the Father. Losing the real Christ, man sinks back again to that previous position, where an infinite gulf separated his spirit from God. The previous errors develop themselves the more powerfully, as through his apostasy from the truth he has incurred the greater guilt; the ground of these errors having formerly been mere ignorance of the truth, but now a wicked denial of it. Moreover, this same tendency of natural reason in opposition to the Divine,—though at first only mingling its sceptical and obscuring influence with the conception of what Christ is,—must yet, true to its own nature, go on in a progressive and more complete development and expression of itself, extending that influence over the religious sense in general. And thus, in every view, is sustained the truth of the Apostle's words, that he who denies the Son, the same has not the Father; but he who confesses the Son has the Father also.

We must not overlook what is further implied in these words; viz. that with confession, in the true sense of the word, there must be connected also a HAVING of that which is presupposed as the object of confession, of faith, of knowledge. He who confesses the Son, in the true sense of the word, he who knows him and believes on him, also HATH him. He stands in the most intimate fellowship of life with Christ, and through him in the same fellowship with the Father. Through this fellowship he knows God, as He can only through this be known, through this his self-revelation in the consciousness of such as in the Son have the Father also,—the Father, to whom none can ever rise by mere effort of thought, apart from a union of the life with him. And thus, whoever detaches himself from this union with Christ and denies him, having him no longer present in his life, thereby renounces also union with the Father. He can no longer know him whom he no longer HAS, with whom he is no longer connected through fellowship with Christ.

As these words of John are confirmed by the whole history of the human spirit, since the time they were written ; so does the present age furnish a peculiarly emphatic witness of their truth. The study of passing events serves, in no small degree, to elucidate the deep meaning of these pregnant words; as they, on the other hand, become specially important to the higher interests of our own times, when we learn how to apply them. We see, that as those radical errors in the conception of Christ's person have reappeared in the same anti-christian tendencies which John opposed, and men have departed from the true Christ; the same radical tendency of the natural reason gradually led on to the misapprehension and denial of God, whom Christ has revealed to us as the Father. It was a tendency which at first, while thus limiting and mutilating the doctrine of Christ, yet sought to maintain its hold of the doctrine of God as the Father, to whom it ascribed the influence of Christianity. But, as we have seen, it was continually impelled by its own nature to overstep these boundaries. First, that intimate filial relation to God as Father was lost; only the general reference to God as the Unknown, the God afar off, remained. Then was the God of heaven, the living personal God, also lost. The deification of the world,—opposing itself to everything supernatural in the Divine, to everything which can be perceived only by faith, and cannot be apprehended by the senses, or by the natural reason confined as it is within the limits of the world,— widened its grasp continually, and developed more and more in denial and destruction its anti-christian power. What at first was professedly only a matter of knowledge, became more and more an element of life. And thus will the declaration of John forever continue to be verified. As Christ is the centre around which all turns, and in reference to the most vital contrarieties in opinion and life this only is of account,—what is the relation to Christ; as we have all, or lose all with him; so the distinction comes out with continually increasing clearness, between having Christ and with him having the Father, or losing the Son and with him the Father, and at the same time all that is divine, all wherein the God-related spirit can enjoy possession of itself, can find its true life.

The Apostle concludes this warning by again enforcing the exhortation, that they hold fast and faithfully preserve what they have received; so should the gifts of grace also remain theirs. "Let that therefore abide in you, which ye have heard from the beginning. If that which ye have heard from the beginning shall remain in you, ye also shall continue in the Son, and

Ch. ii. 24, 25.]

in the Father. And this is the promise that he hath promised us, even eternal life."

Here again in the original Greek, the "Ye" is placed first ("Ye therefore," which we cannot imitate), in emphatic contrast with those heretical teachers. For as these, through their apostacy from the original truth, had again estranged themselves from that fellowship with God as the Father, which is received through Christ; so on the contrary, should the church be distinguished from them by a faithful adherence to that original teaching, and by so doing abide also in fellowship with the Son and with the Father. What they have received from the beginning is to remain IN them; being something abiding, not a mere external thing, which like an empty sound had passed by them. As they have received it into their inward life, so should it ever remain deeply imprinted in their spirits. And as it is through the preached word, received into their hearts, that they have attained to fellowship with the Father through the mediating Son; the indwelling of this truth in their hearts is made the condition, on which they should continue to abide in fellowship with the Son, and through him with the Father. This continuing IN the Son and the Father, we must endeavor to apprehend in the full significance of the term. This IN can be exchanged for no other word. It declares that their life has its being in Jesus as the Son of God, and through this, in the Father whom he has revealed as such, and with whom he has brought them into fellowship. In the Gospel of John, the two things are always presented as connected with each other, as involved in each other; viz. the abiding of believers in Christ and his abiding in them. The communication of Christ to the believer,—wherein the whole christian life has its root,—and the continuance of this communication, appears therefore as something dependent upon their susceptibility for this divine gift, upon the free surrender of themselves to Christ. So soon as they, through the bent of the will, abandon their original relation to Christ, will Christ also depart from them. All hangs upon the unconstrained susceptibility, the direction of the will in man. Hence, whatever may be the enjoyment of divine grace in the christian life, the requirement is still binding on man to watch unceasingly over himself, lest through his own fault he should again lose the heavenly gift which he has received. The means on their part for continuing in fellowship with Christ is, in John's view, holding fast the doctrines originally made known to them. By this he does not mean merely retaining them in the memory, in the understanding; but so holding them fast that this truth shall remain an indwelling and determining principle of their inner life. As an encouragement to fidelity, he shows them what on this condition they have a right to expect. He sums up the whole in one all-embracing promise,--the eternal life which Christ has promised to those who abide in fellowship with him; for, as he has before said, in Christ has this eternal life itself appeared personally in humanity. There is, for the God-related spirit, no other blessedness than this life for which he was created, and in which alone he can find satisfaction for all the wants implanted in his godlike nature. It is called The Life, absolutely, inasmuch as it is the participation in that which alone, in the truest and highest, in an unqualified sense, can be called life, the life of God himself; as to the God-related spirit, which can only find in God its true life, the want of it is Death. It is called eternal life, inasmuch as it is in its very nature exalted above all change of time, in its very nature eternal, belonging not to the transitory temporal existence, but to eternity. Where it has once taken up its abode, it can no more be disturbed and interrupted by death; but, victorious over all death, unfolds itself in progressive and glorious development forever. Hence Christ, in the Gospel of John, speaks of it as the fountain which gushes up into eternal life; a river, checked by no barriers, pouring along from the once imparted source, into the eternal and the infinite. And hence it is said, that he who believes in Christ has eternal life; in this Believing, it is his already. The future blessedness promised to the christian is not, therefore, something essentially different from what he has already received in the earthly life through faith, and to be added from without as something new. In its germ and essence, it is contained in what he already has. It needs only to burst from the imprisoning shell, in order to reveal itself in its own inherent glory.

John concludes by a reference to the inward anointing of those whom he addresses, in contrast with those false teachers. "These things have I written unto you, concerning them that seduce you. But the anointing,

Ch. ii. 26, 27.]

which ye have received of him, abideth in you, and ye need not that any man teach you: but as the same anointing teacheth you of all things, and is truth and is no lie, and even as it hath taught you, ye shall abide in him." The Apostle repeats the assurance of his belief, that he need add nothing new by way of guarding them against those false teachers; he need only refer, for adequate instruction in all things, to that inner fountain of divine illumination, that inward anointing. This anointing is here designated, as that which they have received from him; and the reference might be to the source in which it originates, to the Father by whom this spirit is bestowed. But as the pronoun here employed, without any more definite application, always refers in this connection to Christ, that reference is to be retained also in this passage. What is asserted is therefore this: the communication of this Spirit is procured through the mediating Christ; as imparted through Christ, it is said to have been received from him. Just so this Spirit is at one time designated as he who proceeds from the Father, whom Christ sends from the Father, whom the Father bestows for the sake of Christ; and at another, as the Spirit which

Christ imparts to those who believe on him, as the Spirit of Christ, so that Christ's spiritual coming to believers is a coming in and with this Spirit. If now we proceed in accordance with Luther's version, it is here John's first and special object to say,—that what this inward anointing teaches respecting all things is the perfect truth without mixture of error, and they needed therefore only to adhere faithfully to it. In this view, the development of thought proceeds on regularly in what follows. Still it may be asked, whether John would have presented so prominently (as something of special importance in itself) the assertion that all, as this anointing teaches it, is true and there is nothing false in it; whether it is not probable, rather, that he throws in as an independent and accessory thought the words,—"and as it is truth and no falsehood,"—and then proceeds (repeating the previous clause in consequence of this interruption), "And even as it has been taught you, so shall ye abide in him." The 'in him' must be referred to him who is here the one object of reference, to Christ. In the assured trust that the church will ever continue to yield itself to the teachings of the Holy Spirit, and being guided by his illuminating grace will ever remain true to the doctrine which they have received, he feels assured also that they will ever abide in fellowship with Christ.

Pausing upon the thought thus suggested, the Apostle now turns to them again with a personal appeal. In a father's tone he exhorts them to steadfast perseverance in this direction of the life, till they attain the final goal. "And now, little children, abide in him; that when he shall appear we may have confidence, and not be ashamed before him at his coming." [Ch. ii. 28.

As the coming of Christ was, from causes already mentioned, then expected as something close at hand, and the eye, overleaping all that lay between, fixed itself upon that event; so the Apostle here overlooks all which is to follow immediately after death, and turns at once to the day of final decision. This he calls the appearing of Christ. In this it is necessarily implied that Christ now lives in his glory with the Father, he and his glory still hidden from the world and manifest only to believers; that, in his appearing, what is now thus hidden shall be revealed. Christ in his glory shall then become manifest to all, as now he is manifest, through the medium of faith, to the believer. Placing this goal before the eye of believers, the Apostle exhorts them to abide so faithfully, through the direction of their life, in that fellowship with Christ to which they have been admitted, that they may be able in that day to appear before him their Judge, with a quiet and assured conscience. The word here employed in the Greek, indicates an absolute unshaken confidence, as between friend and friend. In such a relation should believers stand to Christ. Conscious of remaining ever faithful to him, and standing in this relation, they will not need to be ashamed in the presence of him to whom their whole life is manifest. But the Apostle here passes from the second to the first person; for involved as he still is in the conflict of the earthly life, he feels himself the necessity of watchfulness. Hence, when speaking of the direction of the life towards this final goal, he does not exalt himself above other christians, but speaks as one who is on a level with them.

This faithful abiding in fellowship with Christ, by virtue of which believers will in that
Ch. ii. 29.] day stand with untroubled conscience

before the Lord, in the sense of John embraces the entire life; including not merely opposition to radical errors in doctrine, but to all sin by which the christian life might be defiled. Thus a new division now commences, with reference to the shunning of everything sinful: "If ye know that he is righteous, ye know that every one that doeth righteousness is born of him."

These words are more closely connected with what follows than with what precedes; and we must therefore here refer the pronoun, not to Christ, but to God. The close connection between the references to Christ and to God, renders this transition easy, without any formal designation of it. It here arises naturally out of the conception, which in all that follows underlies the Apostle's course of thought. The appellation "Righteous" admits indeed of a reference to Christ; and as the subject of remark now is a being of believers in Christ, and their whole life is contemplated as having its source in him, as derived from him and vitalized by him, so also it might be said that they were born of Christ. But the Apostle's uniform manner of conception and expression decides against this view. As he is accustomed to contemplate Christ in his human manifestation,—the incarnate Word; He through whom man is reinstated in fellowship with God, through whom he is raised again to the filial relation to God, and becomes the child of God; so does he contemplate God, as the eternal, original source of the new life imparted through Christ to the believer. It is in this view, accordingly, that he speaks of a birth from God, in contrast with the natural corporeal birth by which one becomes a member of the human family; inasmuch as by this he is lifted out of the customary current of the world, and incorporated with the kingdom of God, in which without divine life there can be no participation. Thus, by the Righteous, we are to understand God. Righteousness is here synonymous with perfect purity, with holiness. Accordingly, the inference is here made, that those who know God as the Holy One must also know, that being through the kindred life imparted by him born of him anew, and called in this sense his children, they must make themselves manifest as such through a righteous life-walk in harmony with him. Two things, an affirmative and a negative, are implied in this declaration. First, that where true righteousness exists, it can have been derived only from this source; that true righteousness can only be attained through a birth from God, as it is only through the power of God that the ruling power of sin can be overcome in man. So Christ asserts, that whatever is born of the flesh needs the moral transformation effected by the Spirit which God imparts. "That which is born of the flesh, is flesh;" it corresponds to its origin, to sinful human nature as estranged from God. Secondly it is implied, that he only who leads a life in harmony with righteousness is born of God; only by this sign can the birth from God make itself known. Where the opposite is found, it furnishes evidence that this birth from God has never yet taken place; that what the Holy Spirit calls the Flesh, comprehending under this name whatever both in the sensual and intellectual nature stands opposed to the divine influence, is still predominant in him. In this connection, as is shown by what follows, the special reference is to God.

CHAPTER III.

[Ch. iii. 1–3.]

FROM the conviction that believers are born of God, and thus are children of God, the Apostle derives the motive necessarily growing out of it, to avoid all that is sinful. This leads him to speak more at large of the dignity of the children of God, and of what is involved in it: "Behold what manner of love the Father hath bestowed upon us, that we should be called the sons of God: therefore the world knoweth us not, because it knew him not. Beloved, now are we the sons of God, and it doth not yet appear what we shall be: but we know that, when he [it] shall appear, we shall be like him; for we shall see him as he is. And every man that hath this hope in him, purifieth himself, even as he is pure."

There can be no more intimate and endearing relation than that of children to their Father, when this fully answers to its nature. How much then must it imply, when creatures separated by an infinite chasm from their Creator, when men estranged by sin from a holy God, are taken into this relation to Him. How great the love he has manifested, by coming near and imparting himself to them, in order to close this chasm, to bring them into fellowship with himself! No higher evidence could be given of the love of God towards his apostate creatures. It pre-supposes the father-heart in God, towards those whom he adopts as his children. Far more is designated by it, in the sense of the Holy Scriptures, than the relation which God as Creator holds to his creatures. It is only in a more general sense that God is elsewhere called the Father of Spirits, from the peculiar relation of spirits as such to the supreme spirit, to Him who is called, absolutely,—The Spirit; being in their nature as spirits adapted to reflect the image of the eternal, the supreme spirit, and therefore akin to Him, and susceptible of a fellowship of life with Him. It is oneness of race, a kindred nature, that unites children with parents; so spirits as such enjoy the special right, over all the rest of creation, of standing in this relation to God, and hence he is called in that more general sense their

Father. But the race of man had through sin fallen from this relation to God; had forfeited that claim founded in their original nature, created after the image of God; were no longer partakers in that life by which they were akin to the holy God, and by virtue of which they might have been worthy to be called his children. It was therefore necessary that He, who from his nature is in the absolute sense Son of God, and who alone is such, should appear in their flesh and blood; that he should impart himself wholly to them, give his life for them, make himself entirely their own and unite them as one with himself; that as he is the Son of God, so they, in fellowship with him and for his sake, might also become the children of God.

But the expression is here peculiar; not, they are children of God,—but shall be so called. It is an indication, how much is implied in the right to bear this name. The name is the sign of the thing, the outward expression of the inward reality. The name may be conferred in advance; the right to bear it may be given, before that which is indicated by the name attains its complete fulfilment and realization. The son, destined to succeed to his father's whole property, his offices and dignities, receives with the right to bear the name of son, the certain pledge that he shall one day come into possession of all. So also in the right of believers to be called the children of God, there is more involved than in what they now, to appearance, actually are. It is their title, given to them of God, to come one day into the full possession and use of all which is indicated by this name,—as assumed by the Apostle in what immediately follows. Since the outward condition of God's children does not here correspond to the dignity belonging to this name, to the glory indicated thereby; the Apostle therefore first directs the attention of believers to this incongruity, that when made aware of it by various painful experiences, they might not become unsettled in regard to what is thus conferred on them, but rightly understand that this must be so,—that it could not be otherwise. They are the object of hatred and persecution to the world; they are in perpetual conflict with it. Are they to be disquieted on this account? No! This is nothing less than one of the vouchers for the great right bestowed on them by the father-love of God, the right to be called his children. It is one of the required testimonials, that they are truly standing in this relation to God. The dignity to which they are appointed, the glory of which they are now the depositories, is one which is hidden from the world. The world is far from surmising the exalted stand-point in the universe, occupied by the christian. The world understands nothing of that by which he is influenced and animated, and bestows on it only hatred and contempt. And wherefore ? As the feeling with which we regard the father is transferred to the son, who follows the example and principles of his father ; as hatred to the father is thus transferred to the son ; so the disposition of the world towards the children of God, is the same as that towards God himself. As the world estranged from God cannot know Him ; as even when professing a zeal for Him, it honors only that, is zealous only for that, which it has made its God, its own self-created idols ; as it knows nothing of the true God, being estranged from him in the temper of the heart ; so neither can it recognize the Father in his children, the image of God in those who bear it. It misapprehends the divine, for the very reason that it is divine. This temper, which separates it from God, is the source also of its hostility to the children of God. When, therefore, these are misunderstood, hated and persecuted by the world, they must not be perplexed and cast down on this account; but, perceiving the causes whence such treatment proceeds, must feel themselves ennobled by it. They must draw, from this encounter with the world, a more deep and living consciousness of that endearing and intimate relation to God, which places them in this position towards the world.

But how are we to reconcile with this the prayer offered by Christ as High Priest of his people (John xvii. 22, ff.), that the glory bestowed by the Father upon him and by him upon believers,—a glory consisting in the oneness of believers with him as he is one with the Father,—may reflect itself in their life, in their fellowship with one another; that they may so testify of Christ, of his divine dignity and mission, as to lead the world to the knowledge of him; that the manner in which God reveals himself in the living fellowship of believers, may lead the world to perceive how much they are the objects of divine love? How are the two things to be reconciled, that what is cause of misapprehension and persecution to the world, should at the same time be the means by which the world is to be led to recognize the revelation of God in his children, to awaken desire after a participation in it? In order to this, we must distinguish a twofold character in that which is called the world. That which makes it such, the source of its hostility to God and his kingdom, —this must be distinguished from that which forms in the world the transition-point to the kingdom of God, the still inherent capacity in man for receiving the divine image, the after-working of original relationship to the Divine. In virtue of the first, he is only repelled by the Divine in believers, and cannot recognize in it the Divine; while through the second, the divine glory, as mirrored in the fellowship of christians, exerts its attractive force to draw men to the Father, and to the Son who reveals him,—the point of connection whereby the Father draws them to the Son.

It is only in the first point of view that the Apostle here speaks of the world; and his words have a special reference to the then existing relations of Christians to the world. It was then as

Jewish or as Heathen, that the world presented itself in opposition to Christianity and to the fellowship of believers, — to the church of God. Something wholly new had made its appearance among men, standing in direct contrariety to the spirit by which the world was governed, to its convictions, its principles, its morals, its tastes, and to the organizations and arrangements of life originating therein. It must therefore be misapprehended, hated, and persecuted by the world. The recurrence of this same thing is still witnessed in heathen countries, where Christianity is first introduced by missions. But it is otherwise with those nations which have already long borne the Christian name; whose whole history and life, developed under the influence of Christianity, are bound up and connected therewith in an unseen, and to many, unconscious manner; nations sustained by Christianity as the life-element from which the national development and culture, the form of national life, originally proceeded. Christianity, when first appearing among a people, stands distinctly opposed to the prevailing opinions, principles, manners, and social arrangements, which had sprung from the root of a totally different religion. But this is not so with nations which have, as we have said, long borne the Christian name. Much which had its origin in Christianity, has become a part of the common national life, entering into its social institutions, customs and modes of thought. Such is that general, world-transforming power of Christianity, forever at work in human history, as seen in a comparison of nations bearing the Christian name with heathen countries whether savage or civilized, especially as represented to us in the history of modern missions.

Do we now, in countries where Christianity has exerted its world-transforming power, find still existing this same opposition between Christianity and the world, and consequently an application here also of the Apostle's words? Or does that spirit, which fills and animates the children of God, here find a point of attachment in everything around them, thus developed from the all-transforming agencies of the Gospel? In regard to this it will forever remain true, that no one can become a child of God by natural birth, or in general, through anything performed externally, upon the body. On the contrary, this is a work which must be wrought from within, through personal faith, and the operations of the Holy Spirit. The saying of our Lord: "That which is born of the flesh is flesh, and that which is born of the spirit is spirit," declares a perpetual contrariety between the regenerate and the unregenerate; and consequently, the opposition between the children of God and the children of the world is one which will forever continue. It matters not whether the world arrays itself in open hostility against Christianity; or whether the latter has so far extended its all-transforming power, that the world itself has to a certain degree become affected by its influence, in many respects assimilated to it under the outward form of Christian culture, and now wages against it a more covert, unavowed, in part perhaps unconscious warfare. Those who belong to God as his children, in whom Christ has been truly formed, who in their whole life and being testify of him and reflect his image, whom he has chosen and consecrated through the Holy Spirit as his instruments in representing and extending his kingdom, these will ever feel constrained to maintain a conflict with all which is of the world and not from God, in order that they may make it subject to the kingdom of God, may through the sword of the Spirit subdue it to the obedience of Christ. Such cannot be deceived by that outward show of Christianity, in which the world, superficially affected by its all-transforming influence, has veiled its own true character. They will therefore have to contend with all that is unchristian here, not less than among a people never before brought in contact with Christianity. What then obtained when these words were written, when even externally the heathen world was distinguished from Christians dwelling in it, must ever continue even when that external distinction has been done away. Hence we see the genuine children of God, in all ages, involved in conflict with the world. In proportion as the Father is not recognized in his love and holiness, must the children, in whom that love and holiness are revealed, be misapprehended also. They cannot but be misunderstood. Often are they despised, or hated and persecuted; and they must then find their consolation in the words here spoken, pointing to that high dignity bestowed on them by the Father, as the true ground of this antagonism between them and the world.

This relation of the world to the children of God may exhibit itself under two forms. Those who have been affected more or less by this general influence, diffused among a Christian people, may be clearly conscious of the source of that superiority by which they are distinguished from all who belong to pagan nations; or they may unconsciously imbibe this influence as an element once introduced into the national development, without acknowledging Christianity as its source. The former are indeed deeply penetrated by a sense of their obligations to Christianity. Though far from recognizing Christ in his divine dignity and glory as the Incarnate Word, they yet acknowledge him as author of the most salutary revolution in human society. They honor and are willing to promote Christianity, as the means of diffusing through the life of every people those general moral influences which they have themselves felt. But they are unable, notwithstanding, to recognize and comprehend those who attach so much importance to Christianity, as a whole, in its own peculiar nature; who claim for it the entire life, requiring that everything should give place to the holy condemnatory earnestness of the Gospel, that everything should bow before it. The animating and impelling principle by which such are governed, remains to them a mystery; it becomes to them a stone of stumbling. Hence arises an opposition between these two classes; an opposition all the more bitter for the very reason, that those who are conscious of that general influence of Christianity upon the formation of their character, suppose that with this they have all they need; resenting it as a heavy offence if more is required of them, if they are not regarded, on account of what they already have, as children of God. Those who confront them with the Gospel in all the earnestness of its demands, are accused of putting something else in its place, of making the way to the kingdom of God too narrow; just as the Jews, having received so much that was akin to Christianity from the Law and the Prophets, and deeming this all-sufficient, hated him in whom they were fulfilled, and reproached him as being himself an enemy to the Law and the Prophets.

If now we turn to the second case, this too we shall find may assume a twofold form. It may be that those who share in spiritual blessings, which the people to whom they belong have attained only through the educating influence of Christianity, do indeed acknowledge this agency; but they suppose, the possession once secured, the nation needs this influence no longer. Though recognizing it as a means ordained by Providence for bringing humanity up to this stage of development, they believe that Christianity has now accomplished its work. Its highest mission was to make itself superfluous,—by cultivating the nations to that state of maturity and self-dependence which they have now attained. This is one case. In the other, not even so much as this is conceded to Christianity. It is not recognized as the source of those blessings, which through its world-transforming influence have become the property of the nations. Their connection with the agency of Christianity is regarded merely as accidental; and a release from its restrictive yoke would, in the view of such, be followed by a more complete and happy national development. But as the fruit of a tree can only prosper in connection with the trunk and root, and with the fruit-producing sap which diffuses itself from the root through the trunk and all its branches; so these fruits also will soon vanish, if connection with their root, which is Christianity, is no longer maintained and kept alive in the national consciousness. Here too will the words of the Lord be verified: "He that hath not, from him shall be taken that which he hath." What is thus torn asunder from the root of Christianity, having become thereby something wholly different, having been deprived of its true nature and significance, will run more and more into the form of decided opposition to Christianity. The world, not being led up from that general reformatory influence of Christianity to its true inward nature, will throw off more and more even its outward appearance, and the concealed hostility will become an open one,—a result which we see fast preparing in our own day. And thus, what is here taught of the warfare between the children of God and the children of the world, and should serve as a ground of consolation in this conflict, will again find its full application in the case of each individual, so soon as he has made his choice between these two adverse forces, which are every day coming into more direct conflict.

While thus contemplating the children of God at their present stand-point of conflict with the world, the Apostle marks the distinction between the present and the future. He leads their thoughts to that still concealed and undeveloped future, which they bear within themselves. We have already, he says, the inward assurance of that which to us is above all else, of which no one can rob us, that we are the children of God. Herein is contained the germ of all which is to be developed in the future, in eternal life, even to the completion of the kingdom of God; but the whole extent of what is thus bestowed, the fulness of the glory of the children of God, is as yet veiled even from themselves, much more from the world which knows them not. We indeed know already, would the Apostle say, what we ARE; but it is not yet revealed what we shall be. As it is said to be a revelation of Christ, when he shall show himself openly in his yet hidden glory; so of the children of God, it is said that they shall be REVEALED, when their glory, now veiled and hidden from view, shall be brought forth to light. Of what shall then follow, the Apostle says: "We shall be like him, for we shall see him as he is."

The question may arise, to whom is the pronoun here to be referred, to Christ or to God? What the Apostle says would be strictly true, and might be said with perfect propriety, in either case. The two stand in close connection also,—indeed each is necessarily involved in the other. For perfect likeness to God is inseparable from likeness to Christ, through which as a mediate agency it is produced; so also, to behold God stands in close connection with beholding Christ, through which in like manner it is effected. We must consider, however,—not what the Apostle might in any connection have said, not what is in itself a truly apostolic thought and in the spirit of John,—but what in this particular connection was present to his mind. The reference to God being here the predominant one, what is comprehended in the idea of his children being the subject of consideration, it is manifestly their relation to God which is here before the mind of the Apostle. To Him, therefore, the pronoun must be referred.

As the image of the father is presented in the son, and the son is recognized by his likeness to the father; so the Apostle makes the full revelation of the children of God, as such, to consist in perfect likeness to their Father. It is implied, therefore, that the dignity of the children of God is still imperfect and obscured, because their likeness to God is not complete,—because they do not yet perfectly reflect the image of God their Father. This likeness to God as their Father, must indeed be gradually developed in their entire nature, after the model image of Christ, whereby everything human in them is to be transformed and glorified into a revelation of the divine nature, is to be made divine. All that has its origin in the old man, and is not yet wholly overcome and rooted out, stands ever opposed to this assimilation of believers to God. The perfected glory of the children of God is therefore identical with perfect likeness to God. That which obscures the one, stands opposed also to the complete realization of the other. In that one thing all is included. Complete likeness to God is, moreover, represented by the Apostle as the consequence of our seeing the Father as he is. We have here a promise, transcending all that the human spirit is able to conceive or hope; as that which is promised answers to the profoundest longings of the spirit thirsting and fainting after God. The immediate, perfect knowledge of God as he is,—this bewilders and confounds all finite conception. It seems irreconcilable with the infinitude of the divine nature, and the narrowness of finite creatures. Under the old dispensation, it had been said that no mortal could behold God; the vision of God was regarded as something, before which the elements of human nature must dissolve away. But now the Eternal Word,—He who was with God and was himself God, the only begotten Son who is in the bosom of the Father and has alone known or could know him,—He having taken upon himself our nature, and God having thereby entered into this most intimate and endearing union with it; the chasm is now closed, which divided between God and the created spirit. Like Christ himself, shall they who stand in fellowship with him, attain through him to the immediate and perfect vision of God, to whom even here below they are united in faith and love.

What we possess, in this glorious prospect, we best learn from contrast with two opposite errors of human opinion, between which Christianity alone shows us the proper medium. The one bearing the name of Deism, is seen in the vain effort to reach, through the idea of an unknown and far off God, the true conception of that felicity, a longing after which is so deeply implanted in the spirit of man. While allowing to the glorified soul progressive development in perfection, to move onward from world to world, it still leaves it forever at an infinite distance from God; the idea of such a perfect, immediate vision of God is far beyond its flight. The other error is that of Pantheism; which, knowing not the God who is at once near and afar off, the God everywhere present who is at the same time God in Heaven, mingles God and the universe into one (as does also a false mysticism); annihilating the personality of the created spirit, it resolves it wholly into God, thereby destroying likewise the idea of the living God himself, who is not a God of the dead but of the living.

On the contrary, the promise of the Gospel presents to us, as the aim of the created spirit ripening to perfection, an immediate and perfect intuition of the Divine Being, with the removal of all those temporal bounds in which our present conscious ness is yet confined. It will be a knowledge of God no longer fragmentary, no longer borrowed from the imperfect mirror and the broken rays of this our temporal consciousness, but as He is in himself, in his essential nature; a knowing of God so immediate that, as the Apostle Paul says, we shall know Him as we are known of Him, as He is known of himself. Still, we shall remain forever distinct from him, in a glorified personal existence; otherwise, it would not be eternal life, but mere annihilation. What John here certifies is this: that in the perfect intuition of God lies the ground of our own personal perfection; that as personal existences, created in the image of God, we are to become perfectly like him. The two are placed by John in the closest connection; the perfect intuition of God and, as proceeding therefrom, a perfect transformation into his image, the oneness of life between the beholder and the beheld. The beholding of God must react upon the beholder, transforming him into that which is the object of contemplation, assimilating him to that which he beholds, —and the perfect perception can proceed only from affinity of life. It implies the removal from the life as from the perception, of all which might separate, a perfect unity between the two. Life and perception are here entirely one. So in our Saviour's words: it is the pure in heart who shall see God; by which he too expresses the sum of all blessedness. And as progress in the knowledge of God, proceeding as it does from fellowship of life with God, is dependent upon the progressive purification and development of the christian life, the life of likeness to God; so at the last consummating point, are perfect intuition of God and perfect likeness to God made coincident with each other.

Throughout this Epistle promise, and exhortation to that which is made the condition of the promise, engrafting themselves one upon the other, are found constantly in close connection. So also here, upon this highest promise follows the exhortation based on the condition of its fulfilment. The present and future, the beginning and end, are united by an indissoluble bond. All which is to be perfected in eternal life must already be possessed here in the germ; and by an ever-progressive development out of the germ, must it attain to that final limit of complete maturity. Since now perfect likeness to God consists in perfect holiness, it is through progressive sanctification in this life the way must be prepared for that final consummation, the unobstructed vision of God in perfect likeness to him. Hence John says: that he who has this hope towards Him, the Father,—

the hope that through Christ's promised grace, he shall attain to that glory of the children of God, which consists in perfect likeness to the Father and in the perfect vision of Him as He is, —he will be impelled by such a hope to become holy as Christ is holy, after the model image of Christ which is ever before his eye. He will purify himself, more and more, from all that obscures the reflection of that holy image; that when made like to him who is the perfect likeness of the Father, he may attain in him, through him, and with him, to the vision of the Father as he is.

This exhortation is continued in the following words. "Whosoever committeth sin transgresseth also the law: for sin is the transgression of the law. And ye know that he was manifested to take away our sins; and in him is no sin. Whosoever abideth in him sinneth not: whosoever sinneth, hath not seen him, neither known him. Little children, let no man deceive you: he that doeth righteousness is righteous, even as he is righteous."

Ch. iii. 4–7.]

It is obvious from the Apostle's mode of expression, when urging upon Christians this earnest striving for holiness, this shunning of all that is sinful,—that he must have had cause for it in the adverse influence which some were exerting, and from which there was reason to apprehend a diminution of moral earnestness, a laxity of moral judgment in the church. The Apostle is warning his brethren against certain seducers. These were the promoters of that externalized and formal Christianity, of which we have spoken in the Introduction. Already, at this early period, had such appeared in the churches. Unable to comprehend the full extent of what was included in separation from heathenism, they taught that no more was required, than the abandonment of idol worship with all that pertained to it, and a profession of faith in one God and in Jesus as the Messiah; without recognizing that the Christian life as a whole, in its entire consecration to God, belongs to this separation from heathenism. From the Jews, chiefly, proceeded these superficial and outward tendencies in religion, which rested in a mere external faith, external profession, and external fulfilment of the law. These are the vain words against which Paul warns his Ephesian brethren (Eph. v. 6), when declaring that the wrath of God comes upon the children of disobedience, not merely on account of idolatry, but also of all the sins connected with it. Here now the Apostle asserts with special emphasis, that all sin whatever is unrighteousness (as Luther translates it), or as it should be in accordance with the Greek original, contrariety to law, transgression of the divine law. We might naturally infer from this, that the Apostle was dealing with such as did not comprehend the idea of the divine law in its whole dignity and majesty, as embracing all which is requisite to the full realization of the divine will, as being the full revelation of God's holiness in the mirror of its demands on man; such as explained the commands of God in a gross and merely external manner, which rendered it easy to satisfy their demands without coming thereby any nearer to the true nature of holy living. Such a conception of the Law is condemned by Christ in the Sermon on the Mount. It was from the stand-point of such a superficial conception of the Law, that the rich young man in the Gospel (Matt. xix. 17, ff.) could suppose that from his youth he had fulfilled all its requirements; a conception which has often been reproduced in the church, and with the uniform effect of making obedience to the Law easy, of lowering the requirements of Christianity to each one's life, and thus enabling him the more readily to appease his conscience. In christian self-examination and self-knowledge, all depends upon a right understanding and clear view of the nature of the Law, which must be ever present before the eye of the believer, as the mirror in which to contemplate himself and his life. The careful daily study of that holy interpretation of the Law, contained in our Lord's Sermon on the Mount, will above all else aid us in this duty.

Such, then, had made their appearance in John's sphere of labor, as thus externalized and degraded the conception of the divine Law; lowering the standard of moral judgment, and recognizing only in various outbreaking sins transgressions of that law. It was necessary, therefore, that John should oppose their influence by holding up sin in its character as sin,—all sin as equally transgression of the divine Law. In judging of the moral character of men, regard should indeed be had to differences of gradation in moral development; and of this the Apostle himself will by and by give us occasion to speak. Yet is it of the greatest importance to a right view of the true nature of sanctification, and for that strict self-examination which is the condition of all progress therein, that we first understand the equal dignity of the divine Law in all its commands; that the obedience it requires is absolute, and embraces the whole life. There is here no distinction between great and small; all sin, as proceeding from the same fountain the depraved creature-will, that which the Scriptures call the flesh in opposition to the spirit, as violation of the divine will, transgression of the divine law, is on the same level. This is the precise point of view established by John in these words.

He then proceeds to show, how irreconcilable is the tendency here rebuked with the nature of faith in Jesus, as the Lord and Saviour; that this faith cannot maintain itself without the earnest striving for sanctification, without the shunning of all sin; what a contradiction in the very nature of things it would be, to desire still to remain in the service of any sin, while professing adherence to Jesus as the Saviour. He takes for his starting-point: Jesus has appeared to take away our sins. It is here represented as the highest aim of the appearing of Christ, to take away all sin from humanity, and (the same idea under the positive form) to found a kingdom of holiness in man. This thought is, in itself, a sufficient demonstration, that its origin is not of earth but of Heaven, the demonstration of its own divinity. It is a thought which could never have arisen in the sin-polluted mind of man. He who could conceive it, would thereby already have demonstrated his superhuman greatness. To be able to express such a thought, in the midst of a sinful race, involves the consciousness not only of its superhuman origin, but also of superhuman powers to achieve its realization. It marks a new era in history; that henceforth, for those who appropriate to themselves the work of Christ and enter into fellowship with him, Evil and Sin are as if they were not, as if wholly and forever taken away. Not only shall sin no longer have dominion over them, but former sin shall be as if it had not been, as if annihilated. In regard to the expression, "to take away our sins," a comparison with the original Greek, and with John's language elsewhere, leads us to refer the conception underlying it to Christ. It is He, who by entering into fellowship with man's sinful nature, and thus acquiring a living sympathy with all the misery brought upon it by sin, became conscious in his sufferings of a connection with the sin of humanity. Through his fellowship with that nature which he had adopted, he bore the guilt by which humanity was burdened, and felt it as his own; as indicated by those words upon the cross: "My God, my God, why hast thou forsaken me!" It was thus that he took upon himself and bore the sins of men, and therefore he is said to have taken away our sins. So the sin of the people was, in a symbolical and typical manner, laid as it were upon the sacrificial victim to be borne and expiated by it. But in order that Christ might thus take away the sins of man, it was requisite, as the Apostle subsequently indicates, that in himself there should be no sin. He must be the Sinless, the Holy One, in order as such to suffer for the sins in which he had himself no share; to take them away, and set over against them a life of perfect holiness answering to the divine law; to be able, in the fulfilment of that law, to do for all and in place of all, what all mankind should have done each for himself.

Since then it is as the Holy One that Jesus has taken away the sins of men, the Apostle infers that none can stand in fellowship with him, who perseveres henceforward in the way of sin. He declares, in the most absolute manner, that he who abides in fellowship with him sinneth not. To sin, and to abide in fellowship with the Holy One, who appeared for the very purpose of taking away sin, are things irreconcilable. To belong to him, is to be separated from all sin. The life which exists in fellowship with him excludes all sin. This assertion is subsequently repeated by the Apostle, in order to enforce it with the strongest emphasis, in the negative form: "Whosoever sinneth hath not seen Him, neither known Him." This seeing indicates, as we have before noticed, not bodily sight which cannot here be meant, but inward vision, a seeing with the eye of the spirit. From the distinction here made between seeing and knowing, it is evident that something more is meant by seeing Christ than by knowing him; as indeed elsewhere John is accustomed to represent by sight a higher stage of knowledge, that immediate spiritual perception which rises above mediate knowledge. If through the preaching of the Gospel the knowledge of Christ has been attained, there will follow that higher spiritual intuition of

Him, as manifested in his divine-human life, as He was and is. Such a living image of Christ, enchaining the soul, must be ever present to the spiritual gaze of the believer. But this can only be the case with him, whose life-walk is in harmony with this holy model. He who continues in sin, though he may outwardly have confessed Christ, can never truly have beheld this image; nay, he is still far even from knowing him as the Holy One who appeared to take away the sins of man. Such an one, in place of the true and living Christ, has devised for himself another and fictitious one.

Accordingly, John adds a protest against the vain words of those who lower the demands of the Gospel upon the christian life, representing a mere outward profession as that whereby christians are separated from the sinful heathen world, and entitled to contrast themselves as righteous with the sinners of Heathenism. He asserts, on the contrary, that it is only through the practice of righteousness, through a life-walk conformed thereto, that one can prove himself a righteous man. This, however, by no means harmonizes with the doctrine, that only through the fulfilment of righteousness, only through a course of action, one can become righteous. In all that is here said, there is presupposed that righteousness which has its root in fellowship with Christ, the new life proceeding from him and formed after his holy image. What he would enforce is this: that this inward righteousness,—originating in fellowship with Christ, and distinguishing the new stand-point of life from the former one,—can not be present without revealing itself in the outward life; that as the image of Christ the Righteous, the Holy, is transferred to the inner life of the believer, no one can stand in fellowship with him without showing himself, in his life-walk, to be righteous even as Christ is righteous.

It may appear strange, that the Apostle should so absolutely and unconditionally exclude all sin from the christian life; should seem to assert that it must correspond, in entire and unspotted righteousness, to the holy image of Christ. And yet, in what precedes he has given his readers to understand, that the christian life is one which still needs a purifying process. But it was here the Apostle's first object, in opposition to that laxness of moral views, that compromise with sin, to bring before the mind the full scope of what is involved in the essential nature and idea of Sin and of Righteousness; to exhibit, in its whole strictness and majesty, the claim upon the christian life arising from fellowship with Christ, from faith in him as the Redeemer. This is the same point of view which Christ takes in the Sermon on the Mount. The christian life, as such, in its essential nature and idea as a life of righteousness after the image of Christ, is in itself the opposite to all sin; and in this view, no difference of moral gradation can be made, although in the actual life such gradations are found to exist. It was the first object to bring out clearly, in the full import and extent of their contrariety, the stand-point of the old and that of the new man. From such a view it will always follow, that the determining tendency of the christian life, of the will in the christian, can be no other than holy and averse to sin; that only the after-workings of the former relation of sin, of the old man, oppose themselves to what is now his determining and controlling tendency.

It was here then the Apostle's object to draw the separating line between these two rad-
Ch. iii 8.] ical tendencies, in reference to holiness and sin, in its full breadth and force. Hence the un-

conditional contrast in which he presents those who abide in fellowship with Christ, those who are born of God, the children of God,—and those who are of the devil, who make themselves known by their lives as children of the devil. What then does he understand by the devil? He designates him as the one who sinneth "from the beginning." If we take the expression, "from the beginning," in an absolute and unlimited sense, and follow it out to its necessary results, we must understand by Satan a spirit in his origin and essence the opposite to the holy God, evil in his very nature, in his whole being and essence the representative of evil; and consequently two original Principles of Being, a good and an evil, must be admitted. But from a comparison with the Apostle's whole mode of conception, and with his ideas of the creation, it is clear that such a view is wholly foreign to him; for he derives all existence simply from God and his Word, and consequently can recognize no Being co-existent with God. Since, moreover, he regards God as absolutely Light, to whom all darkness is alien,—as the Holy One from whom nothing evil can proceed,—he must, while recognizing God as sole creator of all existing things, assume that all things as they proceeded from Him were created good. He cannot, therefore, admit that an originally evil spirit was, as such, created by God. And farther still, the Johannic conception of sin is inconsistent with such an idea of a sinner from the beginning, of a being originally evil. For the idea of sin implies transgression of the divine law, by a spirit created to fulfil the law, one in whose consciousness the divine law was present as a law for himself. It is rebellion of the creature-will against the divine will to which it should be subject. All this is comprehended by John in the idea of sin when predicated of man. In all this there is implied a spirit created by God originally good, who through the misuse of his own free will rebelled against the divine will. And thus also the supposition of an originally evil Principle is seen to be inadmissible. We must accordingly understand by the expression, "sinneth from the beginning," not that the devil sins on evermore from the beginning of his existence as a spirit, but from the time when, through the apostacy of his will from God, he became what he is, the Devil; SINNING, through the steady persistence of his will in a course at variance with his original nature, a variance involved in the idea of sin, having become his second nature, his element of life. The expression, "from the beginning," is justified moreover on this ground: that the origin of all sin is from the devil; that through him sin first entered the universe, and the first beginning of sin in the human race also was brought about by his intervention. Hence all sin is an imitation of Satan, a reflection of his image, the work of the same spirit, of that selfish tendency in the creature by which it renounced its natural dependence on God, made itself law, end, centre to itself, instead of referring as its destiny required the whole life to God alone, and making him its law, end and centre. This tendency having first proceeded from the Devil, he is consequently regarded as its representative; all which is done from this disposition is referred back to him, and viewed as the work of the spirit which shows itself operative in him, which first came into being in him. But it is characteristic of John to seek only the practical-religious point of view, to apprehend everything in its bearing on the christian life, its influence upon sanctification,—and to refrain from questions relating merely to matters of knowledge without practical importance. He therefore pursues no farther the inquiry, what the devil originally was in relation to the rest of the spirit-world. He only exhibits what is here of practical weight, viz. the connection of all sin with him from whom sin first proceeded,—with that sinning of the devil from the beginning. It is no mere matter of speculation, it is something practically important,—important in respect to the consciousness of sin,—that we go beyond its present manifestation in man, and behold in Satan its essential nature. Thus while viewing sin as the act of a spirit gifted with higher powers, created originally good, we shall become more clearly aware of its true nature, as a revolt of the creature-will against the supreme will of God which all should obey, as a voluntary transgression of the holy law given by God to all rational beings. Learning thus to understand Evil in its whole fathomless depth, as guilty estrangement from God, we shall thereby be guarded against the error, so prejudicial to moral earnestness, of regarding evil as merely an infirmity, an overpowering of the Rational by the Sensual ;—

as nothing more than a product of the sensual nature in man.

With this aim,—to show the incompatibility of all sin with the christian life, and arouse the christian to the conscious necessity of avoiding all contact with sin, as something diametrically opposed to the position of the child of God, to the life which is in him,—John refers every sin, without distinction between great and small, to the same origin, the one radical tendency expressed in all sins, to the devil who sinneth from the beginning. By sinning, one puts himself on an equality with the devil, shows himself to be one of his adherents, to be governed by his spirit. That which constitutes the characteristic of the devil is the operative principle in all sin, viz. this same radical tendency of self-will in the creature resisting the holy ordinance of God. Since now the Apostle derives all sin from the devil, and in all sin recognizes the kingdom of the devil; as in all the evil which reigned in the human race until Christ's appearing he sees the influence of that kingdom, the progressive working of the disorder introduced by the devil into the world; he therefore says, that the Son of God has appeared to undo, to destroy, the works of the devil. The expressions, "to take away the sins of men," and "to destroy the works of the devil," are employed by John with the same general import. After having exhibited sin in connection with the devil, these expressions could now be interchanged. As he here contemplates evil, not merely as manifested on earth, but in its more general connection with the development-history of the universe, of which indeed revelation unveils only such a fragment as is demanded for our practical religious necessities; so also does his designation of Christ's work of redemption, include that more general reference to the history of the universe, and of the kingdom of God in its widest sense. It is here represented as the highest aim of the appearing of Christ, to destroy all which is the work of Satan, all evil,—the triumphant establishment of the kingdom of God on the ruins of Satan's kingdom. Since then Christ appeared to do away all sin as the work of the devil; it clearly follows, that only he who renounces all sin as the work of the devil can share in the work of Christ, can receive in himself the fulfilment of the purpose for which Christ appeared.

Whilst he thus shows the total contrariety between the children of God and the children of the devil, between him that doeth righteousness and him that sinneth, the Apostle says: "Whosoever is born of God doth not commit sin; for his seed remaineth in him; and he cannot sin, because he is born of God." John here first certifies a matter of fact; he states a practical proposition, viz. that he who is born of God,—as being born of God,—sinneth not. The ground of this is stated in the declaration which follows, that in such the seed of God remaineth. The figure of seed, so often employed in the Scriptures, is usually taken from husbandry. Thus in the parables of our Lord, the word of God is compared to the seed, the soul to the ground in which the seed is scattered, the difference of susceptibility for receiving the word of God to varieties of soil. But this, obviously, is not the allusion here. It is not men represented as recipients of the seed, and deporting themselves variously in respect to its reception; it is the believer begotten from the seed. The allusion is manifestly to the seed in human generation, as in John i. 13. The seed of God is the divine life derived from God and imparted through Christ, from which proceeds the

[Ch. iii. 9.

new birth, regeneration, and which constitutes those to whom it is imparted children of God. Having by the reception of this divine life been born of God and become children of God, so long as the divine seed, the new divine life abides and continues operative in them penetrating their whole nature, they cannot but remain children of God and manifest themselves as such. Since now this seed from God stands as the exact opposite of the life which is kindred to that of the devil, to all which is sin ; it is obvious that the children of God sin not, since this new life, the very thing which constitutes them children of God, excludes from itself all sin. Having stated this practical proposition, he proceeds to prove that it must of necessity be so, that it cannot be otherwise. Such an one cannot sin. It is in the nature of the case impossible that he should sin, because he is born of God ; because this being born of God stands in direct contradiction with sin. Sin cannot proceed from it, can find no point of connection in it. As nothing Undivine, but only what is Divine, can proceed from the divine life, so from those who are born of God, as such, there can proceed no sin.

John now places these two classes of men in contrast with each other: "Herein is manifest who are the children of God and who are the children of the devil." [Ch. iii. 10. Thus he divides the whole human race between these two diametrically opposite classes, the children of God and the children of the devil. But is there, then, only this one distinction among men? Is there nothing intermediate, are there no points of transition, between the two classes? If so, it would be impossible to explain, how children of God could be formed from children of the devil, how a transition from the one class to the other could be effected. And yet John assumes such a possibility in the recognition of the fact, that such as served sin and belonged to the kingdom of Satan, to the kingdom of the world, have through faith in Jesus as the Saviour withdrawn therefrom, and have become children of God. By saying that the Son of God has appeared to destroy the works of the devil, he says virtually, that he appeared in order to make those children of God who hitherto were children of the devil. There must then exist a point of attachment, whereby those who are as yet children of the devil become susceptible to the influence of the Son of God. There must somewhere be a ground for the fact, that some remain children of the devil, while others receive the seed of God and thereby suffer themselves to be made children of God. Or are we to say, that this ground lies not in the previous differences of susceptibility in men, but only in the sovereign agency of God; that it is alone the work of transforming grace whereby this difference is produced, and the children of the devil are re-created into children of God? But this is in contrariety with what John says, of the divine Father-love towards the whole human race which it seeks to redeem, of the scope of Christ's work of redemption which takes in all humanity; that the object of his appearing in humanity is to destroy all the works of the devil, to make an end of evil universally. It is not therefore in the divine purpose taken by itself, but in the treatment of it by men themselves, that we must look for the cause why some attain, while others do not, to a participation in that which the love of God has proffered to all. John could not, moreover, have spoken of a judgment everywhere connected with the preaching of the Gospel, and going side by side with it (as in John iii. 19), if all men deported themselves alike towards the preaching of the Gospel; if God himself, by his almighty agency, alone made the difference between them; if this difference had not its ground in themselves, being brought to light through the judicial power of the Gospel by means of the various positions taken by men in respect to it,—the sifting process effected by the Gospel. Thus we are led by John himself,—though he only presents in general the contrast between children of the devil and children of God, the regenerate and the unregenerate,—to add to this radical contrariety still another distinction, whereby it becomes possible that from children of the devil can be formed children of God. The Gospel of John contains many an index to the clearer recognition of these differences, these intervening steps. From that being BORN OF GOD which can alone be effected through the agency of the Gospel, through faith in the Son of God, is to be distinguished a preliminary state which is designated as a BEING OF GOD,—a BEING OF THE TRUTH (John xviii. 37); whereby is meant that susceptibility for what is divine, for the truth, which leads those who possess it, before they are yet born of God in that higher sense, to follow the call of the Gospel when extended to them. To this addresses itself that DRAWING by the Father which takes place in their souls made thus susceptible through the bent of the will, and by which they are led to the Son. The judgment, the sifting attributed to the Gospel, is effected simply by the development through its agency of the already existing but hitherto concealed diversity among men, in respect to the bent of the will. This is exhibited in the difference of their bearing towards the Gospel, according to the difference of their susceptibility for it; some hating and resisting the dawning light, on account of its contrariety to the darkness which they love and do not desire to forsake, and to the works of darkness which thus exposed are brought into condemnation; while others joyfully accept the light after which, consciously or unconsciously, they had already longed. (John iii. 20, 21.)

We have seen that in the children of God, although their determining tendency is that which has its origin in the birth from God, that of the divine life, yet all is not as yet in harmony with this tendency. From that which characterizes them as children of God,—that which belongs to the animating principle in them, to their new spiritual self, their new regenerated personality,—must be distinguished that which proceeds from the after-working of the former state. So also in those, who under that general classification still belong to the children of the devil, must be distinguished something which proceeds not from him; something which is to be ascribed to their original descent from God, the obscured but still underlying image of God, which darkened though it be has not ceased to exert its influence. And according as men, through that in them which is of the devil follow the spirit of the devil, or through that in them which still proceeds from the obscured image of God follow the leading of God, will result a division among those who seem collectively to belong to the children of the devil. But why then does John make only this general distinction? For this reason: that it is of practical importance, first of all, to show in the strongest possible light the contrariety between the new christian stand-point and the former one of the old man, that each may be fully aware how he is to distinguish himself from all others as a child of God. The obliteration of this distinction has uniformly exerted the most pernicious influence in respect to the demands upon the christian life, to the strictness of self-examination. It is all important that we learn first to separate light and darkness, the Divine and the Undivine, totally from each other; to repel all reconciliation and agreement between these fundamentally opposed directions, as viewed in the whole strength of their contrariety. Unconditional decision is here required. It is important that we learn to recognize, in all evil, this determining tendency by which the children of the devil are manifested as such, in order that we may be secured against the danger of yielding in any manner to the evil, even when disguised under seeming good; lest hurried along farther and farther we at length wholly succumb to the power, which when first approached we did not recognize, and which now over-masters us because we did not then sufficiently resist it. It is for this reason so important to our own security, as an incitement to constant watchfulness over ourselves, that the distinction here made between the children of God and the children of the devil,—and this distinction as manifested in the outward life,—be apprehended by us in its full force and ever borne in mind as a matter of living consciousness. If we contemplate history, not as developing itself in gradual manifestations and with its final decisions yet concealed, but as it is presented to the divine view; it may indeed be said, that those who are adapted and destined, through their still latent susceptibility, to become children of God when reached by the preaching of the Gospel, are already present to his omniscient eye as his children. Thus contemplating what is gradually developed to human view, by the judicial potency of the Gospel, as being ever open to the eye of God, we shall be able to explain those intervening and transitional points in that general contrariety, and to find in them a distinction plainly involved in the Apostle's view.

To bring out this generic distinction still more strongly, John now adds a specific mark by which it may be recognized: "He that doeth not righteousness is not of God, neither he that loveth not his brother." The Apostle here resumes the general distinction, in order to trace back righteousness in the abstract, to that concrete which is always contemplated by him as the soul of all righteousness,—that which is in itself the fulfilment of all righteousness, the one thing which suffices in place of all, viz. Brotherly-Love.

This forms the transition to what follows, the representation of love as the distinguishing the characteristic mark of the christian relation: "For this is the message which ye have heard from the beginning, that we should love one another. Not as Cain, who was of that wicked one, and slew his brother."

Ch. iii. 11, 12.]

Here again, in his peculiar mode of conception, John passes over the manifold gradations in actual life, and apprehends the moral opposites in their most sharply defined contrariety, as it is founded in the essential nature of the inward disposition. With him, this root of the inward disposition is the all in all; and accordingly he contrasts hatred with the principle of brotherly love. He recognizes no intervening stand-point. Where love is wanting, selfishness is the governing principle, making the individual the centre of all, referring all to itself; and hence the effort to remove out of the way whatever stands opposed to its own selfish interests. It can tolerate no competitor, nothing which is not subservient to itself; and hence it becomes hatred towards another, when through him these selfish interests are endangered. Hatred too, he apprehends at the culminating point of manifestation, since out of hatred proceeds murder; and accordingly he names, as the representative of those motives of conduct which are opposed to love, him who first actualized such a disposition, and who is exhibited in the Scriptures as the first who shed another's blood. Thus the Apostle everywhere apprehends moral opposites in the deepest root of the disposition. To Love, ready to surrender life for another's good, he opposes Hate, which for itself would sacrifice the life of another. Where love is not the animating principle, there rules selfishness with hatred in its bosom; and hatred, at the culminating point of its manifestation, is murder. In the germ, the disposition, murder exists there already. The germ needs only to be fully developed in order to become murder. In the want of Brotherly-love, in hatred, we behold the root whose fruit is murder. Thus the highest moral tribunal regards not the act, but condemns in its first germ the disposition out of which the act proceeds. Before this tribunal every emotion of hatred appears as murder. John here follows the standard of moral judgment employed by Christ in the Sermon on the Mount. And thus the children of God, whose animating spirit is love, are set in contrast with those who are of the evil one, the children of the devil, in whom hate governs as in Cain their representative.

The Apostle is led by this to contemplate Christians in their contrariety to the world. The transition is suggested by the contrariety between Cain and Abel. "And wherefore slew he him? Because his own works were evil, and his brother's righteous. Marvel not, my brethren, if the world hate you." As Abel is the type of the children of God, Cain the type of the children of the devil, so in their relation to each other is exhibited the relation of Christians to the world. As Cain hated and murdered Abel on account of the contrariety between the godly and the ungodly disposition, so does the world hate and murder the children of God on account of the same contrariety. The world and the children of God are, like love and selfishness, in perpetual conflict with each other. Hence it need not surprise Christians to find themselves hated by the world; they must ex-

Ch. iii. 12–15.]

pect it beforehand, as a consequence of the contrariety of their spirit to that of the world. It is the stamp of the divine life, whose impress constitutes them the opposite of the world. Hence the words which follow: "We know that we have passed from death unto life, because we love the brethren. Whoso loveth not his brother abideth in death. Whoso hateth his brother is a murderer: and ye know that no murderer hath eternal life abiding in him." To John, the love of God alone appears as life absolutely; and the true life of the God-allied spirit can consist only in fellowship with God, in participation in the divine life. All life apart from this fellowship,—the life of the spirit abandoned to itself, referring only to itself,—being an estrangement from that which is and can alone be the spirit's true life, and is for the spirit Death. The world, as estranged from God, has therefore fallen a prey to death. Christians also were once, as belonging to the world, subject to the same death. Being separated from the world by faith, and becoming partakers of fellowship with God through Christ, they have passed from death unto life. While yet here below, they possess in themselves this true divine life; and as the seeming life of the world, which is but death, makes itself known by the want of love, by the selfish nature, hatred; so on the other hand, love is the characteristic mark of the true divine life. Herein therefore must the contrariety, between those who have attained to the true life and those who are still in a state of death, make itself manifest. He who loves not his brother, says John, though he calls himself a Christian, belongs still to the world. Love is wanting, and therefore also the divine life whereby the children of God are distinguished from the world. Such an one has not passed from death unto life: he abides in death, like the world to which he belongs. What he calls faith, is not that direction of the spirit whereby one passes from death unto life, and is not therefore what in the true sense can bear the name of faith. In John's view, it is not by assent to certain articles of belief that genuine Christianity, the distinction between what is Christian and what is Unchristian must make itself known,—but in the life, in love. Here, however, must be borne in mind the connection of ideas peculiar to John's mode of conception,—viz. that love proceeds only from faith, is something spontaneously evolved from personal experience of the redeeming love of God in Christ. He asserts that where there is not love, there can be no participation in that true life in its nature exalted above change and death, containing in itself the germ of a development for eternity and hence called eternal life. And this he proves by substituting for NOT TO LOVE its equivalent, HATE; and by applying to the germ of hatred in the heart, what is true of murder, which is only the highest expression of hate. He assumes, as already known and admitted, that no murderer hath eternal life; where this disposition exists, eternal life can have no place. Perhaps John here alludes to a spiritual conception of the divine sentence, that he who sheds the blood of another shall die the death. To him, all life estranged from God is death,—is the opposite to that true divine life which already is eternal life. What is predicable of murder is, from the standpoint of that highest tribunal which takes cognizance of the intention, to be applied to the germ of murder already existing in hatred,—in the want of love.

Our attention is directed to that connection be-

tween faith and love, of which we have spoken, in
Ch. iii. 16.] the verse immediately following: "Herein perceive we the love of God, in that he has laid down his life for us, and we ought also to lay down our lives for the brethren."

What John designates as love, is only that which springs from inward experience of the redeeming love of God; which feels itself constrained to imitate the redeeming love of Christ, as exhibited in his life; that love to God which pours itself out in brotherly love, after the example of Christ. By this example John brings to view the true inward nature of love, and the way in which it must manifest itself in the life. What love is, says he, we have already learned in the example of Christ who gave his life for us. So also with us, must love prove itself to be true by our readiness to give up all, to sacrifice life itself for the sake of the brethren.

But since everything depends on keeping the
Ch. iii. 17, 18.] distinction clearly marked between appearance and reality; since all which is genuine can be imitated in its outward aspect, and become mere appearance; John feels himself obliged to warn his brethren against this tendency,

even in regard to that which is peculiarly opposed to all seeming, and is adapted above all else to demonstrate the true nature and the reality of the christian life, viz. Love. He contrasts that brotherly-love which proves its existence by act, by sacrifice of self, with that of which there is a mere show in words, and where the words are convicted of falsehood by the act. "But whoso hath this world's good, and seeth his brother hath need, and shutteth up his bowels of compassion from him; how dwelleth the love of God in him? My little children, let us not love in word, neither in tongue, but in deed and in truth." Where brotherly-love does not exist, and show itself by acts for the relief of others' necessities, there love to God is also wanting.

[Ch. iii. 19–22.

Having thus distinguished between truth and appearance in respect to love, requiring that love which is truth; he now connects this with the general fact, that the whole christian life must have its root in truth,—with the universal contrariety between truth and appearance. "And hereby we know that we are of the truth, and shall assure our hearts before him. For if our heart condemn us, God is greater than our heart, and knoweth all things. Beloved, if our heart condemn us not, then have we confidence towards God. And whatsoever we ask, we receive of him, because we keep his commandments, and do those things that are pleasing in his sight." John has shown, by a single example, in what way the truth of the christian life whose essence is love, must approve itself. This Christ has also done in the Sermon on the Mount (Matt. xvii. 12): "Whatsoever ye would that men should do to you, do ye even so to them; for this is the Law and the Prophets." These words are by no means adapted to express the peculiar nature of christianity as a whole; nor should they be used for this purpose, as has been done by some through misapprehension of the nature of the Gospel, and of the import of these words in their connection. Were this all, then truly Christ needed not to have come. To enjoin the command,—this is an easy matter; but does not bring with it obedience to the command. The great point is, how to attain to a conformity with this command; and all turns upon the question, from what temper of mind does the fulfilment of it proceed. For even the wisdom of self-love could suggest, that we must be willing to do for others what they desire of us, in order that we may receive the like from them. Thus it would only be the course of prudent calculation, far from that which Christ established as a law for the life. But our Lord's design in this passage, as also that of John in the above example, is to contrast true righteousness whose essence is love, with a pretended righteousness; and accordingly he directs attention to the test, whereby the true nature of love is to make itself known, as opposed to a love merely assumed for show by such as are deceivers of themselves. The test is this: are we constrained by love to do for another, what we in like circumstances would desire that he should do for us? Such is also the test of love here presented by John. By this test, says he,—viz. when our conduct actually harmonizes with the disposition presupposed in us as christians,—we may know that we are of the truth. In the mode of conception peculiar to John, he regards truth not merely as a matter of knowledge, but as something pertaining to the moral temper and the life. Thus, as in the children of God he assumes a being of God, so does he also a being of the truth. Christ calls himself, absolutely, the truth; in him the truth has appeared in a personal form, and has entered into the life of humanity. His whole life is truth, the only life which is perfect truth, wholly one with itself as it is one with God. Thus believers also, in proportion as they have received him into themselves, are of the truth. In the world all is appearance; with christians all should be truth. And the touchstone here proposed, whereby they may know whether they are of the truth, is this: does their life, their conduct, really harmonize with what they acknowledge from the christian standpoint as the law of their conduct,—with what they have professed?

If now, says the Apostle, our whole life in profession and conduct is thus of one piece, is in accord with itself, we shall be able to quiet our hearts before God. Under the name of heart, John comprehends all the various capacities and modes of action belonging to the spirit, without applying the particular designations coined by more cultivated languages for the separate faculties. These distinctions have indeed their propriety; and so has also the neglect of such a division, the indivisible conception and contemplation of the spirit in the totality of all its powers and actions. It indicates to us how closely all is connected together in the life of the spirit. This is important for the right conception and formation of the christian life, both as it directs the attention to the inmost and deepest root of the spiritual life, all being here determined by the moral basis, the bent towards God or the world, towards good or evil; and also as it is the christian's work, the task assigned him, from that highest principle the one determining tendency towards God, to mould the whole life in all its capacities and relations into an all-embracing unity. In this passage, by heart John understands that faculty of the spirit, which elsewhere is designated as the conscience. He speaks of a quieting of the conscience before God, inasmuch as in the conscience the voice of God our judge reveals itself; bringing us before the eye of God as the judge of our life, and making him present to the soul. It is that tribunal of conscience referred to by Paul (Rom. ii. 15), where he speaks of the thoughts of men as accusing or excusing their dealings one with another. And a condition of the inner life is here presented, wherein man can bring quiet to his conscience in view of God the holy judge; wherein he need not fear the accusings of conscience, through which speaks the judicial voice of God: inasmuch as conscience can convict him of no discord between his profession and his course of life, but he is conscious to himself of fulfilling the conditions of salvation ordained by God.

The Apostle then illustrates by contrast the high value of such a possession, that of a quiet conscience in harmony with itself. If our conscience convicts us of inward falsehood, makes manifest to ourselves the contradiction between our life and our profession; we must be convinced, that as we cannot deceive our own hearts, cannot falsify, or silence the voice within us, still less is it in our power to deceive God. God is greater than our heart, is the Omniscient One; and what cannot be kept concealed from our own conscience, will certainly not remain hidden from his eye, whose all-penetrating glance nothing can escape. The accusings of our own conscience thus reveal to us the condemnatory sentence of God against us. Thus the Apostle directs us to something in our inward being, from which we can obtain the surest knowledge respecting ourselves and our relation to God; by which we may be guarded against all corruption through the praise of others, who look only upon the appearance, against all the deceptions of vanity and self-love; something which is ever present, teaching us to distinguish between being and seeming, between the real and the apparent character of our life. It summons us to collect ourselves from all the distracting influences of the world; to withdraw deep into our inward selves, and there before that holy incorruptible tribunal, to test ourselves, to judge, and to mould our lives accordingly.

As then, says the Apostle, if our own heart condemn us, we thereby know that God so much the more condemns us; so on the other hand, if our heart condemn us not, this is a pledge that neither does God condemn us. We have the most assured and joyful confidence towards God as the witness of our integrity.

A reliance upon human righteousness, as availing before God, can by no means be intended here. This would be in contrariety with the whole teaching of the Apostle in this Letter. So far from this, he assumes the filial relation to God grounded in fellowship with Christ as already existing, and as being the source of that joyful confiding trust, in which the believer rises to God as his Father. He is merely pointing out the conditions, under which alone believers can hold themselves entitled to appropriate all that is involved in that filial relation. It is then, and only then, when their life in truth accords with this relation to God as their Father, and so all in them is truth.

The Apostle then dwells particularly upon one of the privileges belonging to that filial relation, and in which it is specially recognized, viz. the position towards God as their Father in which believers stand through prayer,—the filial relation in prayer. As sons, whose filial relation has suffered no interruption, can with childlike trust and confidence ask all from their father; so believers, whose life is of the truth, who are conscious of no disturbance of their filial relation to God through unfaithfulness on their part, can ask all with childlike trust and confidence from God their Father. And as the child knows beforehand, that the father will grant to him all that is conducive to his best good; so do believers also, while in this temper of heart asking God their Father, know that he grants all they desire, leaves no request unheard. It is all the same as if they already had what they ask. By such a certainty of being heard is their prayer accompanied. The ground of this certainty, according to the Apostle, is this: that they obey the commands of God, and,—as he more exactly defines it,—do those things which are well-pleasing in his sight; that is, what is truly good, what appears such in the sight of a holy God. This has reference not merely to the external act, but to that also from which alone the practice of righteousness in external acts derives its true significance, the disposition of heart from which the act proceeds. It must be a disposition corresponding to the divine law, such an one as God desires, well-pleasing in his sight; one which has God for its end and aim, which has no object but his glory. It is clear, therefore, that the connection of prayer with the christian life as a whole is here presupposed; that prayer is not something isolated and distinct from the rest of the life, but proceeds from the same holy disposition which governs the whole life, and expresses itself in every action. In order that the whole life may be of the truth, it is necessary moreover that this disposition, this direction of the spirit towards God, since it proceeds from fellowship with Christ, should in every work show itself as something derived through him.

What we have now said removes an objection, which, without a more careful consideration of the words, might arise from the unconditional promise that every request shall be heard. For the object of prayer might be something, which would not really promote the salvation of him who desires it; something not in harmony with the councils of God's universal government. Shall aught therein be changed by the caprice of man? But this difficulty is at once relieved when we contemplate prayer in the connection here presented, prayer as proceeding from the whole filial relation to God, from the disposition which determines and controls the whole life. This is no other than the spirit of filial submission to God, of concord between the human and divine will. The condition, which is afterwards expressly insisted on by the Apostle, follows of itself from this connection. Prayer too can be reckoned among the things well-pleasing to God, only so far as submission to his will accompanies every request; and hence the absolute promise that it shall be heard. Moreover, a relation so intimate of believers to God as their

Father is presupposed, that from the same fellowship with him in which their whole life has its root, proceed also their prayers. The believer prays, in fellowship with Christ, for that which Christ himself would have prayed for in his place; for that which the spirit of Christ, in moments of peculiar spiritual elevation, discovers to him as suitable, and impels him to ask. The same God, who through his Spirit inspires the prayer, grants also the fulfilment of it. All has its source in the same reference of the life to God. This is what Christ designates as prayer in his name; and the hearing of such prayer is therefore promised unconditionally.

Having previously spoken of obedience to commands in general, the Apostle now resolves [Ch. iii. 23.
the whole into obedience to that one command in which all is contained: "And this is his commandment; that we should believe on the name of his Son Jesus Christ, and love one another, as he gave us commandment."

The law of the Old Covenant began by instituting commands for the conduct. But the power so to conduct was wanting; and this no law could impart to man. Hence the Law could serve no other purpose than to bring man to the consciousness of his moral inability, of his discord with God and with his own better nature, to the consciousness of spiritual death. Here now, on the contrary, all commands are resolved into one; and this has reference not to a DOING, but to a BELIEVING,—the command of the Father that we should believe on the name of his Son Jesus Christ; should believe on him in the relation in which he is presented to man by God as his only-begotten Son, as He through whom alone we can come to the Father, the Redeemer from sin, the Lord to whom henceforth should belong the whole life. So Christ, when asked by the Jews what they should do that they might work the works of God, gave no other answer than this: That they should believe on him whom God had sent; implying that in this was contained the source and sum of all. (John vi. 29.)

Belief, however, is a matter of conviction. How then can it be commanded a man, to make this or that an object of conviction to himself? This stands not within his own power, it depends not on his own will; for conviction is an involuntary thing. God would have instituted no such requirement, had not He, who is to be the object of belief, so corresponded to the requirement in his appearing and his life, as necessarily to become the object of belief to every truth-loving, salvation-seeking spirit. In this command there is presupposed the impression, which the whole life of Christ must make upon him who contemplates it in the right spirit; the impression of Christ as designated and accredited by God himself, through the manner in which he dwelt in him and wrought in him. So also in the words of Christ just referred to, this is alleged as the ground on which God can require faith in him: "For him hath God the Father sealed;" the works which the Father had given him to perform being the tokens of that sealing. While it is here assumed on the one hand, that God has thus accredited him in whose name he requires belief, and therefore can require it; it is also presupposed that he has so formed the nature of men as that He cannot but make on them this divine impression,—cannot but reveal himself as He to whom their God-allied nature attracts them, and in whom alone they can find satisfaction for all their higher wants; of whom their God-related nature itself bears undeniable testimony, that to him they belong, that he alone can free them from sin and all their misery, can alone impart that true life which they need. There is presupposed the original and continued connection of the God-related soul with the God in whom it lives and moves and is; and hence that drawing of the Father by which the souls of men are led to the Son. This command of God is, consequently, no other than what arises of itself from the relation of Christ to the human soul. It is no arbitrary requisition. What is required by the truth itself, by those divine historical facts, according as they do with the capacities and laws of human nature, with its deep-implanted wants,—this here takes the outward form of a command of God. All this, however, whereby this command is shown to be the expression of an inward divine necessity, could be presupposed as already known, and needing no farther confirmation. For the Apostle was addressing churches already long established in Christianity; who had found, in their own experience, manifold evidences of the inward necessity of this belief. To such personal experience the Apostle makes his appeal in many passages of this Epistle. They had long known this as a command divinely enstamped upon their souls, constraining them to believe on the name of Jesus. Now as in this one command all others are included; so of necessity, as single commands to be enjoined each by itself, they are made superfluous. In that one command was bestowed, moreover, the ability to obey all others,—the motive-power for the fulfilment of all which the Law requires. Thereby had the Law been converted from an outward to an inward law, having its root in the inner life. The Apostle, therefore, expresses only that one command; which, having for its basis faith in Jesus who had offered up his life for the salvation of man, contains all others in itself and renders them superfluous,—the one command proceeding from Christ himself, LOVE ONE ANOTHER!

As it is by keeping the commands of Christ that faith in him must approve itself, so also is this the condition of abiding in fellowship with him. [Ch. iii. 24. "And he that keepeth his commandments dwelleth in Him, and He in him: and hereby we know that he abideth in us, by the spirit which he hath given us." Thus it is by obedience to the commands of Christ as contained in that one command, we attest our voluntary abiding in fellowship with Christ; this being the necessary condition on our part, in order that we may continue to enjoy the communication of Christ, and that he may abide in fellowship with us. This reciprocity is always presupposed; the keeping of the commands of Christ as depending upon that mutual fellowship, and as being also the condition and the evidence of this continued fellowship.

The Apostle then appeals to that, whereby this continued fellowship manifests itself to the consciousness of each; to that internal fact of a conscious divine life, imparted by Christ through the Holy Spirit. That we live in fellowship with him, we know by the spirit which he has given us,—that invisible pledge, manifesting itself to the inward experience, of uninterrupted union with him. Thus when about to part from his disciples, no more to be with them in his personal bodily presence, he promised that he would be invisibly near and present among them, no less truly than during his earthly manifestation. The proof of this his actual presence among them, should be the communication to them of his Spirit. This should be the medium of union between believers and their Saviour, until vision takes the place of faith; till that immediate view of Christ, enjoyed by his disciples in the familiar intercourse of his earthly life, is restored in heightened glory to believers. It is to this inward experience that the Apostle makes his appeal with these churches, and to it the inward experience of believers in all ages bears witness. Here, then, are conjoined two characteristic marks of fellowship with Christ which cannot be dissevered from each other; the one inward, perceptible to the immediate inner consciousness,—the other belonging to the outward life, but presupposing the former, of which it is at once the outward expression, and the condition of its continuance. The first is,—Participation in the Spirit promised by Christ; the second, Obedience to his commands, which is the fruit of that Spirit's agency, and in which such participation makes itself apparent. This being the Spirit's work, is also, as the evidence of this work, the condition of its continuance; all divine gifts being conditioned upon the faithful use of what is bestowed, according to the words of Christ: Whoso hath, to him shall be given.

CHAPTERS IV. V.

Throughout this Epistle, the exhibition of truth and the reprehension of opposing errors alternate the one with the other. Here the point of transition lies in what he had just said, viz. that in the case of all believers, participation in the influences of the Holy Spirit is the pledge of continued fellowship with Christ. This leads him, since there was much which falsely claimed to be from that spirit, to direct attention to the difference between its genuine operations and such as were only pretended, only a deceptive imitation. This connects itself with his previous warnings against false teachers.

These teachers, as is clear from the traits subsequently ascribed to them, professed to enjoy the special illumination of that Holy Spirit who is the source of life to all christians. They spoke with an irresistible enthusiasm; they claimed the character of prophets. All who assume the office of teachers in the church, should be organs of that Holy Spirit who is the pervading vitalizing principle of the church. As it was this Spirit, whose vital influence is presupposed in all as christians, without which no one could testify of Christ; so all, who would be received as teachers in the church, could only speak as instruments of this Spirit, and they were fully entitled so to speak. What they taught, however, must approve itself as truth, by its harmony with that which the same Spirit revealed to all. John himself, in a passage which we have already considered, appeals to this inward test in every believer. In the operations of this Spirit, however, there were to be found many gradations. It might be more the divinely enlightened reason, with its calmly progressive development of truth, which predominated in the teacher's mode of instruction; or it might be more the immediate influence of sudden inspiration by the Holy Spirit, seizing upon the mind with irresistible power, or revealing to the inward christian sense, in moments of extraordinary activity, new and higher views of truth of which the recipient felt himself constrained to testify. This latter was the peculiar characteristic of the prophets, in distinction from the ordinary teachers in the church. A like difference in the various spheres of christian inspiration, in the gradations of the divine and human, obtains in all periods of the church. As it is the same Holy Spirit which governs the church in all ages, and the unity of this Spirit connects the church of all ages with that of the Apostles; as the relation of human nature in all its various powers to the Spirit which animates them, and the laws according to which that Spirit works, remain ever the same; so also will his influence at all times manifest itself in the same generic forms and with the same gradations. Hence, a careful observation of history will show, in other times, a similar distinction between prophets and ordinary teachers in the church, between the prophetic gift and the ordinary gift of teaching; a distinction between such as are to be compared with the teachers, and such as more resemble the prophets of the apostolic church. The apostolic church cannot indeed, nor was it intended to be, reproduced as a whole in exactly the same literal form. Yet since it must serve, as to its ruling spirit and its leading principles, for the model of all subsequent christian development, it were much to be desired that we could more closely follow its example, in distinguishing between these different gifts, and in the training and application of them to the various circumstances and wants of the church.

The apostolic age differed from later periods of the church only in this: that as Christianity then first made its appearance in humanity, as the divine world-transforming power, there was a greater predominance of that immediate divine impulse and inspiration; the appearing of prophets, and the various manifestations of the prophetic gift, belonged more to the ordinary phenomena of the church. But as, from the very first, corrupt human nature mingled its disturbing and adulterating influence in all the manifestations of the divine; so with this genuine inspiration there connected itself a false one, with the suggestions of the divine Spirit those of an undivine. Enthusiasm for the truth was counterfeited by enthusiasm for error; delusion and fanaticism had also their own prophets; false prophets mingled with the true. Error in doctrine, proclaimed with all the ardor of a false inspiration, wrought through the influence of that enthusiasm the more power-

[Ch. iv. 1–3.

fully upon the popular mind. Hence there was needed for christians some decisive test, whereby they might be secured against the influence of this deception, and be enabled to distinguish between true and false inspiration. This is furnished by the Apostle in the following words: "Beloved, believe not every spirit, but try the spirits whether they are of God: because many false prophets are gone out into the world. Hereby know ye the Spirit of God: Every spirit that confesseth that Jesus Christ is come in the flesh, is of God: and every spirit that confesseth not Jesus, is not of God. And this is the spirit of Antichrist whereof ye have heard that it should come, and even now is it already in the world."

Under the term spirit, the Apostle here comprehends two things outwardly alike, but differing in their inward and essential nature,—viz. true and false inspiration, what originates in the suggestions of the divine spirit, as well as in those of the undivine. He who judged by no other test than appearance merely, must suppose he witnessed in all these outward manifestations the same power of inspiration, revealing itself in words of resistless fervor. And here a twofold error might be committed. Christians might either yield themselves credulously to all which claimed to be the revelation of a higher spirit, allowing themselves to be hurried away as the blind instruments of every influence; or, detecting the suggestions of the undivine spirit and seeking to avoid its delusions, might be thereby led to suspicion and distrust of all such manifestations, of every kind of inspiration. As there was a false confidence of unquestioning credulity, so might there arise also a morbid scepticism of mistrust, whereby the influences of the Holy Spirit might be obstructed in the church, and the kindling flame of inspiration be at once extinguished. Against both these errors, Paul thought it necessary to warn the church at Thessalonica. (1 Thess. v. 19, ff.)

The same danger which then threatened the christian life, must, by virtue of the uniform law in christian development, be constantly repeated; and the healthful christian spirit, alike far from blind credulity and from suspicious and unloving distrust, must trace out for itself the right way between these two extremes. This finds a special application in times which resemble the apostolic age; viz. when Christianity,—though not indeed making its first entrance into the world, yet rising anew from victorious conflict with the hostile forces of superstition or of scepticism,—begins to work with a new power; when a new outpouring of the Holy Spirit is preparing the way for itself, and gives tokens of its coming; in all times of special religious awakening, or of a spiritual excitement which affects the religious sphere. In such times, there will always be found some who are caught by everything unusual; who give ear too readily to everything which assumes the language of religious zeal; who behold the Divine in everything which proceeds from a state of peculiar mental excitement, and claims to be the work of the Holy Spirit. Others, on the contrary, detecting this infusion of foreign elements, suffer themselves to be thereby made distrustful towards all religious awakening. Instead of trying the spirits, they class them all together and reject all; and thus, as far as in them lies, they extinguish also the divine flame, and prevent the growth of that new religious life from which a new creation was to be developed. The warning of the Apostle not to believe every spirit, his requirement to test the spirits, includes a caution against both these errors.

In his caution not to believe every spirit, it is implied that we are not to reject all which claims to be the voice of the Holy Spirit; but should feel a confidence that here is in reality something divine. Hence he requires us to try the spirits, as a means of learning to distinguish the true from the false, what proceeds from a divine spirit and what from an undivine.

But though the Apostle has in view both errors, it is here his special object to warn against the delusions of false prophets, and to furnish a test by which these should be recognized. What he here says tallies with his previous warning against the seductions of false teachers. So also the mark, for distinguishing between the true and the false, is in both cases the same. As we have before seen, the preaching of Jesus, as the divine-human Saviour and theocratic King, is the centre of all. To acknowledge Jesus as the Christ, this in John's view is synonymous with acknowledging him as He who appeared in the flesh,--the Son of God manifested in the flesh,—the eternal Word in his humanization,—the eternal divine life-fountain letting itself down into human nature, and revealing itself in visible human form,—the truly divine and human, in harmonious union. In this is involved the rejection of that spectral sublimation of the Idea of Christ, already mentioned; of all which tended to separate the only-begotten Son of God from Him who has appeared in the flesh,—to obscure the unity between the divine and its manifestation in the flesh. That one divine fact, John makes the centre of all. It was, as we before remarked, the grand point of controversy in that age, as it is the one around which gather all the vital questions of the present time.

Here again there is no other test of true faith, no other law for christian union, than steadfast adherence to that one fundamental fact of the appearing of the Divine-human Redeemer. In all which proceeds from this belief, the influences of the divine Spirit should be acknowledged. Hence it follows, that provided faith in this one fundamental fact be the soul of the christian life, no minor differences of creed should be allowed to disturb christian unity; that mistakes and alloys of christian truth, which trench not on this one fundamental fact, should not hinder us from recognizing the divine stamp in him whose faith and profession have their root therein,—that the bonds of christian fellowship should not thereby be sundered or loosened. Steadfast adherence to this one foundation is the mark of being from God, of the spirit derived from God. Of course, he who adheres to it is in fellowship with God, is a partaker of the divine life, is animated and led by the Spirit of God; and from it will securely proceed the purification of the whole life, both in knowledge and practice. Thus the Saviour, comparing himself to the vine and believers to its branches (John xv. i ff.), says that these branches are to be more and more cleansed in order that they may bring forth the more fruit. That is: believers, abiding in fellowship with him, will thereby continue to partake of the divine life diffused from him through all his members; and being thus, in the divinely ordained and directed development of that life, more and more purified from the foreign and undivine which still obstructs it, will bring forth more and more of its fruits in their whole life and conduct. This then is applicable to all such, as through adherence to that one radical fact are branches of the true vine; and in them will be experienced, in their faith, views, and practice, the quickening energy of that divine life, which spreads from the vine-stock through all the branches, cleansing away all that is foreign.

But while John presents both the affirmative and negative aspect of this characteristic mark, it is here his special object to enforce the negative; to warn against all manifestations of that spirit which does not acknowledge this radical fact, but either denies or mutilates it. Whoever so taught was to be at once rejected. No other mark for the designation of the undivine, the antichristian, the false, should be needed for the believer. In all such manifestations the Apostle recognizes the spirit of Antichrist, whose culminating point, self-deification, was to precede the triumphant revelation of Christ in the last time. In all which denies or mutilates this one ground-fact, he bids us discern the tokens of that approaching Antichrist, whose spirit is thus shown to be already in the world and preparing for his full manifestation. He calls upon believers to watch for, and at once and totally to reject, all such manifestations; lest, being gradually drawn aside from the one foundation, and yielding themselves to the delusions of that antichristian spirit, they might at length come wholly under its dominion.

Having thus taught how to distinguish the revelations of the spirit which is from God, and of that which is not from God; the [Ch. iv. 4–6. Apostle holds out a solace for believers under their conflicts with the representatives of that ungodly spirit: "Ye are of God, little children, and have overcome them; because greater is he that is in you, than he that is in the world. They are of the world: therefore speak they of the world, and the world heareth them. We are of God: he that knoweth God, heareth us; he that is not of God, heareth not us. Hereby know we the spirit of truth, and the spirit of error."

Truth and Error have each their peculiar history of development. As in the continued development of christian truth, the Holy Spirit is ever revealing itself in the inward consciousness of the believer,—that Anointing spoken of by John; so does Error, proceeding side by side with this revelation, mingle therewith its own disturbing and adulterating influence,—rending single truths from their connection with the whole system of truth, and giving them the stamp of error. These are the two currents, proceeding from the ever operative spirit of Christ and from the spirit of the world; the latter mingling with the revelations of the former its own disturbing element, and imitating them with a deceptive outward seeming. If we compare the Johannic with the Pauline age, we shall perceive, notwithstanding the common foundation on which the church rests and the common participation of the Holy Spirit, that each period had its own peculiar contrarieties of truth and error. So must we in every period seek to distinguish, by the light of the divine word, what proceeds from the Spirit of Christ and what from an unchristian Spirit of the Age, disguising itself under the outward appearance of Christianity. As then, the higher conception of the essential nature of our Lord Jesus Christ's person, the truth respecting the incarnate Word, received a special development through John, and a wider diffusion of light on this important subject of christian knowledge distinguished the Johannic age; so also was this development of christian truth accompanied and corrupted by the one-sided conception of the anti-christian spirit. Every form of error has its time; and it is owing to the peculiarity of the time, that certain errors especially predominate. Those who still adhere to the whole simple truth, may be perplexed at seeing these errors increasing with seemingly irresistible power, and perverting many from the pure truth. This was the case in the age of John. As the peculiarity of Paul's time was the judaistic tendency, mingling law and gospel together, and seeking to bind Christianity within the limits of the old dispensation; so in the Johannic age, it was this corruption of the pure doctrine of the person of Christ. Then were brewing the elements, which burst forth unrestrained in the agitations of the second century. John seeks to inspire those, who might be thus perplexed, with courage and confidence. He begins with reminding them that they are born of God, that the Spirit of God dwells and works in them, is their teacher, uses them as his instruments to testify of the truth which he has made known to them. Hence, comparing them with the teachers of error, he draws the conclusion: "Ye have overcome them." He does not say, Ye shall overcome; but represents this as a fact already realized. Inasmuch, namely, as they are the children of God and are led by him, they have thereby in fact already overcome those who are animated by the opposite spirit. It is that victory of the divine over all that is undivine, which is inherent in the very relation of the one to the other, as represented by the Apostle himself: For a Greater, a Mightier, is he who dwells and works in you, than he that is working in the God-estranged world. God is mightier than the undivine spirit, and against him it cannot prevail. In the assurance of the victory of God's omnipotence, over all which arrays itself against him, they are assured that, virtually, they have already overcome their adversaries. This anticipated victory of christian truth over anti-christian error, requires indeed time for its realization. Their faith must outstrip the course of history; and in the assurance of faith, they even now possess the certain decision of the conflict. They may look into the future with cheerful confidence, since the final result is already present to their christian consciousness. The course of history only brings that to light, which is inherent in the very relation of the spirit, by which they are animated, to that which animates their adversaries. These adversaries they would never be able to overcome, had they not, by virtue of that inward relation, overcome them already. That they have already overcome,—this is the very thing which is to be made manifest. When Jesus bids his disciples be of good cheer, it is not because he will overcome the world, but because he has already overcome. (John xvi. 33.) By his re deeming life and sufferings he has, once for all, broken the might of Evil. Its kingdom is henceforth as if it were not. It may still prevail in many forms; yet this is but a passing show.

Christ, then, having once for all overcome the world, believers are the witnesses of this his victory, the instruments by which it is to be spread throughout the world. Now in this assurance of having overcome their adversaries, it is implied that they are themselves assured in the truth; that unmoved by these assaults they stand firm, while all around them wavers; that they confidently look forward to the full and final triumph of truth in the world. But it by no means follows, that their adversaries will be so overcome, as that they themselves shall be convinced of their errors and abandon them. For this is something which cannot be forced upon man from without. It depends upon his own free susceptibility, his own free submission to that spirit which animates the preachers of the truth. Hence they are not unsettled and perplexed, when, for the moment, error prevails to an extraordinary degree in the world. The Apostle shows, that this cannot be otherwise. There is, he says, no agreement possible between them and their adversaries. What belongs to the inner nature cannot but come forth to light; the spirit, the temper of mind, cannot but express itself. As is the tree, so is its fruit. Those false prophets, says the Apostle, belong in their spirit, their inward temper, to the world. Hence they teach what corresponds to this worldly spirit and temper; their earthliness of mind is mirrored in their teaching. So long as they are thus minded, it cannot be otherwise; and all attempts to convince them of their errors, will be repelled by the adverse tendency of their spirit.

By this he also explains, how it is that with so many they find admission. The world eagerly receives that which is kindred to its own spirit. Thus is brought to light the essential contrariety between those who are of God and those who are of the world. Those who in spirit and temper belong to the world have no susceptibility for the divine, and cannot receive what is made known by those who are animated by the Spirit of God, the teachers of divine truth. But, " he that knoweth God, heareth us." The knowing of God might here mean that general preparatory connection with him, of such as feel the drawing of the Father by which they are led to the Son, and thus show a susceptibility for the pure divine truth. But it may also apply to those who are already grounded in the christian faith, and remain true to the christian knowledge which they have received; and hence are able to recognize and to distinguish the genuine preachers of truth, by whom they are led on still farther in christian knowledge. The attitude thus taken, towards teachers of truth and teachers of error, becomes a sifting process among christians themselves; separating those who are truly born of God, who in spirit form the opposite to the world, and those who still belong to the world although externally united to the christian church. Thus, in this sifting process, is manifested the inherent essential contrariety between the spirit of truth and the spirit of error, between the undivine spirit and the spirit of God.

From belief, the Apostle again turns to its practical application to the life; and here again

he refers all back to Love, as the animating principle of the christian life. His language
Ch. iv. 7, 8.] rises with this view to a loftier tone: "Beloved, let us love one another: for love is of God; and every one that loveth is born of God, and knoweth God. He that loveth not, knoweth not God; for God is love."

This is not a command to love. It is not the Apostle's aim to bring before believers new motives to mutual love. His aim is this: to show them what must necessarily follow from a certain presupposed fact; the necessary mark of a certain existing state; the effect which cannot fail when the cause from which it proceeds is actually present. He would produce in them the conviction, that just so certainly as they are the children of God, as life from God exists in them; so certainly must this reveal itself in mutual love. The want of this love would show that they were not children of God,—that life from God was not in them. The proof he adduces, that as children of God they must love one another, is this: love is from God, and therefore every one who loves is born of God. Love is here represented as something divine, something which points back to the eternal fountain of love in God, a ray of divine life. It is love which constitutes the absolute opposite to the life, to the stand-point, of the natural man; to that which is supreme in him, when his whole nature has completely developed and expressed itself. The natural man makes Self the centre and end of all. Love impels man to go beyond self, to renounce self; to make the interests of others his own, to share with them all that he has, to give himself to them, to live for them.

Where now something of this impulse is present in the soul, man thereby makes himself known as the image of God; it is a mark of that higher life which proceeds from God. Single instances of such love may be found, we admit, even where that life from God which John describes does not yet exist, where the birth from God has not yet taken place. Still, even these bear witness of a power which is foreign to the natural man as such,—a ray from the primeval Source, a mark of divine lineage. As such we cannot but recognize them, whether derived from the new divine life introduced by Christ into the world, from the general influence of society and education,—through which many divine impressions from Christ may have been received, by such as have never yet opened their hearts to his influence,—or whether we find them existing apart from all connection with Christianity. In either case, we cannot but discern in them the features of that image of God, which, though obscured by sin, still gleams out through darkness; the marks of that original divine lineage, of that general connection with the God in whom we live and move and have our being.

In this passage, however, the apostle is not speaking of such emotions, breaking forth singly in opposition to the prevailing selfishness; but of a state, wherein this love is the governing principle of life. This is what he designates as the necessary mark of children of God, since love is from God; and hence, where this love is the ruling and animating principle, it is evidence that its possessor has this principle from God, is born of God. We have often observed, that in the Apostle's view all true knowledge of God proceeds from the life, the fellowship of life with God. So also here, "being born of God," and "knowing God," are classed together. To the affirmative declaration he immediately subjoins the negative, drawn from the same premises; viz. that he who loves not is far from knowing God, from being in union with him. He had before said, that love is from God; thereby referring to him as the primal source of all love. But he now goes farther and says: God is love. Love is his essential nature; God and Love are coincident terms. Love absolutely, whose essential nature is to love, whence therefore all love proceeds, is the designation of God himself.

It is a thought full of meaning, which the Apostle here expresses. He indicates thereby, that Love is the clearest embodiment which we can vision to ourselves of the incomprehensible God. It is personal spirit only that is capable of love. To an impersonal existence love cannot be ascribed; unless something else is understood by the name, than what it is adapted to express. When God is represented as Love, we are led thereby to regard him as the Being, from whose nature it is inseparable to reveal and to impart himself, to diffuse beyond himself the bliss which he enjoys. Inasmuch as he is himself the sum of all excellence, the highest good, he must first be himself the object of his love. Thereby begat he the all-perfect likeness of himself, the only-begotten Son, who is the object of his absolute love.

Such is the import of Christ's own language, in his prayer as High Priest of his people. (John xvii. 24.) Knowing himself to be one with that Eternal Effluence of the divine glory; and feeling himself called as man to a share in that glory, because of the Eternal Word dwelling in and animating him; he speaks in that prayer of the glory which the Father's love had bestowed upon him, before the foundation of the world. This love moved him, for the purpose of revealing and imparting himself, to bring into existence the whole creation; in which every being is by itself a revelation of God as Love, while each enjoys its own appropriate measure of happiness. Hence too he created, as the aim and end of all creation beside, rational beings for whose sake he would thus reveal himself; who were themselves adapted in their nature to receive this his revelation from without, to become partakers of his self-communication, to enter into fellowship with him, to receive into themselves his image, and to reflect it in their conduct. Love moved him, when man had estranged himself from this his highest destiny, to send the dearest object of his love, the only-begotten Son himself, to appear in human nature; and to bestow him in whom he thus appeared, wholly upon man. He too, as being the all-perfect image of him in whom God had from eternity mirrored himself, now becomes the absolute object of his love in humanity; that love which extends itself from him who is the eternal Effluence of the divine glory, upon him who is the Effluence of that glory in time and in humanity. He is therefore called, absolutely, the beloved Son of the Father,—He in whom the Father is well-pleased. This can be said of no other; since only that which perfectly presents to the Father his own image, that wherein he beholds himself, can be absolutely the object of his complacency. And from him the love of God extends itself to all who stand in fellowship with him, who reflect his image as it is more and more actualized in them, and who to the Father's all-foreseeing eye appear as already bearing his image, as entirely one with him. In him we have the perfect revelation of God as Love; in his whole manifestation, in his life and death, we learn to know God as Love.

To the revelation thus made in humanity, of God as Love, the Apostle then refers in the succeeding words. "In this was [Ch. iv. 9–10 manifested the love of God towards us, because that God sent his only-begotten Son into the world, that we might live through him. Herein is love, not that we loved God, but that he loved us, and sent his Son to be the propitiation [reconciliation] for our sins."

Here, overlooking all else, John fixes his eye upon that highest fact, in which the love of God reveals itself most gloriously; his love toward those, who after being by this love made capable of its highest communications, being created in its image, had rendered themselves unworthy of it. To a world of sin, thus alienated from the God of love, he gave that highest gift,—Him who is called, as no other can be, the Son of God,—that through him he might bestow on the sinful race of man that high destiny for which it was created, and which it had lost through its own guilt; to impart to the dead in sin that true blissful life, which should endure forever. In this fact, says John, we perceive the true nature of love. It was not our love to God, that called forth a return of love in him. His own love moved him to that highest proof of love, to send his Son into the world, that those who were alienated from him by sin, and through sin arrayed against him the Holy One, might be rescued from this state of ruin,—to send him to be the reconciliation for our sins. From these words it is evident, that we are not so to conceive of this reconciliation, as if God the hater of men as sinners had now, at this particular time, become reconciled to them through Christ. On the contrary, the work of reconciliation presupposes that love in God, which moved him to adopt this plan, to be actualized at an appointed period; the eternal love of God as the ground, not the result, of this reconciliation. Hence also, the New Testament never speaks of a reconciliation of God with man, but only of a reconciliation of man with God; indicating that God, as love, ever desires to impart himself to man, that the hindrance is in man himself. To those who are estranged from God by sin, he must, from the relation which they consciously hold to him, appear as the angry Judge, whose just vengeance they have incurred. Since then, no man was capable of raising himself out of himself into another relation to God, the hindrance must first be removed by God himself; and the medium, through which this was effected, is called by John the reconciliation for sin, the sin-offering for man.

It is plain, therefore, that the changed relation to God of which man becomes conscious, presupposes a divine act independent of himself, whereby this has been made possible. To this also pointed the sin-offering in the Old Testament, to which John seems to allude. It was intended to awaken in the human spirit the conviction, that no man is of himself able to close that gulf, which separates the sinner from God. As God is love, so also is He holiness; as is taught by John when he says, that God is Light, excluding all darkness, —meaning that he is Holiness, excluding all evil. As The Holy, he reveals himself in a moral government of the world corresponding to his holiness. This requires a perfect actualization of the holy law by man; only on this condition, can the holy God impart himself to humanity in the revelations of his love, can come into fellowship with it, can become to it the fountain of bliss, of eternal life. But to this stands opposed the universal prevalence of sin in man. Hence Christ, the Holy, must perform for all what they cannot themselves perform; must restore harmony in God's moral government, by himself satisfying its demands on man. In the laws of this moral government, the connection of sin with misery as the punishment of sin, was forever fixed. Christ as man, in actualizing the holy law, submitted himself to its conditions in this respect also,—to this connection of sin and misery, which weighed down the human race. In his suffering, he took upon himself their guilt and made it his own; his all-devoting love entered into the whole feeling of man's guilt and wretchedness; as expressed in that cry, when, in the fulness of his sympathy for humanity, he felt himself one with it in its load of guilt: My God, my God, why hast thou forsaken me! All which men had to bear he took upon himself, and in his holy life and sufferings, imparted to them all that was his. This it is which constitutes the turning point in the relation of man to God; that whereby sin ceases to be the separating wall between man and God,—the reconciliation (expiation) for sin, as it is termed by the Apostle. Herein we perceive the true nature of holy love.

Having thus spoken of the revelation of God's love in the reconciliation effected by Christ, the Apostle again makes a per- [Ch. iv. 11.

sonal appeal to believers: "Beloved, if God so loved us, we ought also to love one another." Such love in God, the Apostle would say, must beget in those who have experienced it a return of love. But this love, enkindled by the revelation of the redeeming love of God, must manifest itself in mutual love, on the part of those who are conscious of being objects of God's love, of having experienced it in themselves. From the consciousness of this love of God to believers, must necessarily spring mutual love towards each other. It is one holy flame of love, passing over from God to man, and extending itself to their mutual relation to one another.

In connection with the declaration that God is himself love, the Apostle sets forth the

Ch. iv. 12.]

high import of love as the bond of fellowship between God and man: "No man hath seen God at any time. If we love one another, God dwelleth in us, and his love is perfected in us." In the words, "no one hath seen God," must be contained the reason, why it is only through love we can be certain of his dwelling in us. "Us," we may regard as meaning the whole body of the church. "Seeing," we may first take in the sense of bodily sight. We become conscious of the presence of a visible being, by seeing him among us. But the invisible God cannot be so united with us. He cannot dwell visibly among us; there can be no visible manifestation of deity, such as was expected by the Jews and was once desired by Philip. (John xiv. 8.) What John would say, therefore, is this: No one has ever seen God by the bodily sense; a denial which, in John's mode of expression, involves the assertion that he cannot thus be seen.

It follows, therefore, that the church can be united to the invisible God only by a spiritual bond; and only thereby can have the assurance that he abides with and in them, that he dwells in continued fellowship with them. And this spiritual bond is Love. As God is love itself, and all love radiates from him; so must the union of the church with him be manifested hereby, that he works in them as the spirit of love, that Love rules in them as the animating principle.

If, however, we compare other expressions of John, it becomes a question whether the word "seeing" is to be taken here in the sense of bodily sight. He is accustomed, as we observed above, to express by the original Greek word, likewise a spiritual beholding, perfect, immediate knowledge.

In this sense he says (John i. 18), "No man hath seen God at any time; the only-begotten Son, who is in the bosom of the Father, he hath declared him." If now we take the word "see" as it is plainly used in this passage, it involves still more than what we have said: viz. that no man has ever had an immediate perception of God, has ever attained to perfect knowledge of him, neither can he thus be known by men on earth. We cannot therefore be assured of union with him, by his having become to us an object of perfect knowledge. Did it depend on that, he would remain forever beyond our reach. The incomprehensible Essence, no one has known or can know. But as God is love, we are assured of union with him and of his dwelling in us, by his abiding self-revelation among us as love; through love we abide in union with him who is love. In love we have his true essence, so far as it can be the object of perception to man on earth. Union with God through love precedes that perfect vision of God, promised us for the life which is eternal. In this union with God through love, we have already more than we are able to develop in the form of knowledge.

Herein, then, is contained the weighty truth:

that only through love we can become conscious of God, can be convinced of the reality of his being and nature,—love being in itself the reflection and the product of his nature. And hence the more a man has shut his heart against love, the more he is sunk in selfishness, the less can he know of God. But genuine love to God, that which is enkindled by the revelation of God's love to believers, and has God for its source, can only attest itself as such by the mutual love of believers for each other, since this is its necessary working and effect.

That God, through his indwelling and vitalizing love, abides in union with believers, means the same as that his Spirit dwells in them: [Ch. iv. 13. for his Spirit, imparted to believers through Christ, is itself the fountain of love which can originate only in God, the Spirit which dwells and works in God himself as love. They cannot be conscious of a fellowship of spirit with him, if love, the mark of that spirit, shows not its living agency among them. Hence the Apostle appeals to their experience of the influences of the Spirit imparted by God,—the token and pledge, that as they continue to surrender themselves to fellowship with God, God likewise abides in inseparable fellowship with them. "Hereby know we that we dwell in him and he in us, because he hath given us of his Spirit."

He now returns to that, which he ever contemplates as the ground of the whole Chris-
Ch. iv. 14–16.]
tian life and of salvation, the ground of the whole church and of all its divine inward experiences, since upon this depends all and with this is given all,—the testimony respecting the Son of God, whom the Father has sent as the Saviour of the world. Of this he bears testimony, with the confident assurance of an eye-witness: "And we have seen and do testify, that the Father sent the Son to be the Saviour of the world." But with those who had been so long acquainted with Christianity, he needed not to appeal merely to his own sight and experience. They were not to be dependent upon his personal testimony. The fact, to which he bore witness, must long since have fully attested itself, in their own conscious experience of fellowship with God attained thereby. But he would, again and again, impress it upon their hearts, that firm adherence to this fact must ever be the ground of all true fellowship with God. For faith he then substitutes confession;

since faith must approve itself by an open confession of the Son of God, without fear or shame, in opposition to the world which ignores him and hates his followers. "Whosoever shall confess that Jesus is the Son of God, God dwelleth in him, and he in God." Assuming in christians this fellowship with God, which is the fruit of true adherence to faith in Jesus as the Son of God, he speaks not merely from his own personal experience, but as if uttering the experience of all: "And we have known and believed the love that God hath to us. God is love; and he that dwelleth in love, dwelleth in God, and God in him." The Apostle recognizes a reciprocal relation between knowledge and faith. The divine fact, which is the object of faith, must be in a certain manner known in order to be believed. But it is by receiving through faith this divine fact into the heart and making it properly our own, that we first become truly acquainted, in the experiences of the inner life, with the object of faith; and therefrom develops itself the true knowledge of that object, not as something external to the spirit, but as being through this inward experience a part of itself. In the spirit enlightened by faith, knowledge is developed; and faith, through the knowledge derived from this inward experience, receives in turn a higher import. We believe in the love of God toward us, because we know it by this inward experience. This is the kind of knowledge here meant. But in thus knowing God's love for us, we come to know God himself; and in that way in which he can most perfectly be known, for his nature is love.

Abiding in love is represented by the Apostle, as the condition and the token of abiding in fellowship with God. By love he doubtless means, as the connection shows, primarily the love of God as revealing itself in Christ the Saviour of the world, and making itself felt in the hearts of believers; and as then, by the light of faith becoming an object of knowledge. They attain to a conscious knowledge of that which is their life-element. But their hearts cannot be filled with this overflowing love of God, without producing in return that love to God, and to the brethren, which has its root therein.

The Apostle then characterizes the habitual temper of mind, which exists where
Ch. iv. 17, 18.] this abiding in the love of God has

reached its maturity. "Herein is our love made perfect, that we may have boldness [joyfulness] in the day of judgment; because as he is, so are we in this world. There is no fear in love; but perfect love casteth out fear: because fear hath torment. He that feareth, is not made perfect in love." This fellowship of life with God has for its fruit, a confidence in him, undisturbed by fear. By the word which Luther here translates "joyfulness" is indicated such a relation to another, as allows us to walk with him in free familiar converse, to tell him without reserve all that is in our hearts, to turn to him in all our concerns with perfect confidence. Such a state of joyful assured confidence, disturbed by no fear no apprehension, in which under all circumstances and necessities we turn to God, is the one here indicated. Particularly is excluded fear in view of a future judgment of the holy God, before whom no sin can find allowance. To him who stands in this relation to God, the day of judgment is indeed ever present; and it is no false or light-minded security by which he is raised above it. But that final decision has for him no such terrors, as for those who have in God a stern judge to fear; who feel themselves estranged from him by sin, and are therefore conscious of the wrath of God. He looks towards that day with joyful confidence, for he knows that he has no judgment to fear; that through the love of God revealed to him in Christ, of which he has the assurance in his inner being, he is exempt from judgment. True, he is conscious of still inhering sin. He has a sharper eye to detect its presence, than those who have made less advancement in the development of the christian life. But even sin has for him lost its sting. He knows that God has forgiven him; and as he feels and knows himself to be united through love with the God who is love, he is certain also that this still inhering sin can no longer separate him from God; and that God, through the Spirit which he has given him, will purify him more and more, will carry on the begun work to its completion. It is not the believer's own worthiness, or perfectness, which John regards as the ground of this confidence. Were that the foundation of his trust, it would rest on a very frail support, soon betraying its worthlessness under the temptations and conflicts of the earthly life. It has an immovable foundation,—the revelation of the love of God in

Christ, through which the believer knows himself to be one with Christ. Christ is indeed in heaven, and the believer still belongs outwardly to earth. Yet, through his oneness with Christ, who is to him as present as if still living on earth, he is conscious that he stands in the same relation to God as Christ himself; that, belonging to Christ as a member of his body, he can no more be separated from God than Christ himself; that in him he has become the object of divine love, divine complacency. And thus, in Christ's relation to God, he has the pledge of his own. This is the immovable ground of his confidence.

The Apostle here contrasts two religious states. The one is this fellowship of love, of sonship to God which has its root in Christ; when as a child of God, man is conscious of holding the same relation to him, which Christ as Son bears to the Father. In the other, God is viewed as the stern judge, the object of fear; the apprehension of divine punishment weighs down the spirit. So elsewhere in the New Testament, the filial relation to God and the slavish relation are contrasted with each other. It is true, indeed, that where this fellowship of love has already commenced, doubts and apprehensions, arising from the former slavish relation, may still mingle in it their disturbing influence. But the Apostle points out a stage of the christian life so high, where love has so gained the preponderance, that fear is wholly banished. No terrors of impending punishment disturb the joyful confidence in God. He would, indeed, by no means banish that holy awe, which impels him who lives in the consciousness of still inhering sin, to watch continually over himself, to shun everything which might mar his fellowship with God. He will be led to do this, by the power of that very love in which his life has its root; and in this there is no "torment," at that high stage of the christian life, where all is possible to Love.

In order to impress on christians the obligation of brotherly-love, John again reminds them, that through God's love to them their own love was first enkindled; and then goes on to show, that in love to God is necessarily involved love to the brethren. "We love him because he first loved us. If a man say, I love God, and hateth his brother, he is a liar: for he that loveth not his brother whom he hath seen, how can he love God whom he hath not seen?"

Ch. iv. 19, 20.]

The appeal thus founded on that conscious christian fellowship, to which both he and his readers have been admitted, presupposes this love to God as something possessed in common, originating as it does in their common experience of God's redeeming love. But so certainly as this love exists among them, will it reveal itself as such in its effects. It is easy to say, I love God; the point is, that this love should manifest itself by its unmistakable signs in the life. The witness to this presence of God's love in men, is Brotherly-love. He who says he loves God, and yet hates his brother, is called a liar, since his professions are proved by his acts to be lies; for in John's view, hatred of one's brother and love to God mutually exclude each other. We must here remember, that with John there is nothing intermediate betwen love and hate; it is either love to the brother, or hatred of the brother. With him therefore, "to hate the brother," and "not to love," are one and the same; since where love is wanting, the selfish disposition already contains the germ of hate.

But is it not strange that John should ask: How can he who loves not the visible brother, love the invisible God? For he always regards love to God as the primary, and love to the brother as the derived affection; self-sacrificing brotherly-love as originating in love to God, that alone being able to overcome the selfish principle in man. But if from the cause, we may deduce its necessary and spontaneous effect; so on the other hand, from the effect we may reason back to the cause, and regard the effect as evidence of the cause. Love to God is in itself an invisible act, seen only by him who looks upon the heart; but the effects of this love, as they appear outwardly, are seen by man. Whether there is true love to God must be determined, therefore, by the presence or absence of Brotherly-love. Hence John's conclusion: How can I believe that he truly loves God, in whom I see not the visible evidence of this love? The visible here bears witness of the want of the invisible. And moreover, man as a creature of sense, is more readily affected by the visible than by the invisible. If we conceive of love as a capacity inherent in the God-related nature of man, and pointing back to its primal Source in God who is Love; yet, for this capacity to raise itself to the Invisible One, more is required than to awaken it into action through the impression made by his visible image in man. How is the invisible object of love to exert an influence upon him, whom the visible leaves unaffected?

Such being the necessary connection between these two relations of love, the Apostle adds: "And this commandment have we from him, That he who loveth God, love his brother also. Whosoever believeth that Jesus is the Christ, is born of God: and every one that loveth him that begat, loveth him also that is begotten of him." [Ch. iv. 21, v. 1.

This necessary connection between love to God and Brotherly-love, John deduces from their common sonship to God, from the equal relation of all to God, and their inward relationship of life to one another. He begins with faith,—faith in its true import. By faith he understands, not what James calls a dead faith. It is not the mere admission of certain historical facts, as one believes any historical narration of the past, without being at all affected thereby in his inner life. It is not the tenacious adherence to certain articles of faith, received into the understanding and memory as a matter of custom; in regard to which the liability to doubt is less, the less there is felt of a living interest in them, the less their influence penetrates below the mere surface of the spirit. Faith, in the Johannic sense, presupposes all that is in volved in the acknowledgment of Jesus as the Christ, in knowing him for ourselves as such. It implies the recognition of the Crucified One, as Sovereign in the kingdom of God, as Redeemer from sin. There is, therefore, implied that deep conviction of sin and longing for deliverance from it, that deep feeling of the necessity of redemption, without which faith in the Redeemer is not possible. There is implied faith in his resurrection, as the divine attestation that Jesus the Crucified is the Redeemer of sinful man, and Sovereign in the kingdom of God; in his ascension to heaven, by virtue of that glorified divine life, exempt from the conditions of mortality, to which he has attained; in his continued fellowship, in this his glorified superearthly state, with believers on earth. In this faith there is presupposed true spiritual fellowship with Christ. For faith is nothing else than that conviction, which, having passed through every stage, from the sense of sin to the acknowledgment of Jesus in every revealed relation, embraces in itself the sum of all; the act whereby the soul, renouncing itself, and joyfully accepting the offered union with this Jesus as its Redeemer and Lord, gives itself wholly away to him, that it may belong no more to itself but to him alone. Hence, of every one who believes in this sense, John says, that he is BORN OF GOD. This he regards as something which cannot proceed from the life inherent in the spirit itself; which can only be the result of a divine power entering the heart, a work of God in man, a divine fact. Where this has taken place, there must exist a divine life; for it is that whereby the being, hitherto wholly centred in himself and sunk in earthliness, receives a new existence whose fountain and root is in God, becomes in the true sense a new man born of God. As man, by natural birth, enters the world and takes his place among the beings who belong to it; so by this fact is he raised to a wholly new, a higher existence. As by natural descent, the son derives from his father a being like his own and reflects his image; so the believer, by virtue of this new spiritual birth from God, by virtue of this new divine life which he has in common with God his Father, is called a son of God. And thus he reflects, by virtue of this divine life, the Father from whom it proceeds. Hence John says that he who loves God, from whom this divine life is derived, must, on the ground of this same descent, this relationship and likeness, love him also who is born of God, in whom exists this same divine life. In love to the Source of the divine life, is necessarily included love to all who are partakers with us in this life. All who are united in this fellowship as children of God, must for that reason feel drawn towards each other, must understand and love each other, as in no other relation among men.

"By this we know that we love the children of God, when we love God, and keep his [Ch. v. 2, 3.] commandments. For this is the love of God, that we keep his commandments." As love to God must manifest itself in love to the brethren, so must it also in obedience to the divine commands. All these are, indeed, summed up by John in the one command whose requirement is love, which is the fulfilment of all.

He then shows what it is which imparts to believers strength to fulfil all these com- [Ch. v. 3–5.] mands. "And his commandments are not grievous [difficult]. For whatsoever is born of God, overcometh the world; and this is the victory that overcometh the world, even our faith. Who is he that overcometh the world, but he that believeth that Jesus is the Son of God?"

These are the highest of all commands, those instituted by Christ himself, and by him alone perfectly fulfilled; the commands developed by him in the Sermon on the Mount, the ground-traits of an all-transcending holiness, such as has been reached by no system of human ethics, and before which every human spirit must bow in deep humility. And yet we hear John saying, that these commands are not difficult. But as the highest of all moral requirements, they should be the most difficult of all. How then are we to understand it, when John says that these commands are not difficult? He must himself have learned by experience, that they are not hard to obey. Not in the commands themselves, not in their relation to other moral commands, must lie the ground of his assertion; but in the changed position of man towards the divine law. What was once difficult, nay impossible; this has now, by virtue of his moral transformation, become easy. He himself assigns as the reason, that all which is born of God overcomes the world. From the fact then, that believers have received strength to overcome the world, he deduces the consequence that these commands are no longer difficult for them, difficult as they may be for him who has not received that strength. We can therefore infer from this, what is requisite for fulfilling these commands, which is the victory over the world. Only in conflict with the world can they be fulfilled. What makes their fulfilment difficult to man, is the entanglement of the spirit in the world; the power of the world over the spirit, the worldly bias, the earthliness of spirit, whereby is stifled the higher God-related nature of man, which accords with the divine law and for which that law exists. The power of the world, is the power of all that is not of God. To him whose spirit is ruled by the world, who feels himself drawn to the world and finds in it his highest good, to him the commands of God appear difficult. Since now, in the strength of that divine life which believers have received the power is given which overcomes the world John says that all which is born of God overcomes the world; and since, through this world-conquer-ing power, all hindrances to the fulfilment of the commands are easily overcome, he says that for believers these commands are not difficult. They possess the power whereby the difficult is made easy. So Christ invites to himself those who feel weighed down, who cannot breathe freely, by reason of the burden of the Law, saying: "My yoke is easy and my burden is light;" made light by fellowship with him, by the power which he imparts.

John then shows what it is, by which believers are freed from the power of the world, transformed from children of the world to children of God, made partakers of the divine life, and thus enabled to overcome the world. This is faith in Jesus as the Son of God. It is worthy of note that he does not say: faith is that whereby we attain the victory over the world; nor, faith is that which will overcome the world. He says: faith is itself the victory, which has overcome the world. In these words lies a deeper meaning, whose full import we must endeavor to unfold.

Faith is itself a victory already achieved over the world; it has its being only as a victory attained in conflict with the world. For when the divine drawing in the heart of man, the drawing of the Father to the Son, incites him to the exercise of faith; the whole world then rises against him, to hinder him from attaining faith. What in man is of the world and is in union with the world, resists the incipient faith. Hence the manifold counter-influences, which make it at first so hard to believe. Hence the power of those doubts, which withstand faith. Thus faith itself is a victory over the world. And having thus come into being through victory over the world, having once for all overcome the world; in it there resides the divine power, against which the world can effect nothing. Faith, once for all, has overcome the world; and therein is given the victory which in all succeeding conflicts with the world, attests itself by the fulfilment of the divine commands. The whole subsequent christian life, if it holds fast the faith in its quiet healthy process of development, is nothing else than a continuation of the victory over the world once attained in faith. As Christ, in the words already quoted, says not that he WILL but that he HAS overcome the world (John xvi. 33), and bids believers rejoice in this assurance; so faith, by virtue of fellowship with

Christ, shares in this his victory over the world. Since now there exists no other power through which the world can be overcome, it necessarily follows, that only he overcomes the world, who believes that Jesus is the Son of God.

From this we learn the important lesson, that all true reformation of the world can proceed only from this faith, from the energy of the divine life residing therein. We cannot, therefore, but be distrustful of all attempts to cure the evils of the world, which build not upon this one foundation. Even though they may accomplish many single reforms, yet a radical cure of the disease is not to be effected by such means. For that which is everywhere the obstacle to the fulfilment of the divine commands,—the world, which stands opposed to all that is of God,—that remains unweakened in its strength, the fountain whence all evil continually springs anew. Though at single points the world seems to be overcome, it avails nothing. The world may be overcome by the world, and its power remain as before; it has but assumed another form. The conquest of the world, as a whole, can be achieved only through faith in Jesus as the Son of God, only through the might of his Spirit; and this must first be effected before the world can truly be overcome in all its single forms of evil. So Christ himself represents all attempts to extirpate evil from humanity and from the individual man as futile, if the inward might of evil be not first broken by the power of the mightier, which is Christ,—by the finger of God. (Luke xi. 20, comp. Matt. xii. 28.) Hence he says of such attempts to subdue and banish evil otherwise than by his Spirit, that though apparently producing by other agencies effects similar to those of the Gospel, they are yet not for him but against him. So far from laboring with him, in the one divine work of founding the kingdom of God in its unity among men, their tendency is to lead men away from this unity, away from the kingdom of God. This is the most corrupting of all delusions, under the most dangerous of all disguises; professing, by apparently similar results which proceed from another spirit, to supply the place of that work which can be effected only by Christianity.

John then adduces three tokens, by which Jesus as the Son of God has revealed himself; Ch. v. 6–8.] indicating at the same time three combined relations, in which he presents himself to the christian consciousness, as the One incarnate Son of God. "This is he who came by water and blood, Jesus the Christ; not in water only, but in water and blood. And it is the Spirit which beareth witness, for the Spirit is the truth. For there are three that bear witness: the Spirit, and the water, and the blood; and the three have reference to the One."*

While thus presenting the three tokens by which Jesus as the Son of God has revealed himself, it is at the same time his object to combat those, who (like that Cerinthus and others of whom we have spoken in the Introduction) did not rightly recognize the connection of the divine and human in the person of Christ, the unity of his divine-human person, of his life and of his work,—rending asunder that in him which should be conceived of as one. From the heavenly Christ, who descended from the higher spirit-world and was the true redeeming Spirit, they separated Jesus, who in their view was a mere man, and with whom as man this higher Spirit connected itself at his baptism. The dove, which then descended upon him, they re-

* As translated by Neander.—*Tr.*

garded as a symbol or embodiment of this Spirit. Thenceforth this Spirit, through the man Jesus revealed the hidden God and announced divine truth; it bestowed on him the power of working miracles; but before his Suffering, it forsook him and withdrew again into its own higher regions. To them also, as to the Jews, The Crucified continued to be an offence. They could not understand the mystery of his sufferings; suffering had, in their conception, no place in the work of redemption. They could acknowledge a divinely teaching, a divinely working, but not a suffering Christ. To them, the life of Christ was not a divine-human life from its very beginning. On the contrary, the Divine, whereby Jesus was to be distinguished from all other messengers of God, had at that definite point of time suddenly taken up its temporary abode in him, and had again in a like manner departed from him. The Divine, in the servant-form of the incarnate Son, from his birth to the crowning point of self-abasement in his suffering,—the crowning point also of his moral glory,—was something which they could not comprehend. They sundered the high from the low, instead of recognizing the truly high in the low.

In opposition to such, John now declares Jesus to be the Christ, as revealed not merely in water at his baptism, but also in his Suffering. By water we must not here understand, as some have done, the baptism instituted by him. It is the baptism to which he himself submitted; and at which the dignity of Jesus, as the Son of God, shone forth in the manner described by John in his Gospel. Since the blood has immediate reference to the person of Jesus, being the designation of his Suffering; the water also must designate something which has a personal reference to himself, viz. his baptism. Accordingly, there is here set forth the one reference of his baptism and his Suffering,—that it was the same Jesus, who in his baptism and in his Suffering manifested himself as the Son of God, the Christ. Both must combine in order to make him known as the Son of God; both belonged to his redemption-work.

Still a third witness, a third token by which Jesus reveals himself as the Son of God, is introduced by John; the witness of the Spirit, the Spirit absolutely, the divine or holy Spirit.

In accordance with the relation of the three ideas to each other,—as by the water we must understand something precedent to his Suffering, and by the blood the Suffering which followed his baptism,—so by the Spirit's witness must be understood something subsequent to both. It must be, therefore, those manifestations of the Holy Spirit, which followed the triumphant ascension of the suffering Christ; that continued working of this Spirit, which since its first outpouring has testified, wherever the Gospel is preached, of Jesus as the Son of God; that divine Witness, to which Jesus himself appeals in those last discourses recorded by John. Upon this testimony John lays special stress. It was indeed the witness which must be added to the two other tokens, in order that the Jesus who was baptized and had suffered, might be accredited, in a manner perceptible to all, as the Son of God. Hence he emphatically adds: "The Spirit is the truth." Truth itself, as revealed in the divine workings of the Spirit of God, of him who is The True,—this cannot lie. And these three bear witness. The Spirit (now placed first by John, since by it the two other witnesses are confirmed) the Water, and the Blood, all have reference to one and the same object, and all concur in revealing and accrediting Jesus as the Son of God.

The reading, followed in the above translation and explanation, must certainly be regarded as the true one. It has the authority of the oldest manuscripts in its favor, while the commonly received reading has grown out of explanatory additions to the text. It is also favored by the connection, in which these additions appear as something wholly foreign and discordant; for in this connection, the writer is concerned only with facts occurring on the earth, as signs and evidences that Jesus has revealed himself as the Son of God,—not with witnesses in heaven. Such a reference to the latter would have wholly distracted the reader's attention, from that which it was the sole object of John to set forth in this passage.

In our own age, as already remarked in the Introduction, are repeated those same tendencies, by which are sundered the divine and human in the person of Christ, and the one is exalted at the expense of the other. The divine-human Christ, as manifested from the beginning, in the words of eternal life uttered by him as a public teacher after his baptism, in his miracles, and in his sufferings, is not recognized in his undivided unity. To such tendencies, wherever found, these words of the Apostle are applicable. They apply also to the case of those, who do not recognize as actually true and real the harmonious image of this Christ presented in the Gospel record, and convert the true historical Christ into a vague form of mist. If his baptism and his sufferings are events of the past (though in their import and influence still making themselves ever present) yet it is otherwise with the witness of the Spirit. This is something belonging not merely to the past. True, in the wonderful period when John wrote this, it was manifested in an extraordinary manner. Yet in that unceasing, connected agency with which it continues to work through all time, it still remains a present witness for ourselves. The church being the perpetual organ for the operations of the Spirit, the progress of its history has been continually adding, even down to our own time, a succession of new witnesses to those of the past, through which we as christians live in connection with that witness of the Spirit in the apostolic age. The more widely Christianity diffuses itself among the savage races of humanity; the more various the modes in which it reveals its all-subduing all-transforming power, and the forms which it calls into being from the moral putrescence of human life; the more often it goes forth victorious from the conflict with superstition and unbelief, to new and still more glorious conquests; so much the more is revealed the witness of this Spirit, which is the Truth. If the same Spirit, which then imparted to the preachers of the Gospel the power to testify of Christ through their word, their life, and their blood, is now working through them in a greater number of nations than at any period since the apostolic; if through this Spirit, martyrs have again been raised up among heathen nations to seal their faith with their blood, as seen of late in the Isle of Madagascar; this is but the continued and renewed witness of that Spirit. What is now being wrought, through foreign and domestic missions, is part of that same witness, and connects itself with all which had been testified by that Spirit, and which it continued to testify, when these words were written. And on this will we ever take our stand, in opposition to those who seek to veil the historical Christ in a cloud of mist: that the Spirit, which is the Truth, testifies of him whose image they would obscure, of that Jesus who, in water and in blood, revealed himself as the Son of God.

He then shows how much is involved in this divine witness, in the emphatic words: "If we receive the witness of men, the witness of God is greater: for this is the witness of God, which he hath testified of his Son."

Ch. v. 9.]

That which he has called the witness of the Spirit, is here designated as testimony given by God himself; and this divine witness is contrasted with all human testimony, which is ever liable to mislead. If we receive anything as true, upon the testimony of men whom we have reason to believe, how can we but follow this unerring witness of God? So is this continuous divine witness, extending through all times, something more reliable than human testimony. This factual witness of God himself, everywhere seen in the practical workings of the Gospel, shows us the same image of his Son delineated in the Gospel narrative, and thus attests it to be true, beyond all reach of doubt. It testifies of the same Christ mirrored in the Gospel history. It is, as John says, the Father's witness of the Son. This, in the preceding passage, had been represented as belonging to the present. It is now spoken of as something completed, the witness which the Father has already given of the Son. Looking back upon the past, on these operations of the Spirit as a whole, he regards them as a testimony already closed. But as extending into his own time, they are a present witness. And thus we also, from the stand-point of our own age, may appeal to it as something at once past and present.

The Apostle then shows that it depends on man himself, to receive or to reject this testimony; and that when received, it is necessarily converted from an outward to an inward witness. "He that believeth on the Son of God, hath the witness in himself: he that believeth not God, hath made him a liar, because he believeth not the record that God gave of his Son." [Ch. v. 10.

For him, who through that outward witness of the Spirit has been led to believe on the Son of God, it is no longer mere outward testimony. It has become a part of his own inner life. What God first testified to him from without, is now by means of his faith testified inwardly to his own living consciousness. He bears the divine witness in himself. It is the Spirit's testimony in his heart. Through his own inward experience of the divine life is it certain to him, that Jesus is the Son of God.

But he who believes not God in his testimony of his Son, has thereby made him a liar. By this very unbelief, he practically declares those divine facts, which testify of the Son of God, to be false witnesses, and in effect makes God a liar. If through the operations of his Spirit God thus testifies of his Son, and yet he is not received as the Son of God; what is this but saying, that God contradicts himself, while thus by these divine facts accrediting him as his Son who is not so? Unbelief cannot recognize God in his workings, as him that is true. It stamps the divine as the undivine. It can see in the ways of God nothing but contradiction.

From these words of John we may deduce a truth most important for our own age. That Jesus is the Son of God, as he has declared himself in his history, is attested by no resistless proofs, for such as will not recognize the witness in what God has wrought through the Gospel; for such as, having no susceptibility in themselves for receiving it, do not yield themselves with an humble and receptive heart to the witness of the Spirit, that it may thereby become to them an inward witness. It is the individual character and disposition that must here make the decision. It belongs to the individual will to decide, whether one will yield himself to that witness of the Spirit, or rather than this, will account God in his workings a liar.

Having thus spoken of the testimony whereby Jesus is accredited as the Son of God, the Apostle now shows more particularly what is its import in reference to believers, what this attestation that he is the Son of God implies, and assures to them. "And this is the record, that God hath given to us eternal life, and this life is in his Son. He that hath the Son, hath life; and he that hath not the Son of God hath not life." [Ch. v. 11, 12.

Through this witness, whereby Jesus is accredited as the Son of God, he is made known as the One who alone can impart a true, eternal, divine life of bliss to man. By sending to us his Son, God has in him bestowed on us the fountain of this eternal life. Hence this witness includes also that gift of eternal life. In the Son is grounded this eternal life; all life, apart from fellowship with him, being only death. It follows, that he who has received the Son, has in so doing experienced in himself that true life; while he, who through unbelief shuts himself out from Christ, shuts himself out from the fountain of true life, and from that life itself.

To reawaken this in their consciousness, he repeats, is the object of his epistle. This is to him the first and the chief thing. In it is included all which is necessary for the inner man; since this true divine life comprehends in itself, all which man needs for time and eternity. It is the exhaustless source of satisfaction to the spirit, so formed, so constituted in its very nature, that it can satisfy itself with nothing less than God; can find its true life, its true happiness, only in that fellowship with him which is bestowed alone through his Son. "These things have I written unto you, that ye may know that ye have eternal life, who believe on the name of the Son of God."*

Ch. v. 13.]

This then was the Apostle's object, that believ-

* As translated by Neander.—*Tr.*

ers might know how much has been bestowed upon them in their faith. True they must, as believers, have known this from the beginning; but then, in human life, all things slide so easily into the mechanical form of habit! The current of life sweeps us along; and though one may indeed abide in the faith, yet he may lose more and more the vivid consciousness of the treasure therein imparted to him. Hence he must ever draw anew from the divine life-fountain opened to him through faith; the consciousness of that which he has therein received, must be continually revived and invigorated; and from faith must the knowledge of that, which was first received in faith, continually develop itself anew. There can be no halting here. Unless the fountain of faith is itself dried up, there must proceed from it a progressive development. Hence he writes to those who have already long believed, as if they were now first to learn, that by believing in Jesus as the Son of God they became partakers of eternal life. Their joy in that divine possession was to be continually renewed and increased. They were again and again to be reminded, that no power of earth can bestow upon them anything higher, anything more; to be thus warned against the treacherous arts of those false teachers, who sought to unsettle them in their faith, commending to them something else as the truth or as a higher truth; to be thereby established in this faith, under all temptations and conflicts.

He then proceeds to remind them of one especial blessing, the fruit of this relation to God into which they have entered through faith. "And this is the confidence that we have in him, that if we ask anything according to his will, he heareth us. And if we know that he hear us, whatsoever we ask, we know that we have the petitions that we desired of him."

Ch. v. 14, 15.]

Thus John regards it as the fruit of faith, that God is no longer to them a God afar off. The chasm is now closed which separated man from his Creator,—from Him who is over all worlds, God in his infinitude, in his incomprehensibility, in his holiness. They now hold a filial relation to him, enjoy continual intercourse with him, in all their necessities can turn to him with filial confidence as to a father and friend. In him they have ever at hand one in whom help, counsel, and comfort are to be found. It is this living relation to

God as our Father,—continually mediated through faith in Christ as the Son of God, through conscious fellowship with him,—which constitutes true Christianity as a matter of the life. To this child-like confidence, leading us to prayer and enjoyed in prayer, the Apostle attaches a high import. Prayer he makes the soul of the whole christian life. Having previously said, that prayer in the name of Christ is ever heard by the Father; he now adds the condition, that we pray according to his will. The one is involved in the other, as we have already shown. He who prays in the name of Christ, is moved and guided by the Spirit of Christ in prayer. He can ask for nothing, but that which is in accordance with the will of God; can with assurance ask only that, which the Spirit of Christ makes known to him in prayer, as corresponding to the Father's will. When this certainty is wanting, his prayer will always be accompanied with the condition, that the desire arising in his soul and taking the form of prayer, may have for its object something which the Father approves.

From this we are not to conclude, however, that prayer in itself can have no definite effect, since whatever is grounded in the will of God must happen in any case. Nor are we to suppose that prayer, by bringing man into this living relation to his Source of being and his Father, therein alone accomplishes its whole work upon the inner life; that its whole influence is seen in the holy temper of mind which it produces, and which naturally flows from the elevation of the soul above itself and the world to God, entering into living intercourse with him, and losing itself in him. It is true indeed, that herein consists one of the chief blessings of prayer; but this is not all which prayer effects. And even this effect would not be fully realized, if prayer were not something more than the mere objective contemplation of the Divine. For it presupposes the assured consciousness, that the relation to God into which we enter by prayer is a living personal relation, as of one individual person with another, in which both are mutually acted on; that he perceives that, which our spirit in directing to him its feelings and thoughts would have him perceive. In this it is necessarily implied, that our prayer for a definite object will not be in vain. This the Apostle indicates, when he speaks of a hearing of prayer. Prayer is the soul's necessity, breathed forth to

God with filial confidence and submission, in the consciousness of that living relation to him as father; it must therefore, in rising to God, find satisfaction in reference to that which is the object of want. True indeed, prayer cannot in the proper sense constrain the will of God,—a thought which is excluded by the very nature of this filial relation to him. But the actualization of the divine will excludes not intermediate causes; and among the chief of these is prayer. Passing beyond the outward and finite of the earthly world, as presented in space and time; beyond the natural connection of phenomena; as an invisible spiritual force, it penetrates with its agency to the very heart of the invisible world. Itself the breath of love, its workings are in unison with the laws of the invisible kingdom of love. It belongs not to that which can be mechanically estimated, —like all that is highest, and deepest, and innermost. Prayer is the highest act of the God-related spirit, entering into that living relation to God for which it was created. Prayer, grounded in fellowship with Christ as here represented by John, presupposes that power derived from God, whereby the soul is winged for this its loftiest flight, whence it receives this its highest energy of burning aspiration. This power tends back to the Primal Source from which it flows. It is a special gift, bestowed on man as a member of the invisible world, whereby he may lay hold on the invisible. It is one of his homeborn rights; enjoyed already here, as pertaining to that heaven where he belongs, and which shall one day be his home. So certainly will prayer be heard, that christians, while they pray, should be inspired with the assurance that what they ask is virtually received already.

From all for which as christians we may pray, John now selects a single object of prayer. Ch. v. 16.] This must, therefore, appear to him to be specially connected with the peculiar nature of the christian life. "If any man see his brother sin a sin which is not unto death, he shall ask, and he shall give him life for them that sin not unto death. There is a sin unto death: I do not say that he shall pray for it."

True prayer as grounded in fellowship with Christ, must proceed from the christian life as a connected whole. That which is the animating principle of the whole christian life, must also be the animating principle of christian prayer. The prayer of love, is that which binds all christians together as brethren. Hence the Apostle singles out that sympathy of fraternal love, which expresses itself in prayer. As this sympathy must first respect the spiritual necessities, which to each are his own highest concern, and as the need arising from sin must seem to each his brother's greatest need; so will his sympathy expressed in prayer, his ardent desire to help, have special reference to this need, which he feels himself constrained to bear with his brother. It may indeed happen, that those who are strict toward themselves practise the same strictness toward others also, despising and repulsing them, when they see in them any sin. But this is not that zeal in sanctification, which is in harmony with the christian life. Conscious as he is himself, that he owes all to redeeming grace, that the divine life in himself is still mingled with much that is impure; the christian cannot but be lenient in his judgment when he sees others fall, while he thus feels his own weakness, his own continual need of redemption. And here, especially, is shown the power of that love, which feels as its own the brother's need. Accordingly, John calls upon christians first of all, to help with their prayers the brother who has fallen into sin. He assures them, that to the fallen brother,—in whom the divine life has been impaired through sin, who by yielding to temptation has fallen from the unity of this divine life,—that to such an one God will restore this divine life in its original vigor. They may thus, through the intercession prompted by love, become instruments in restoring to life a fallen brother. Could they render him a higher service of love!

But how are we to understand John's limitation of this requirement, in the exception, emphatically repeated, of sins which are unto death? Should not then the claim for help be greater, the greater the brother's spiritual need? Should limits be set to that gushing love, which pours itself out in intercession? Should not prayer for the brother be so much the more required? To make this clear, it is only necessary to understand what kind of prayer John has in view; what he presupposes as the condition on which prayer is heard, and how he distinguishes from other sins the sin which is unto death.

True, the divine life, in its essential nature, excludes all sin,—as John has already shown. Sin and death, according to the Holy Scriptures, are closely connected ideas. But the divine life in believers, as we have already seen, develops itself in continual conflict with the after-workings of the earlier life of sin. Numerous disturbances of the divine life may thereby ensue, interruptions of the christian development, which yet do not undermine this life itself as the controlling principle, but only repress it at particular times and in certain manifestations. The ruling tendency of the will is still directed towards holiness. Sin is hated and abhorred; and though its after-workings are still felt, it is only as something foreign cleaving to the true self, whose animating and controlling principle is love. In such a case it is only necessary, when one falls under single temptations, to call again into action the controlling element of the divine life existing in him, in order to overcome the principle of sin. It is of such cases the Apostle speaks, where there is true repentance and longing after continued sanctification; and hence, where the conditions and the susceptibility are not wanting, for that which is to be obtained through a brother's intercession. It is of such persons he speaks, who are in a state of grace, and have not apostatized from their christian calling; who still deserve the name of christian brethren, and hence have a claim upon all the aids of christian love, which one brother can render to another. An intercession is meant, which in the nature of the case can respect only such persons; and it is presupposed that all, who are connected by the bond of christian brotherhood, will mutually intercede for one another.

It may be, however, that an individual has fallen into such a state, as absolutely excludes the presence of the divine life in him; an evidence that he who seemed to have passed from death unto life, has again fallen under the power of death. Such an one may never in reality have attained to the true life. The essence of living faith, as delineated by John, may have been ever wanting in him. He may have only seemed to be a christian, without being truly so; having received only the baptism of water, not the baptism of the Holy Ghost. Christ may never have been actually formed in him; and at most, he may have experienced only transient emotions of the higher life. Or it may be that such an one, after having truly received through living faith a divine life and become a new man, has fallen from this state, has estranged himself from it, and sunk back again into his former position. This could not indeed happen at once; but yet,—through want of watchfulness over himself, through negligence and sluggishness in the conflict with after-working sin, through a false security, a presumptuous reliance upon grace or a false self-reliance,—it might be brought about gradually, and through many downward stages. Now where such a state existed, it showed itself in acts; in such sins as no one, who remained true to the christian relation and faithfully applied the imparted means of grace, could possibly have committed. Such persons were excluded from the fellowship of the church, in accordance with the principles of church relationship in that age; as is assumed to be necessary by the Apostle Paul, in a case like this occurring in the Corinthian church. John could not mean, that it was forbidden to pray for such as had thus fallen. For in regard to the first case,—there is no ground apparent, why those who had not yet been truly converted, and at most had felt only occasional impulses towards Christianity, might not become susceptible to the farther operations of grace and be brought under their influence. Or if we take the second case,—of such as had culpably lost the life imparted by grace; we can find no reason, why they might not have regained it through true repentance. It is true indeed, that this was rendered far more difficult by their misuse of the means of grace, and by the increased moral blindness induced through their own fault,—which is referred to in the sixth chapter of the Epistle to the Hebrews. When John calls Christ the Reconciliation and the Intercessor for the sins of the whole world, he certainly meant not to exclude one belonging to either of these two classes, provided only that repentance could be reawakened.

In this connection, however, he is speaking of intercession for christians, for such as have not trifled away the forgiveness of sins through Christ. Hence, in this connection, those must be excepted who have fallen into what John calls "sin unto death," in the sense explained; for in their case such intercession would be inappropriate, since in them the conditions and the susceptibility for it were wanting. Had he not made this distinction, he would have given the false impression, that one who commits such sins may still abide in Christianity; as if christians and those who are not christians could be known, the one from the other, by no distinctive signs in their life-walk. He would thus have required the church to regard such persons as still christian brethren, since they were to be embraced in the common supplication for all christians. He would have made those persons themselves more secure in their sins, and led them to a false reliance on the intercession of others. With christian love, the unsparing condemnation of sin must go hand in hand. A love, which overlooked all distinction among sins, would have been no true love.

How unlike John it would have been, to withhold from one ever so debased the consolation of forgiveness through Christ, and to withdraw from him the sympathy of his love, is seen in the beautiful tradition, (which there is no reason to discredit) of that fallen christian youth, who had become chief of a robber-band, and who by John's love was rescued and brought back to the Lord.

But while he thus demands even for the sins of brethren the offices of christian sympathy and love, he deems it important to [Ch. v. 17, 18.

avoid thereby effacing the essential contrariety between the christian life and sin, and to summon the christian to continued conflict with sin. "All unrighteousness is sin, and there is a sin not unto death. We know that whosoever is born of God, sinneth not: but he that is begotten of God, keepeth himself, and that wicked one toucheth him not."

He deems it necessary to add this warning, lest some might be led, by the distinction which he had made among sins, to think too lightly of any sin; lest christians should suppose they had done enough, if they only avoided such outbreaking sins. Here again he refers to the fact, that the Principle in all sin is the same. All transgression of the divine law, all which proceeds from the Selfish in man, as Sin, is in its radical principle one and the same thing. It is only in reference to the outward manifestation, that such a difference among sins can be made, that the sin unto death can be distinguished from other sins. To this end he reiterates the truth, that the divine life stands in contradiction with ALL sin; and that one, as born of God and possessing that divine life which is opposed to all sin, keeps himself separate from all sin. Such an one, faithfully cherishing the divine life which he has received, and watching over himself, has nothing to fear from temptations to evil; he has the power to withstand Satan in all his influences. There is nothing in such an one on which he can fix his hold. As he was compelled to retire from the Redeemer himself, finding no access to him with his temptations; so will he be compelled to leave unharmed, those who stand in fellowship with the Redeemer. Herein are included two things: first, the duty of all such as have become partakers of the divine life, to guard against all sin whatever, without regard to gradational differences; and secondly, the proof of the fact, that such as have fallen into sins which are unto death are not born of God. From this it is evident, that if they were actually born of God, they could only, by neglecting to watch over themselves, have again fallen a prey to the power of evil, which they must otherwise have withstood.

This leads the Apostle to exhibit yet once more, before he closes his epistle, the essential contrariety between christians as born of God, and the sinful world. [Ch. v. 19, 20. "And we know that we are of God, and the whole world lieth in wickedness. And we know that the Son of God is come, and hath given us an understanding that we may know Him that is true: and we are in Him that is true, in his Son Jesus Christ."

The Apostle, now about to take leave of his readers, once more impresses on their hearts what christians must ever hold in living remembrance, if they would not prove faithless to their calling,—their relation to the world. As born of God, as partakers of the divine life, they form the opposite to the world, of which John says, that it lies under the dominion of Evil. The divine life in them constitutes the entire and irreconcilable opposite to the evil which reigns in this world. Out of the fulness of the divine life in his own soul, the aged John looks back upon a long life, during which he had witnessed the constant progress of evil in the world, developing itself in an ever-ascending scale. He must now look to his near departure out of this world, whence he was to be called into the home of the Good, to Christ. But his spiritual children he left behind in this world of wickedness, exposed to the taint of its corruptions. He reminds them, that by virtue of the divine life within them, they should constitute the opposite to this wicked world. Hence they should be ever watchful over themselves, guarding against all inward contact with the wickedness which is in the world, and by the power of their inward divine life preserve themselves pure from its contaminating influence; ever bearing in mind their position and calling, to maintain a conflict with the evil of the world, to be themselves the salt of the world.

As The True, John designates him who alone is to be called God. The world knows him not, is in a state of estrangement from him. It is included in the very idea of the world as such, that it gives to another the honor which belongs to God alone, that it serves false gods. But believers are, in their inward life and spirit, separated from the world by this,—that the Son of God has come, and has given to them the perception, whereby they know the true God. John here assumes that man, as he is by nature, in his natural tendencies, cannot by the natural understanding attain to the knowledge of God; that the spirit must first be freed from the worldliness in which it is ensnared, a new God-related sense must be awakened, in order that he may thereby, with the eyes of the spirit enlightened, know the true God. John himself, though he had been brought up in Judaism, and taught from early life the knowledge of God; yet ranks himself here with Gentile believers, as one to whom the Son of God first imparted that inward sense, whereby he might know God. He thus implies that he knew him not before; that the light of the knowledge of God first dawned upon him, when Christ called him from the world to himself. Here too is recognized the fundamental truth, that it is only through the Son the Father can be truly known. Hence it is evident, that one may acknowledge God, may think that he knows him, may have a kind of dead faith in him; while yet he is far from knowing him, wanting that God-related sense through which only he can be truly known. 'From him that hath not,' says our Lord, 'shall be taken even that which he seemeth to have.' So may those, who have only this dead knowledge of God, this form without life, find it wholly swept away by the overpowering force of the spirit of the world. And being thus made conscious of their lack of any principle superior to the world, whereby they can withstand its power, and of their wretchedness in this state of estrangement from God and subjection to the world; they may be led to seek for that new inward sense, which the Son of God can alone impart, and whereby alone they can attain to the knowledge of the true God.

This true knowledge of God has its root in the life, in fellowship with God; and this can be mediated only through his Son. Hence John reminds his christian brethren, that they are in the true God; that they live in fellowship with him, by virtue of their union with his Son; that it is therefore only in this abiding union they can persevere in fellowship with God, and retain the knowledge of the true God. Thereby alone will they be kept separate from the world, and guarded against its influences. The Holy Scriptures do indeed recognize, even in this our fallen state, a certain BEING IN GOD, as the inalienable inheritance of the God-related, God-descended spirit. So Paul, in the seventeenth chapter of the Acts, says: 'In him we live, and move, and have our being.' But that consequent drawing from God and towards him, grounded in this moral relationship to him, leads not to that living, true knowledge of God, which can sustain itself in conflict with the world. Such a consciousness of the unknown God, of the

God afar off, soon gives way before the overwhelming tide of the world; in the midst of a world lying in wickedness, it becomes blinded and confused through the influence of worldly temptations. Man cannot, by this dawn of a higher consciousness within him, maintain his faith in his own divine origin, and in the God of whose being it admonishes him. The scattered rays, whose light has penetrated the darkness of a world lying in wickedness, are again obscured; from the world ascends an impenetrable cloud, which enwraps his spirit, and forms a separating wall between him and the Divine. All else is unavailing, unless that divine drawing lead his submissive spirit to the Son, to be by him made free, and endowed with that inward sense whereby the true God is known.

John now closes this truly noble Epistle, with the admonition: that, persevering in union with Him the only true God, through his Son, and in that fellowship of eternal life received from him, they keep themselves pure from all contamination with Idol-gods. "This is the true God, and eternal Life. Little children, keep yourselves from Idols."

Ch. v. 20, 21.]

It might be a question, whether the word 'This' refers here to God, or to the incarnate Son in whom he has revealed himself. In either case, the practical import of the words is the same. The connection, however, leads us to regard the reference to God as the prominent one, since God is afterwards contrasted with Idols. The Apostle has just been contemplating Christ as the Mediator of this fellowship with God. Hence we must suppose, that in conclusion he sets forth this one prominent thought: This God, with whom believers thus stand in fellowship through Christ, is the only true God, and hence is the primal source of eternal life; through him alone, therefore, we can become partakers of eternal life, in which is contained the Sum of all Good, as the highest good for the God-related spirit. In him, therefore, we have all which we need for time and eternity. It is true indeed as we have seen, that Christ as the only-begotten-Son of God, is called by John the eternal Life which was with the Father, and which has appeared on earth in order to impart itself to man. With these words he commenced this Epistle. But it is also appropriate, that in closing he should point to the Primal Source, to Him who is himself that eternal Life, which has poured itself forth into the only-begotten-Son, and through him into humanity.

But in order to hold fast this highest possession, christians must guard themselves from all contamination with the idols worshipped by a world lying in wickedness. This admonition was, in its present form, intended for such as lived in a world devoted to Idol-worship. Was then this admonition intended only for that age? Has it no application to our own time? If we well consider what John understands by that knowledge of the true God, which can be attained only through the inward sense derived from him and imparted by the Son; it will thence be evident, that where this sense is wanting, and with it that true knowledge of God, the human spirit, though it may profess to believe in God and suppose itself his worshipper, is yet far from him, and is a worshipper of idols. The world as such ever has its idols, to whom it gives the honor due to the true God alone. In a world which lies in wickedness, the children of God will ever be surrounded with idols; and they can insure the possession of their highest good, only by remaining true to their God, by keeping themselves aloof from all contact with the idols of the world. Specially appropriate is the application to our own age, whose ruling tendency is deification of Self and deification of the World; an age of conscious apostacy from the only true God,—of a conscious idolatry of the World and Self. For us, especially, there is need of the warning with which John closes his Epistle: The God whom Christ has revealed, is the true God and eternal Life; beware of taking part in the Idol-worship of a world lying in wickedness!

THE END.

www.ingramcontent.com/pod-product-compliance
Lightning Source LLC
LaVergne TN
LVHW021230110826
845150LV00002B/294

9781425563288